MW00787619

WORKING
IN DEPTH

WORKING IN DEPTH

A Clinician's Guide to Framework and Flexibility in the Analytic Relationship

ELLIOT ADLER, Ph.D.
JANET LEE BACHANT, Ph.D.

JASON ARONSON INC.
Northvale, New Jersey
London

This book was set in 11 pt. New Century Schoolbook by Alabama Book Composition of Deatsville, Alabama, and printed and bound by Book-mart Press, Inc. of North Bergen, New Jersey.

Library of Congress Cataloging-in-Publication Data

Adler, Elliot.
    Working in depth : a clinician's guide to framework and
flexibility in the analytic relationship / Elliot Adler and Janet
Lee Bachant.
      p. cm.
    Includes bibliographical references and index.
    ISBN 0–7657–0160–X
    1. Transference (Psychology) 2. Psychoanalysis.
3. Psychotherapist and patient. I. Bachant, Janet Lee. II. Title.
    [DNLM: 1. Psychoanalytic Therapy—methods. 2. Transference
(Psychology) 3. Professional–Patient Relations. WM 460.6 A237w 1998]
RC489.T73A35 1998
616.89′17—dc21
DNLM/DLC
for Library of Congress   98-4564

Printed in the United States of America on acid-free paper. Jason Aronson Inc. offers books and cassettes. For information and catalog write to Jason Aronson Inc., 230 Livingston Street, Northvale, New Jersey 07647-1726. Or visit our website: http://www.aronson.com

To Helen

and Roy

Contents

Acknowledgments

There are several groups of people whom we wish to acknowledge collectively. For obvious reasons it is difficult to single out individuals for special recognition, though many are truly deserving. First, our patients. They have been a continual source of stimulation, challenge, and gratifying engagement. We have felt privileged that they have honored us with the trust to enter their lives in such intimate depth. Second, our students. The continual effort to formulate and synthesize our understanding in ever more precise and useful forms has motivated all our teaching and writing. Our students were particularly close to us during long hours of writing. We are mindful of the persistence and dedication they display in pursuit of analytic ways of knowing, especially at a time when such understanding may not always dictate the most expedient or lucrative choices. Third, our teachers, both those at whose feet we have sat and others whose wisdom was encountered only on the printed page. We hope that our efforts do honor to their legacy.

In our labors, we have drawn upon the encouragement, support, and advice of a number of colleagues, a few of whose names we are compelled to single out. Arnold Richards has encouraged this project with unselfish advice, critical readings, and practical suggestions. To be validated and valued by a teacher of his erudition helped strengthen our resolve, even when our words threatened to dissolve in our minds like so much cotton candy. He has earned our deepest gratitude. Helen Adler has patiently listened to numerous drafts and redrafts of virtually every word of text. She has been unfailingly appreciative in her response as well as incredibly thoughtful and tactful in offering substantive suggestions. Peter Buirski and Arthur Lynch have both been intellectual selfobjects for the authors. Their critical readings and faith in our ability have provided invaluable encouragement. We are also grateful for the close and perceptive editorial reading of the first draft of this book which Catherine Monk undertook. We have taken the majority of her suggestions, and know that it is a better book for her effort. Ken Barrish contributed a careful reading of three chapters of this work and a number of his specific ideas have been incorporated into the text. We thank the Training Department of the Postgraduate Center and the Psychoanalytic Society of the Westchester Center for the Study of Psychoanalysis and Psychotherapy for providing us with congenial forums to present selected previews of our book.

Our families deserve far more than acknowledgment. Helen and Roy, Rachel and Julian, Rod and Miriam have all made sacrifices to see our project reach fulfillment. Yet they have remained unfailingly encouraging and eager for our success. Above all, their love has sustained us.

Collaborating on a project of this magnitude, involving literally millions of separate decisions taken over a period of several years, is a curious journey indeed. Looking back from our final destination, we confront a rather miraculous phenomenon. Through a process of discussion, writing, editing and revision (twice repeated), we have arrived at a place where both authors will affirm virtually every concept, conceit, word choice, and grammatical gesture that has been wrought. Though each may identify the mark of his or her own handiwork in places, it gives us pleasure to hope that we have succeeded in bending our two independent minds to the task of creating a harmonious and consistent whole. We owe each other a debt of gratitude that we can feel this way after having come so far.

Elliot Adler
Janet Lee Bachant
August 1998

Introduction

Psychoanalytic understanding does not come easily. Emerging slowly, amid exhilarating false starts and apparent dead ends, it taxes the hearts and minds of those who practice "the impossible profession." The tensions that therapists are called upon to manage in daily practice arise from countless sources, as knowledge wrested from transference, countertransference, and resistance is brought to light in a turbulence of disowned desire and fear. These tensions are inevitable and essential aspects of the clinical encounter—understanding another person in depth is not something we can do at a distance. Only sustained, intimate, and emotional engagement with self and other enables us to navigate these dark waters.

This book starts from the recognition that emotional involvement permeates the core of analytic work. This engagement is not a given and does not stand alone. It is fostered within a thoughtfully conceived and skillfully executed framework that has multiple dimensions. An enduring interest in searching out every obstacle to understanding is a defining aspect of psychoanalysis; it initiates a deepening process of relatedness that can take us to the uncharted recesses of a person's most private being. The desire to nurture the internal freedom of our patients, and to support their aspirations to a meaningful life and the highest development of their innate potentials must be allied with clinical vision and technical dexterity to realize the promise of this extraordinary voyage. In the course of treatment, patients will be challenged to question cherished assumptions and confining defenses. The immensity of these risks, a constant current the therapeutic process must contend with, can never be minimized. The balance between the requirements for emotional safety and the dangers inherent in change must be continually assessed and attended to. Ideally, this balance should be built into the very structure of the therapeutic process.

This book articulates one vision for achieving such a balance. We have directed our contribution to a wide audience, striving to address the concerns of those new to analytic work as well as the aspirations of our more experienced colleagues. Our approach is informed by contemporary perspectives on the theory of technique, while honoring the legacy of several generations of remarkable analytic thinkers. In the course of formulating our ideas, we have struggled repeatedly with the question of how far and in exactly what ways the classical foundations of psychoanalytic technique have evolved or have been fundamentally altered by current perspectives and conditions of practice. In addressing these questions, we have eschewed the obscurities of metapsychology as far as possible, seeking instead to ground our reasoning in the pragmatics of everyday clinical experience. Our primary concern has been to articulate the essential ideas and attitudes that inspire a psychoanalyst to approach the treatment situation with coherent purpose and technical flexibility. How can we best guide the analytic process to its potential depths?

At the center of every therapeutic endeavor is the manner in which the relationship between its participants is organized. A pivotal structure, the psychoanalytic situation generates a unique kind of relatedness that makes possible the most profound exploration of human motivation. Organized around the patient's expressive freedom and the analyst's ability to listen, the analytic situation creates a synergistic mode of relating that facilitates emotional engagement in depth. This unique relationship generates the momentum to destabilize neurotic organization and impel crucial integrative and maturational processes. It absorbs, crystallizes, and resolves the tensions emanating from the arduous tasks of psychic growth. In its wake, we embark upon an incredible journey of discovery that traverses the reaches of conscious awareness and the depths of unconscious experience.

The analytic situation is itself an interactive framework that mirrors the structure of individual experience in significant ways. Psychoanalysts recognize that patterns of organizing experience established early in life are extremely enduring and resistant to change. This internal psychic framework, a set of fundamental assumptions, proclivities, and ways of processing experience, both facilitates and impedes maturation. It enables us to make reliable predictions and useful adjustments to crucial aspects of the psychological environment without having to invent ourselves anew with every shifting circumstance. Arising, however, amidst the cognitive confusions of earliest life, significant elements of this framework remain infused with archaic modes of thought that can straitjacket our functioning. Complementing this fundamental psychic orientation is an adaptive flexibility that permits a person to assimilate and accommodate new experience. Both the fundamental elements of psychic organization rooted in archaic mental life and the adaptive capacity to explore and engage the external world represent counterbalancing influences upon the construction of all experience. The checks and balances delineated by these two factors, framework and flexibility, permeate our functioning and have profound implications for clinical practice.

Our vision of deepening the work involves asking the clinician to keep in mind the importance of attending to the ever-shifting balance between these factors. Each makes vital contributions to understanding the patient's experience. Working in depth involves helping the patient to more fully discern the psychic framework employed to structure the world, as well as identifying and utilizing the patient's adaptive capacities in the service of understanding and integration. These dimensions come together most usefully in the interaction between patient and analyst.

When patients come to treatment, they encounter a therapeutic environment mediated by an analyst responsive to their fluctuating emotional needs. The ensuing interaction can be seen as a prolonged process of accommodation between the patient's foundational framework—with its limited adaptive flexibility—and an analytic frame that has circumscribed boundaries and defined requirements. The outcome of this adjustment has profound implications, determining whether a treatment relationship will evolve in which transference and resistance can emerge in analyzable form. When this difficult pass can be successfully negotiated, a psychoanalytic situation is established in which the interplay of archaic and adaptive dimensions of subjective experience can be fully expressed and laid open to interpretive reflection. Vivid encounters merging reality and fantasy, present and past, hope and fear, contribute to this highly combustible amalgam. As the analyst becomes immersed in the adaptive and archaic dimensions of a dyadic transference–countertransference field, the resources of the particular analytic couple will be repeatedly tested. In the face of intense instinctual stimulation and repeated emotional provocation, we will continually strive to return our focus to the fundamental analytic task of explicating the internal world and adaptive struggle of the patient. Our appreciation of the daunting challenge that this entails rests on an understanding of the analyst's multiple functions as an embodiment of the analytic frame, a protector of the analytic situation, a provider of emotional sustenance, as well as an interpreter of unconscious meaning.

We have sought to represent the analytic endeavor with a balance of realism and idealism. In selecting illustrative clinical vignettes we have avoided the temptation to project an image of the competent analyst as an all-knowing expert who foresees every shift and turn of events. We are well aware that even the experienced clinician inevitably gets entangled in the web of a complex interaction that only gradually yields to comprehension. Developing psychoanalytic understanding is never easy, but our belief that there are teachable dimensions of this process has inspired us to write this book.

1

Getting Started

The initial weeks of analytic therapy are a stressful time in which both the procedures and the goals of a complex collaborative endeavor must be jointly negotiated. In a cultural milieu that seems increasingly impatient—if not downright suspicious—of long-term psychodynamically oriented modes of treatment, it is essential that an analyst have a clear understanding of the heightened significance of these early interactions and arrangements in order to navigate a therapeutic course toward a profound psychoanalytic engagement. To a contemporary practitioner, Freud's (1913) genial advice for initiating a psychoanalytic process has a somewhat quaint air: a product of a more graceful era perhaps, an era in which an analyst was granted the immanent authority to lay down fundamental rules, a period when the urgent rush of time did not whistle so loudly about one's ears. Sitting back and "clearing away" misunderstandings as they arise with respectful attention seems too genteel a prescription in this era of tightly managed care and crisis intervention. Psychoanalysis is no longer the only show in town and it has suffered significant losses in prestige and cache after encountering a seemingly endless run of bad press. Under these circumstances, an analyst's initial position is more apt to be on the balls of the feet, rather than serenely receptive—alertly poised to react with definitive swiftness to any emergent crisis.

In the following discussion we review the beginning phase of psychoanalytic treatment, emphasizing what we consider the essential attitudes, clinical perspectives, and practical arrangements that predispose both analyst and prospective patient to build an abiding structure that approximates a psychoanalytic situation (Chapter 2). It is our contention that approaching a patient with this framework in mind, as well as with the flexibility to respond to specific demands of a unique clinical situation, maximizes the probability of negotiating a workable psychoanalytic relationship.

Many things may, and typically do transpire in an initial session; histories are taken, business arrangements discussed, questions asked and answered. Yet beneath the surface, both parties are asking themselves the same question: "Just who *is* this other person?" This unvoiced query—in increasingly elaborate forms—will continue to propel psychoanalytic inquiry throughout an analysis. To launch this progression, a therapist is always well advised to approach an initial consultation without defined expectation. Preliminary information, either from a referring colleague or an initial telephone contact, often stimulates anticipatory ideas that prove of dubious value in the give-and-take immediacy of a first clinical encounter. Throughout the course of treatment, the foundation of our most reliable clinical judgment resides in information received in context; this is especially so at a first meeting when one may be called upon to make hair-trigger decisions with sketchy understanding. We do better to remind ourselves of some essential goals of an initial interview: giving the patient an opportunity to tell his or her story of distress as completely as possible; evoking the feeling that he or she is speaking to a reliable professional person, capable of compassionate and perceptive attention; discovering if this unfamiliar person is a potential collaborator willing to accompany us on a more extended journey of analytic exploration.

It is worth bearing in mind that the consultee is not yet "a patient." The distinction, sometimes overlooked, is that a patient is a person who has accepted an implicit or explicit contract, however tentatively, to work with a particular therapist in a way that makes sense to that therapist, toward certain broadly agreed-upon goals. The person who comes for a consultation is only exploring a possibility. In practice, therefore, we must always be prepared for an individual to decide that we, or the kind of treatment we favor, is simply not their cup of tea. This does not mean, however, that we cannot question a bias against us. Many people arrive for a consultation with quite specific ideas regarding the therapist they *need* or the nature of the work they *must* accomplish: "I need to find a therapist who will *push* me to be independent. I *must* learn to be my own person." It is possible to greet such an idea respectfully and yet to pursue its premises as far as possible in an initial contact.

Experience does not favor the reassuring notion that patients always know what is in their genuine interest. Analytic investigation of such explicit stipulations often reveals an amalgam of naive insight, reparative longing, and defensively avoidant intention. It has much in common with a particular species of daydream involving relationships of completion, a classification that might include the nearly universal fantasies of an ideal mate, a perfect job or geographical locale, or a financial windfall. As with all fantasies of complete fulfillment, their consummation often exposes the unresolved internal problems they were created to disguise in the first place. If, however, we discover the bridge linking sources of hope and danger in patients' emotional history with the immediate therapeutic context, we may enable them to set aside the urgency of their quest in order to chance analytic treatment with us: "I think I can understand why you are determined to take such a goal-oriented approach to therapy; so much time has been squandered in your lifetime on relationships and projects that seemed to promise everything but ended up going nowhere. You must have believed when you married Jim, or started your business, or turned to teaching, or joined the monastery, that, each time, this would be *the* thing that would give your living structure and purpose—a lasting meaning."

There is certainly no right way to begin a consultation. There are, perhaps, less than right ways. We prefer an open-ended overture, as it allows specific urgencies to be defined at the outset when there is still time to understand something about them. A simple "How shall we begin?"—as good as a number of equally serviceable alternatives—casts a broad net to catch what is lurking near the surface. Of course, "How shall we begin?" already *is* a beginning. It adumbrates a highly condensed program—to be repeated at critical junctures along the way—for an entire analysis. How shall we begin? Where do we go from here? How shall we go about ending? are questions that imply the analyst's collaborative reliance on specific guidance from the patient in order to know how to proceed. They indicate that the patient knows something that the analyst needs to hear before a coherent beginning, direction, or termination process can be initiated.

Less sophisticated patients sometimes balk at this personalized approach until they become accustomed to analytic ways of working. Little is gained by immediately frustrating the conventional idea that "the expert" should systematically structure a consultation. Even a patient's silence or hesitation is informative, however. By concretizing intense ambivalence that is difficult for patients to broach, such reluctance often signals an emergent threat of narcissistic exposure, shame, and humiliation. Gaining access to these concerns and addressing the underlying ambivalence directly can circumvent a flight from treatment. It also gives us an initial opportunity to begin educating patients with regard to the analytic value of a structure of spontaneity, as well as to observe how they respond to this suggestion. A seemingly offhand comment, for instance, explaining that "it's generally more informative when a therapist doesn't ask too many specific questions," may suffice to jump start a stalled narrative. A therapist's encouragement to tell the whole story is often received with reserved skepticism. An unspoken doubt, "I guess she needs to know all this before she can give me the help I came for," may be apparent in a hesitant start. Only rarely does one encounter a compelling thirst for self-knowledge. We all harbor secret hopes of a quick fix, even when we have reason to know better.

Rather than launching into a story of distress, one person may bring forward a preoccupation with payment; another, a concern about privacy; still another, scheduling complications. Though we may be tempted to dismiss these questions as business matters, to be cleared up in due time, experience advises otherwise. Any issue, emphasized above others by priority of position, is thereby tagged with an underlying significance and affective intensity. If we dispatch the question to the end of the interview, we may miss a relatively direct route to the core anxieties and wishes that have been mobilized in anticipation of our meeting.

An overriding principle of early intervention can be stated: the most important things we can understand in the initial session(s) are the hopes, fears, and risks that the person brings to the therapeutic relationship itself. As analysts committed to a relationship of trust and truth-telling, we acknowledge, rather than evade, the actuality of risks confronted by patients undertaking treatment. Some may strike us as well founded, while others may seem quite fantastical. In either case, our success in eliciting and articulating these varied concerns, whether they are focused upon ourselves, our method of treatment, or the broader goals and thwarted ambitions that define that patient's life, will also free the hopeful striving that is necessary to propel such an ambitious project. We realize that these hopes and fears, unconsciously organized, will have to be engaged sooner or later if the analytic process is to move on to a deeper level—to embrace the most difficult obstacles and profound opportunities of analytic involvement. However, overt misgivings about entering treatment are a sign of potentially unendurable tension, forecasting a very brief window of opportunity to address the person's concerns. We cannot afford to sit back and wait for our understanding to ripen; we often need to be interpretively proactive to the point of boldness: "You experienced your mother as an enveloping presence thwarting your growth with her selfless love and hovering. You must fear that your involvement with me in this treatment might turn into one more tender trap."

It is rarely necessary, and sometimes even counterproductive, to go further than clarifying and articulating fears and hopes in these initial interpretive approaches. Explicit reassurance, as such, can be only temporarily reassuring. Patients have every reason to know how superficially we apprehend the intensity of their dread, the bleakness of their spiritual outlook, or the psychic precipice they foresee. Any representation of benign sympathy, intended to ameliorate the sense of threat, will be unconsciously identified as a magical gesture, evoked by the patient's or the analyst's immediate anxiety. Reluctantly, at times, we may be pressed to resort to reassurance, though only when all attempts at getting at the underlying significance of an urgent concern have been blankly thwarted. We take care to offer our assurance in a measured and ambiguous form that suggests rather than asserts our claim outright. Thus, for example, when a patient insistently exposes the morbid fear that he will become helplessly dependent on the therapy, we might say, "It's understandable to have such concerns when one begins treatment. It is seldom warranted, but we will be especially alert to any signs that this is coming about." We make the point, without specifically foreclosing the dreaded possibility, mindful of our evasion. After all, we wouldn't want to banish a patient's morbid fears altogether, even if it were possible. For we know, as the patient does not and cannot at this point, that these dangers are at the heart of what will need to be mobilized in the analytic situation if treatment is to have a truly profound impact on this person's living.

The dilemma at this point is roughly as follows: the analyst is far ahead of the patient in terms of foreknowing the parameters of the analytic process. We understand, in a general way, what is and is not likely to happen. We could, but would not say, "I will not abuse, exploit, seduce, attack, or abandon you as you may fear; but neither will I love you in all the ways that you will long for, nor protect you from danger and discomfort as completely as you would wish. And at some point, probably before you feel entirely ready, I will encourage you to leave the comfort of this analysis to face the trials and uncertainties of life on your own." Patients, on the other hand, are far ahead of us in their knowledge of themselves—their potential for disorienting anxiety, depressive passivity, and regressive disorganization. They might, though probably will not, share with us the relentless nature of their beseeching desperation, the truculent stubbornness of their emotional withdrawal, or the chaotic prospect from their inner world. And it is much too early in the relationship for either party to know what ameliorative resources each may count upon from the potential therapeutic partner. Rather than enter into a conversation that the patient is ill-prepared to comprehend, we try instead, through word and attitude, to convey the simple notion that in the therapeutic situation fears may be considered matter-of-factly, in the course of time. Our nonintrusive curiosity about whatever lurks disturbingly in the background of the initial consultation and our eagerness to address forthrightly whatever comes up is perhaps the most authentic way to offer reassurance to a prospective patient. In such an ambiguous circumstance, there are times when it is wise to allow illusion to prevail until hope can be sustained on more reliable grounds.

The outcome of an initial consultation or, for that matter, of an entire treatment depends as much on avoiding confounding mistakes as on the specific brilliance of one's technique. Therefore, until we have a more confident sense of the person we are meeting, caution is the rule. Realizing that it is the patient who invests the analyst with the prerequisite authority and trust that allows treatment to get under way takes the edge off our own eagerness to make a good impression. An analyst, in an initial consultation, does not have time to earn this trust, but we must take care not to lose it through early false steps. We understand that in conditions of stress and ambiguity, unconscious fantasizing begun long before the initial encounter can play a fateful role in organizing a patients' adaptive reactivity, impelling them to seek out confirmatory evidence of wishful or fearful expectation in small details of our person or office. In effect, this means that manifest indications of responsive attention, reserved curiosity, and subdued compassion represent but a scaffold for the construction of an impression of our therapeutic integrity.

Over time, a therapeutic partnership will evolve, marked by the intricate repetitive patterns that characterize any ongoing exchange between two complex human beings working intimately on a mutual task. The analysis of these interactive structures—of the individual contours and dimensions of this unique therapeutic dyad—will periodically come to the foreground of attention as points of annoyance or satisfaction as well as resistance. Once an analytic situation has been established, this focus presents a useful counterpoint to an investigation of the underlying meanings and unconscious fantasies that the analyst's way of being therapeutic may have evoked. In the early going, however, we are not yet positioned to engage in an interpretive exploration of the dynamic configurations and conflictual meanings that structure the patient's experience of our person or personal style of partnering. Initial subjective impressions of the analyst are generally taken as incontestable realities, and any authority we may claim for exploring the construction of these representations has, as yet, very narrow margins. Without the option of a transferential dialogue, we are wise to adjust our responsiveness in conformity to the patient's immediate requirements for safety or support. The multidimensional analytic space within which a person can re-create and explore the objects and dynamic configurations of an internal world of fantastic meanings, dreams, and transferentially inspired enactments emerges only gradually in an interpersonal context that is reliably structured and personally secure. Our first technical objectives, therefore, must be organized around the goal of establishing and maintaining a structured and reliable relationship through a mutual interpersonal adaptation.

In the beginning, how we conduct ourselves is more compelling than any specific thing we might do or say. We try to be unobtrusively encouraging, so that patients can become absorbed in telling their story, while remaining alert for indications of how our listening is being experienced. A patient's observation upon something in our demeanor or approach, "Gee, you haven't said much," for example, harbors a concern we cannot afford to ignore. A therapist's direct inquiry—"I suppose you are wondering what I've been making of what you're telling me"—may evoke the admission, "Oh, I kind of expected you to have more opinions about things!" This exchange creates a timely opening to explore the patient's ideas about therapeutic influence. Perhaps this patient has the notion that an expert will correct behavior through advice and criticism, or the experience of discomfort with the apparent inactivity of analytic listening may be in the forefront of concern. Sometimes an explanation of our behavior will be the only behavior required: "In my silence I've been working very hard to understand what you're telling me. Once I've sorted things out more clearly, I'll certainly share my thoughts with you!" If this answer doesn't assuage the discomfort with reassuring promise, it may be necessary to adjust the animation, pace, and affective tone of our responsiveness.

Such attunements of activity level or affective tone have little to do with manipulating emotional experience. They are an aspect of all interpersonal relationships, establishing a baseline of interactive comfort, which allows dyadic exchange to progress harmoniously toward a relationship. Depriving a person of this comfortable immediate sense of fit serves no useful function. Fine attunements and further modulations toward a less effortful baseline will take place as the patient's deeper sources of anxiety are recognized and gradually ameliorated through processes of interpretation. In a contemporary analytic framework, the impetus of the analytic process is neither enhanced nor thwarted by frustration or gratification per se, but by the progressive clarification and less guarded expression of personal intention, wish, and meaning. To abstain from a therapeutic activity simply because it alleviates a patient's immediate discomfort is a misguided application of an outdated principle of abstinence, in which undifferentiated frustration of all desire was deemed necessary to generate the specific hydraulic pressure toward uninhibited expression. On the other hand, were it to become evident that the meaning to the patient of the analyst's activity served to ward off fearful images and fantasies regarding the analyst's intentions, we would be guided by that understanding to modulate the affective tone of our interactivity in a timely and careful manner.

One strives to establish an evocative presence, rather than making forced efforts to "connect" by demonstrating unique resources of warmth, compassion, or knowledge. We are maximally evocative when we avoid explicitly declaring our emotional position, when we restrain, rather than withhold, our affective response. Overly eager or solicitous attention is as potentially disruptive as a professional demeanor conceived as blandly impersonal and emotionally constricted. To be professionally personal sounds paradoxical. Admittedly, it takes some experience, as well as self-understanding to be relaxed and spontaneously restrained, under the stress of an initial consultation. It helps considerably to be conversant with the inherent boundaries and possibilities of the analytic therapist's role, so that one may embody these limits, even while displaying the particular expressive qualities that define oneself as a recognizable individual.

The first few sessions give patient and analyst the opportunity to feel each other out. We are aware that these initial interactions are loaded with instructional intent on both sides. Patients are busy informing us not only about who they are and the problems they are struggling with, but about what they expect, fear, and long for in the therapeutic relationship. In turn, through demonstration or explanation, all therapists educate their patients in how to work productively in the kind of therapy they conduct. Good technical form is subtle. One tries to avoid obvious technical clichés or cookie-cutter repetitions—or at least to mold them skillfully into the texture of the situation at hand—though sometimes it is unavoidable. The proverbial "question that answers the patient's question," for instance, is a cliché of analytic technique that has inspired numerous spoofs. Yet even this tired formula serves a function, implicitly defining psychoanalytic inquiry as a process that leads to further questions rather than to quick answers. Those repetitious prods, "How do you feel about that?" "What comes to mind?" "What's that about?" with which we punctuate the narrative exposition, inform patients that complete analytic "data" and accurate understanding are only possible in a context of reflective attention to elaborate shadings of emotional and motivational meaning. If we are teased or reproached occasionally by patients for "sounding just like an analyst" it is because we *are* psychoanalysts; we should not hesitate to explain ourselves or our procedures—without apology.

One of the most important early lessons to impart is greater confidence in the spontaneous, as opposed to the more deliberate, labors of the mind. The encouragement to free-associate need not be annunciated as a forbidding rule or obligation. Showing interest in an obscure narrative detail or parenthetical aside may introduce the expectation that every thought or feeling, no matter how trivial, tangential, or disturbing, is of interest to the analyst, that truly whatever comes to mind is bound to accrue to already established meaning. When directly annunciated, this idea of spontaneity can be best represented as a corollary of an ideal of expressive freedom, that is, an unusual human opportunity. However appealingly portrayed, we never forget that free association carried forward in the presence of another is a profoundly radical proposition, one that the patient will necessarily struggle to circumvent.

A question that can orient our early thinking about the patient's presentation is why he or she has consulted a psychoanalyst at this particular time. What crisis, emotional pain, acute disappointment, or sign of impending danger has precipitated the call to the analyst's office? Furthermore, what thwarted steps have been taken to solve these difficulties before the patient appeared in our consulting room? We cannot always count on too much help from the patient on this. Conscious explanations typically emphasize an immediate emotional crisis, frustration, symptom, or inhibition that is confounding. At an unconscious level, however, seeking professional help reflects an admission of bewilderment and helplessness in regard to underlying dilemmas and conflicts. However skittish the approach, it is rarely resorted to until spontaneous efforts at "cure" have repeatedly proved futile. If we succeed in tracing the history of such efforts, whether in a series of failed love relationships, career moves, or an array of symptom patterns, we may be in a position to awaken the person to what is truly at stake. Such knowledge confirms patients' sense of wisdom at having sought out the consultation, bringing relief while solidifying their commitment to the expense and sacrifice of treatment.

Toward the end of the initial meeting we may attempt to give the patient a brief summary of our experience of the encounter. Ideally, this summary will succinctly capture the essential issues that have been covered, however discursively, in the initial interview. We attempt, when possible, to cast the patient's dilemma in a broader frame, which dignifies specific problems by juxtaposing them to larger existential themes of human existence, love, conflict, ambition, and fate. Done well, it sets the tone for a therapeutic process mobilized around the careful attention of a skilled listener prepared to discover the greater meaning in the circumstantial or particular element. Such a summary statement should lead quite naturally to a recommendation for continued exploration of the patient's concerns— either in subsequent consultations or in an extended course of therapy; for example, "I understand why you are so disturbed by the sexual confusion you've been expressing. After all, until you come to terms with these fundamental questions of identity, it's hard to find a consistent direction or devote your full energy to the challenge of making your way in this world."

It is important to acknowledge, at least to ourselves and sometimes to the patient, that our understanding is quite provisional and subject to emendation. As with all psychoanalytic propositions, the sooner we refine and specify our interpretation, the better: "Apparently, you've moved from one job to another in these past ten years, each time reaching an impasse when you encountered a boss who you could not work with" is an observation still in search of focus. "It would seem that each time you've had trouble and reached an impasse at work, you came to believe that the boss was taking credit for your efforts without giving you the acknowledgment that you deserved" is sharply focused, but without dynamic content. "In each of these impasses, when your boss seemed to be taking credit for your achievements, you adopted a stance of proud indifference, rather than lower yourself to petty squabbling over priority. Unfortunately, this indifference soon extended to each job itself, and you were eventually driven to leave in search of more interesting employment" is more encompassing and satisfying, as it lays out succinctly a repetitive psychodynamic situation. Each successive clarification raises new mysteries, the solutions of which have clear implications for the patient's emotional and economic well-being.

TOWARD ANALYSIS

When all goes well in the initial sessions, we succeed in making patients feel relatively comfortable, giving form and definition to some significant problem areas in their living, and eliciting provisional belief that therapy might offer a beneficial way to ameliorate these problems. Having invited the patient to talk spontaneously, we have earned some time. Where do we go from

here? We bear in mind that any agreement to begin therapy
holds open a window of opportunity that can spring shut in a
flash. The configuration of tension in the patient's immediate
circumstance—an inherently unstable wedge—cannot be counted
on to remain in place. A precipitous shift, brought on by some
decisive action of the patient or an intimate other, can swiftly
reassert a temporarily destabilized neurotic equilibrium. For
the most part, patients' initial agendas are essentially visceral—
to get relief from the anxiety or depression that impelled them to
seek out help. The analyst's underlying agenda, by contrast, is
ambitious and far reaching—to initiate an open-ended exploration of patients' inner life and experience in order to promote the
dynamic changes necessary to shift their neurotic equilibrium.
These goals are only theoretically compatible at the outset. It
requires considerable technical dexterity to negotiate this basic
discordance skillfully.

When should we introduce the idea of analysis, given the
tenuousness of the entire situation? Some psychoanalysts argue
for a forthright approach—an up-front declaration that psychoanalysis is *the* treatment of choice, along with a proposal to
begin as soon as it is logistically possible. While this may be fine
with patients who come specifically seeking psychoanalytic
therapy (often persons with a connection to the profession
already), more often than not a willingness to consider psychoanalysis as an option cannot be taken for granted in an initial
consultation, and thus the recommendation may backfire. In
any case, its effectiveness resides in the personal influence of an
authority who overrides whatever misgivings the patient may
bring to the consultation. Such quasi-hypnotic persuasiveness is
linked unconsciously to latent erotic and narcissistic sources. We
believe that the long-term interests of the treatment are better
served when there is an initial opportunity to develop a therapeutic partnership through incremental encounters with the
uncommon dimensions of psychoanalytic relatedness. This allows for a careful trial of analytic procedures and time for
discordant internal voices to enter the field of debate over

whether to venture upon an analysis. Fantastical fears and expectations will not be disarmed or shouted down. Sometimes they can be balanced by competing voices of reason, hope, and emerging trust.

Before psychoanalysis can evolve into a mutual commitment, a path, long with peril, lies ahead. What ground will be traversed, what obstacles encountered, how long it will take, whether or not a particular patient–analyst dyad will ever get to analysis, are all prospects that are difficult to foretell. The single most reliable piece of advice that experience can offer—be prepared to be surprised—is more cautionary than helpful. At best, like the ambiguous sign "Dangerous road" it alerts the analyst to remain ever watchful and take nothing for granted.

The latent discordance between the analyst's and the patient's expectation is at the crux of many of the coming struggles and crises. An emblematic exchange typically occurs in the first moments of an early session. The patient comes in, sits down, and looks expectantly at the analyst. If no apparent response is forthcoming, the patient presses the unspoken question into words: "What should I talk about?" We have little choice but to answer as our silence in this context would be coercive. Sometimes we choose to evade tackling the implicit issue head on, by proffering a harmless structure: "I'd like to know as much about your history and life as you can tell me." Alternatively, "We talked about Joyce last time, perhaps you could tell me more about John and Mary!" Though this temporizing stratagem may succeed, our preference, again, is to encourage the patient to begin with "Whatever is on your mind." A rebuttal, naturally enough, may be the first thing that comes to mind: "Isn't it better if you ask me relevant questions?" It is opportune to meet such a challenge with a more extensive explanation of our directive: "In my experience, if you can bring yourself to speak freely and spontaneously, we will quickly discover what your most urgent concerns are. If I ask the questions, we won't learn what you need to tell us." With this paradoxical instruction we offer explicit direction without determining the content of the session.

In varied forms, this directive may be used many times in the course of an analysis, whenever a patient is lost, frustrated, or pressuring the analyst for guidance.

There are a small number of patients who balk completely at this invitation to assume responsibility for the content of the session. Their adamant refusal may be rooted in quite profound concerns, such as terror of psychotic disorganization, morbid fear of abandonment, extreme vulnerability to narcissistic mortification, compulsive oppositionalism, or despondent hopelessness. Sometimes an inability to grasp the basic premises of analytic therapy may be apparent in a concrete cast of mind or an encompassing fear of all manifestations of fantasy and imagination. Direct inquiry, "You seem to be having some difficulty accepting my suggestion that you express yourself freely," initiates a conversation that can pinpoint the specific obstacle. Perhaps we would do better to move treatment in a more supportive, structured direction, at least temporarily. Though we would not welcome a radical revision of our horizons so early on, it is preferable to proceeding stubbornly upon a course doomed to mutual disappointment.

One basic concern in these early interactions is to assess the patient's capacity to use psychodynamic treatment as a means of changing his or her life. We do not take a formal inventory of psychological strengths and weaknesses, or rely primarily on psychiatric diagnosis; in recent years, clinicians have successfully extended the resources of psychoanalytic therapy to a wide range of psychopathology. We are less concerned with diagnosis than with motivation. (However, signs of severe psychopathology—major psychoses and schizophrenias, very severe paranoid character disorders, and psychopathy—would raise questions as to the wisdom of treating such a patient psychodynamically.) Our fundamental criteria have to do with the way the patient adapts to the various dimensions of analytic relatedness and structure. These early sessions are, in effect, a test run. We monitor the patient's associations to glean an appreciation of how we are being experienced. Is our analytic presence being integrated as an intrusive threat, a comforting refuge, or a seductive enticement?

The analytic rigors of extensive self-expression, self-reflection, and emotional self-regulation within an ambiguously structured interpersonal relationship are encountered for the first time. If the patient appears emotionally overtaxed—erupting in despair, anxiety, rage, or fear—can we at least explore the triggers of this reactivity in the moment? Ambiguous and incoherent responses are not promising. They suggest a compromised ability to reflect meaningfully upon subjective experience under stress. If the patient suddenly flares up unaccountably at something we have said, we would want to be able to explore how our words were construed and why this person responded with such intensity. "I don't know, you just made me so mad!" is quite vague. "People don't care!" is more informative. "I suddenly felt that you were one more person who just doesn't care about my suffering! You just sat there taking notes while I was spilling my guts" is most promising of all, as it reflects a differentiated awareness of both internal reality and interpersonal context. Through such passages of engagement, both patient and analyst begin to take fuller measure of the collaborator and the collaboration they are embarking upon.

SPEAKING TO A PERSON

From an interpretive standpoint, early sessions typically offer an abundance of possibilities. Without special effort, we usually are in a position to draw a sketch of recurrent aversive themes, problematic issues of character, areas of anxiety and depression, recurrent symptoms, inhibitions in functioning, family dynamics, and so on. Though there is satisfaction in the explanatory breath of our initial formulations, we realize that the closer one comes to the intertwined core of neurotic structure, the more painstaking, problematic, and convoluted every overture toward understanding will become. We should not accord very much importance to these early hypotheses; it is not where the action

is. However neatly our ideas stack up or are eagerly welcomed
by a patient starved for answers, they are merely initial bear-
ings, to be revised, elaborated, turned, and twisted many times
before the analysis has reached a satisfactory conclusion.

It is especially important to reserve judgment regarding the
patient's representations of important persons (Schafer 1983)—
the parents, spouses, siblings, friends, lovers, or former therapists who populate the unfolding story. Though we are naturally
eager for some fixed coordinates in order to organize the mass of
material rushing at us, the patient and the process are better
served when we resist developing defined characterizations of
these important persons. We must hear much and know much
more before we allow vivid images of the protagonists to crystallize in our mind's eye. Indeed, over the course of an analysis,
these images should never fully come together in a definitive
portrait. This would have an inhibitory effect on the engine of
analytic discovery, fueled by both parties' willingness to entertain perpetual revisions of the patient's personal history. Patients' continued fixation on a precise and undifferentiated view
of significant persons in their life story year after year without
commensurate advances in understanding is one sure indication
that they have succeeded in curtailing the scope of analytic
inquiry. It is cause for concerned attention, a clear sign that in
the struggle between the wish to get help and the fear of change,
the latter is triumphing.

We can expect, over the course of treatment, that one-sided
portrayals, either idealized or demonized, will be toned down as
the emotional exigencies that color these visions are softened.
Nevertheless, in the final analysis, we only establish insight
into circumscribed dimensions of these persons' psychological
organization—particular character dispositions (e.g., impulsiv-
ity, shame or guilt proneness, emotional availability, etc.) or
specific unconscious fantasies that intersect problematically
with our patient's psychological organization and development.
Definitive versions of the father, the mother, and the mate
remain elusive; we must content ourselves with portraits that

have areas of light and shadow within a slightly unfocused gestalt.

Out of these concerns, we pointedly qualify early interventions by indicating that our view of the people being presented with such passionate conviction is derivative of the patient's vision. "The picture you have painted of your mother suggests that she played a very vigorous role in keeping you from moving out into the world" is cautiously phrased to place some distance between the patient's characterizations and our conclusions. Some patients may hear this qualification as a lack of full support for their version of the truth and will press us to attest to the fidelity of their view. We do better to explore the patient's need or demand for validation than to remove the qualifiers from our assessments, for we have every reason to anticipate that many assumptions that have been jointly contemplated will be revised radically as new information and chapters of the story are subsequently elaborated.

In speaking to patients, we always take care to address our interventions to a person who just happens to be a patient. Language is the primary medium of psychoanalytic exchange. Though visual, behavioral, acoustic, and even olfactory modalities may make significant contributions, we intentionally employ words to serve many of our purposes: to teach, to soothe, to point, to touch, to hold. We want our words and ideas to be as fresh and memorable as possible. Powerful insights are often drawn in robust language rich with figurative resonance. We speak to particular circumstance, avoiding generalizations that might categorize or depersonalize experience. Giving oneself the challenge of formulating every intervention as if it is the very first time that it has every occurred to us to say such a thing—as if we are creating psychoanalytic technique for this particular patient in this very moment—enlivens psychoanalytic discourse. We can even vary the formulaic, if only slightly. "What comes to mind?" becomes "Are there other thoughts/images/ notions/things in that area/place/neighborhood of your mind/ thoughts/feelings/awareness?" Our expressive vocabulary will also vary with the individual we are speaking to. We might fall into an earthy vernacular with one patient, but maintain a somewhat formal grammar with another, empathically matching the rhythm and form of his or her thought. Intentionally echoing the latent metaphors of the patient's narrative reverberates through hidden wellsprings of unconscious fantasy and emotion. When patients speak of being "flooded" with sadness, we can evocatively refer to their fear of "drowning" in tears, of underlying "currents" of emotion, or "storms" of sorrow.

We employ pronouns carefully and self-consciously. "We" or "our" connotes connection and partnership, as in, "We need to understand more about this," or "We will work together to uncover the obstacles that get in your way." By employing the analytic "we," one suggests a common endeavor shared by a companion through the analytic journey. "We" says, by implication, "you are not alone in what you may experience as a new and frightening endeavor." "I" or "my," on the other hand, connotes separation and possible discord. It draws attention to the analyst's separate, perhaps unknowable subjectivity, as a constant dimension of the analytic surround. Patients will be revealing their self to an alien subjectivity, which however compassionate can never quite share the same point of view. Beginning an observation with "I" or "me" ("It seems to me . . .") prepares patients for a confrontation from outside their immediate perspective.

Attention to how we frame interventions can highlight the patient's active part in structuring the repetitive dilemmas and dramas that define a life, as well as suggesting resources of power or control that may be ignored. A patient who "finds" herself getting involved with unavailable men may respond to the analyst's reframing the observation, "You involve yourself with unavailable men," a locution that pointedly avoids mimicking her passive voice. From the beginning of therapy our interventions should reflect our understanding that persons are active creators of their destiny, even though they may prefer to look at themselves as its passive victim.

It is important to remember that process and person become intertwined and indistinguishable in the patient's unconscious experience. This understanding guides us to words that capture the unique form of the patient's dread in the analytic situation. By personifying the process in our language, we explicitly connect fearful fantasies of anticipation with our selves. Rather than "You are afraid of losing control of your thoughts and feelings, if you don't censor your expression carefully," we might say, "You fear an uncontrolled intimacy in which I'd be inundated and repelled by your emotional mess." "You are worried you could come to depend on analysis so much that you would be unable to make any decision without first coming to your session" is less compelling than "You are afraid that if you aren't very careful, I could take over your life, and rob you of your hard-won independence." "You are afraid of being judged here" is more remote than "You are afraid you will find me a demanding and never-satisfied critic, like your mother, auditing your every thought and deed." In effect, to the extent that we can, we do well to emphasize the person in the process and the process as person.

NEGOTIATING AN ANALYTIC STRUCTURE

The analyst's overriding goal in this early going is to negotiate a procedure of work in a context of safety that makes analysis possible. The patient, on the other hand, is, more often than not, eagerly pressing for confining structure, thematic closure, and symptomatic relief. It might be said that our fundamental challenge is to keep our patients' hope alive while assiduously exposing the wishful nature of their current solutions. Holding firm to a process of open-ended exploration and thematic development calls for adroit maneuvering and technical dexterity. We must juggle the twin requirements of accommodating the patient's immediate need for comfort and safety in the relationship, with our determination to refrain from any actions that might compromise an enduring structure that can contain analytic processes as yet unforeseen. We are mindful that early actions are defining acts, establishing boundaries, forms, and precedents that have an enduring life of their own. Patients, in their anxiety, may characterize elements of this initial analytic stance as rigid or uncompromising, rather than as devoted and responsible. Just how careful must we be and how strictly must we interpret the analytic frame and role? To what extent will giving advice, answering personal questions, or narrowing our open-ended focus compromise our fundamental structure? What is negotiable and what is not?

Such questions, though crucial, are quite difficult to consider meaningfully outside a specific clinical context without sounding doctrinaire. A need for immediate help with a circumscribed crisis—a disturbance of potency, a work inhibition, a marital dilemma—may be pressed with unwavering persistence. Attempts to broaden the focus of inquiry are anxiously or willfully ignored, implicitly challenging our view that the most helpful way to proceed is through careful consideration of the entire context of a person's action, thought, and feeling. Without this broad understanding we feel drawn into adopting a comforting or omniscient authoritative role, for we have little else to offer in the face of the patient's obvious distress. This pull can sometimes be countered by appealing to the patient's autonomy. "Your understanding is what's important here. Once we are clearer about what causes you to feel so overwhelmed and distressed, I'm confident that solutions to this dilemma will be more apparent to you!" It may also help defuse some tension if the patient understands that professional integrity motivates the analyst's choices: "I truly understand your impatience to get a solution to this problem, and if I thought I had any serious answers to give you, I wouldn't hesitate to offer them."

The analyst must be clear that holding ground in the face of such pressing desperation is not an inhumane exercise in rigidity. What is at stake? Couldn't we be helpful in one capacity, and later, when the crisis abates, withdraw that kind of assistance while moving back into a position of neutrality? If we are drawn into adopting a role as "the one who knows what's wrong and how to fix what's wrong" in the patient's life, do we risk foreclosing the potentiality of a more profound reliance upon the analyst and the analytic process? How far must we go in attempting to safeguard the patient's potential autonomy by speaking for the fully mature though latent possibilities that we foresee (Loewald 1960). Martin's case may be useful in considering some of these issues:

Martin was skillful in drawing out his analyst, encouraging him to express authoritative opinions about immediate dilemmas in various personal relationships and stimulating him to engage in psychological speculation about matters that were well beyond the understanding possible at such an early point in treatment. "Do you think it's my anger that makes me so depressed?" "Wouldn't you suppose that my insecurity must have something to do with my mother's miserable relationship with my father?" "Do you think if I marry Jane this feeling of mistrust will go away?" Attempts to phrase interventions in a manner that avoided a definitive mode were often rearranged in keeping with Martin's wish for a directive and opinionated therapist. If the analyst responded in a hedging manner, cautiously generalizing that, "Having a marriage contract doesn't necessarily resolve an insecurity," his patient would report back in a subsequent session that he was grateful that his analyst had "warned" him against going forward with his marriage. In a similar manner, he could extract advice from almost any intervention the analyst made, often accompanied by heartfelt expressions of gratitude for the most helpful way the situation had been resolved. Once identified, this pattern was described to him: "I'm aware that you often take my statements as much more certain and definitive judgments than I intend them to be!" Martin was genuinely bewildered that his therapist would "make an issue" of it. "How else can I get better if I don't use what I learn in therapy!" he retorted with an air of indisputable conviction.

In quite another context, this same patient railed vocifer-
ously against his autocratic father, a man of considerable
worldly accomplishment. His father always seemed to know
how to handle things and apparently never tired of instructing
his son in the ways of the world. "The dogmatic tyrant," "the
God-damned know-it-all-son-of-a-bitch," he sputtered rage-
fully, trying to exorcise his exasperation and shame at always
being made to feel so awkward and inept. When a contrast
was drawn between his bitter resentment at the father's
assuming a role of the one who knows better and his apparent
gratitude toward what he took to be his analyst's unfailing
wisdom and helpful judgment, he blithely acknowledged the
contradiction while seeming to dismiss its significance: "You
are more tactful than he is!" he replied, slyly. Martin was
living out his determination to forge a treatment on the very
lines of his difficulty, to find in his analyst a benign version of
this pernicious parental influence to guide him through life.

Martin's attempt to negotiate a psychotherapeutic contract
based on an idiosyncratic version of help is a complex matter
that should be considered carefully. He invites—almost demands—a therapy conceived along reparative lines; he consciously wants an analyst who will provide a benign antidote to
the pernicious paternal guidance he absorbs from his father. We
recognize, however, that he wants to feel better about himself
without surrendering his dependence on parental guidance.
This vision of cure doesn't disrupt the fundamental framework
of neurotic equilibrium. There are a number of fairly typical
therapeutic scenarios that we discover with regularity, though
careful and detailed exploration always reveals very personalized elements. Some emphasize exposure and punishment as the
vehicle of cure; others, a cataclysmic emotional breakthrough or
breakdown. Still others imagine a form of reparation for injuries
suffered. A variation of this idea involves exchanging roles of
victim and abuser with the analyst. "Now it's my turn to be the
abuser!"

Martin's assumption that the problem of his shameful awkwardness can simply be understood as a straightforward reaction to this paternal impingement, and its corollary, that his insecurity could be lastingly ameliorated by better caretaking as an adult, strikes us as naive, though not entirely misguided. Martin's situation confronts us with a paradox that is at the core of psychoanalytic technique: Actualizing one's wishes in a real relationship with the analyst often suppresses the underlying conflictual and fantastical dimensions of that wishfulness, ultimately truncating the depth and range of transferential experience. Gratification of this kind relieves diverse tensions and masks the deeper meaning of our wishfulness by casting it in a fixed and manifestly limited mold.

There are, to be sure, many legitimate gratifications in analytic therapy. The virtues of holding firm should not be overstated nor confused with frustration as an end in itself. When contemporary analysts have concern about being too gratifying, they are generally expressing reservations about engaging in forms of relatedness that sustain regressive adaptations and self-experience. In this instance, to accede to Martin's agenda would risk confining him—at least with regard to the structure of the analytic relationship—to a childlike state of dependence on an omniscient authority. It may well be too dangerous to reveal the true depths of his dependent longing—or the depths of his equally profound mistrust—to an analyst who acquiesces to this omniscient invitation. Eventually, a suppressed urge for emancipation and escape would erupt in rebellious insurrection against an analytic process that was constructed upon such a confining premise.

In holding firm to an analytic stance, we hope that patients will eventually recognize that the problem(s) that forced them to treatment are manifestations of firmly embedded, conflictual tendencies, widely implicated in many areas of compromised living. Until such time, we do well in this initial phase to allow for some play in the analytic stance we adopt. In general, a piece of advice, encouraging support, or a personal judgment are not, like Krazy Glue, going to bind a patient to a passive and helpless position. Insofar as we demonstrate a willingness to seriously consider the patient's beliefs and requests, he or she will be more amenable to alternative solutions. "I believe that you have a strong conviction about what you need most from therapy. You want to find in me a guiding figure who doesn't make you feel inferior." In clearly articulating Martin's desire, we enhance our stature as a benevolent guide, even while guiding him toward analytic goals. Yet we must be careful to offer this guidance primarily in the service of helping him cope with the difficult task of adapting to the psychoanalytic situation, rather than to his life outside. The analyst both meets his expectations and frustrates them, at least in the forms in which he conceives it.

Meanwhile we keep a keen eye on the ambivalence of his unfolding story, searching out the inevitable contradictions and complexities that are a hallmark of unconscious conflict; the time when his father failed to know it all and disappointed him; the flash of contempt he was "surprised" to notice when the analyst didn't appear knowledgeable about some area of learning with which he was familiar. These represent fissures in the consistent face that he attempts to put on things, points of leverage that can be probed to dislodge unconscious ambivalence: "Apparently you feel an urge to knock me off my throne when I fail to be as all knowing as the know-it-all father you despise." We strive to highlight enigmas and raise perplexing questions in order to enlist our patient's curiosity. It is essential, in regard to his readiness to accept a proposal for analysis, that the patient comes to see that the solutions and answers he keeps grasping at don't avail because he is continually tripping over his own incompatible inclinations.

PRACTICAL MATTERS

We can expect to encounter another set of challenges during the opening phase, which, however mundane, are nonetheless thorny. Problems of time and money often emerge in ways that threaten the viability of the entire analytic enterprise. In this context, Freud's (1900) admonition to view anything that threatens to interfere with the continuity of the treatment from the point of view of resistance is especially pertinent. The problems may be real enough, yet they assume an immediate urgency that crowds out all other considerations.

There are no foolproof ways of dealing with these matters; each situation must be mastered individually. Nevertheless, a few considerations and strategies are worth keeping in mind. The business arrangements and accommodations that are part of an initial analytic contract should not be dealt with interpretively until a relatively stable commitment to a psychoanalytic process has been established. Even then, the question of fee increases (or reductions) are subject to special constraints that do not apply to other aspects of a psychoanalytic relationship. The point is, one cannot both analyze the patient's intentions and negotiate with self-interest at the same time. We always have a personal financial stake in the outcome of such negotiations. This interest is a necessary and legitimate part of the psychoanalytic situation, yet it is probably the only time when the patient's and the analyst's interests are so directly at cross-purposes. Patients understand this, and deeply resent what they may assume to be abusive conditions, even though the analyst is convinced he or she is trying to be "fair."

We are entitled to inquire carefully into the circumstance of requests for fee reductions or special consideration with regard to payment schedules, without feeling an obligation to accede to them. On the other hand, to some degree—at least in the beginning of treatment—we are constrained to accept patients' views of their financial circumstance, even when we have some reason to question the accuracy of these presentations. As psychoanalysts, we know that money is one of the most highly prized and irrationally charged objects in every person's inner world, regardless of one's conscious attitudes about it. It is of utmost importance, therefore, that our decisions legitimately reflect our genuine interest—intellectual and moral—as well as our financial interests. If we are uncomfortable with a proposed arrangement, we should decline it both on personal and therapeutic grounds. It is preferable to be straightforward without superfluous explanation. "Yes, I would be willing to agree to this fee/this delayed payment schedule/exception to my usual policy." One may also add an additional proviso: "Naturally, if your situation changes, we'll have to reconsider things." Alternatively, "I'm not comfortable with this change you are suggesting with regard to my usual policy. I believe this accommodation would not work out well in the long run." Every patient will have powerful feelings and numerous fantasies about one's response to such requests. Tact, however, may prevent us from pursuing them in the context of an ongoing negotiation. They will undoubtedly surface later in the analysis.

The question may be asked, When does a particular accommodation compromise the viability of treatment so severely as to be nonnegotiable? Frequently arising around issues of time and frequency, the salient criterion must be whether the analyst and patient can do meaningful work within the structure being considered. The traditional model of multiple weekly sessions of approximately one hour specifies the conditions that the majority of analysts have found ideally compatible with the ambitious goals and rigorous procedures of this kind of work. Departures from this model make demands upon the analyst that begin to discourage the complexity of our thinking and undermine the quality of our attention. One loses interest in things one cannot deal with adequately. Most importantly, infrequent, irregular, or foreshortened therapeutic contacts interfere with the depth of emotional investment that the patient, if not the analyst, is willing to make in the analytic process. Transference will exist certainly enough, as it is a given of all sustained human relationships, but it is transference as it comes to be expressed within the context of an analytic process that constitutes the unique therapeutic opportunity of psychoanalysis.

In the absence of compelling external restraints, therefore, we do well to regard every proposal to limit the scope of or commitment to the analysis as a manifestation of an unmastered sense of personal danger. However patients represent this (their reluctance may or may not be accompanied by conscious anxiety), we know to look for this danger in the process of the analysis and the person of the analyst. It is the patient's largely unconscious anticipations of process and person that always present us with the most perplexing obstacles to establishing a profound psychoanalytic engagement. When we reflect that the analytic process embodies a call to radical expressive freedom, while the person of the analyst within that process awakens all the (suppressed) potentiality of human relatedness, we realize that the magnitude of anticipated threat will always be formidable. It is, as we have emphasized repeatedly, wise to accord these issues interpretive precedence in this phase of treatment.

SUMMARY

In this chapter we have reviewed the opening phase of psychoanalytic treatment from the perspective of those technical principles and clinical attitudes that encourage prospective patients—typically ambivalent and at emotional risk—to give themselves over to an increasingly introspective process that involves a significant commitment of energy, time, and money. In this process, we have emphasized a respect for the patient's autonomy, balanced by an appreciation of psychodynamic forces outside conscious awareness that predispose a person to flee or circumscribe the scope of that inquiry. Given a limited "window of opportunity," the analyst must make every effort to alleviate underlying anxiety and to free suppressed hope, while demonstrating those working attitudes that embody a psychodynamic vision of the therapeutic enterprise. Attitudes of open-ended inquiry and benevolent understanding, introduced from the first contact as essential structuring elements of psychoanalytic relatedness, stimulate spontaneity of expression. They also elicit resistant counterreactions, as patients, attending to thoughts and feelings long ignored, awaken to the magnitude of their dilemma. Issues of mutual struggle and adaptive accommodation were underscored in this connection, as the patient and analyst work out a structure of relatedness that can grow into a psychoanalytic situation. It was suggested that this framework of negotiation provides an opportunity for the most searching test of the possibilities and potentialities of a psychoanalytic engagement, giving each party a chance to change course if this seems indicated. An interpretive language that emphasizes the unconscious equivalence of person and process was also demonstrated and recommended as the most evocative voice for expressing dynamic conflict in the context of an unfolding therapeutic relationship. The analyst's skill in elucidating these hopes, fears, and risks brought to the relationship is recognized as a crucial factor determining the ultimate path upon which the participants will embark together.

2

Free Association and Analytic Neutrality: The Basic Structure of the Psychoanalytic Situation

This chapter defines and explores a contemporary understanding of the psychoanalytic situation with specific regard to its complex role in fostering and safeguarding an analyzable clinical process. In particular, we highlight the way the truly radical nature of free association and analytic neutrality create an extraordinary therapeutic interaction that is structured into the core of the analytic process.

The analytic situation is a shorthand way of referring to the structural elements that make possible an analyzable therapeutic process. Collectively, these elements form an integral whole whose purpose is to codify the optimal conditions that enable a patient to pursue awareness, self-expression, and personal integration, and for the analyst to analyze. There are both prescriptive and proscriptive dimensions that establish the essential boundaries of the analytic enterprise, conferring context and meaning upon the actions of each participant. It is seen, upon reflection, to be a carefully structured situation in which a spontaneously unstructured relationship can safely and meaningfully unfold. Honoring the boundaries of this structure serves to guarantee the safety of both participants by channeling and absorbing the powerful psychological forces released by the psychoanalytic process, thereby ensuring full development of the transference.

At its heart is an extraordinary interpersonal arrangement with few direct parallels in normal social life, an arrangement most easily described in terms of the reciprocal role requirements of each participant. We must bear in mind, however, that the analytic situation presents patient and analyst with distinct yet integrated tasks that can be isolated for heuristic purposes only. We believe that the juxtaposition of free-association and analytic neutrality are the fundamental structural pillars of the psychoanalytic situation, providing stability in the wake of the regressive and progressive currents of the psychoanalytic process. For this reason, although the psychoanalytic situation serves many important functions for patient and analyst, our discussion is focused on an elaboration of a contemporary understanding of the crucial dimensions of free association and analytic neutrality in structuring the analytic situation.

THE PATIENT'S ROLE

The patient's role is essentially organized around the prerequisites of expressive freedom. This entails an extensive expressive license that guarantees the opportunity—if not obligation—to speak spontaneously without respect for conventional ideas of tact, propriety, or thematic organization. Speaking freely, without self-censorship or undue evasion is a very difficult thing to do in the presence of another human being. As patients talk about their daily concerns and struggle to change, ideas arise that are considered too shameful, frightening, or silly to express openly. What particular patients find difficult will vary considerably, and in itself says a lot that is diagnostically significant. However, it is a safe generalization that the most difficult contents to verbalize will be those that directly concern patients' fears, wishes, fantasies, and feelings regarding the therapist they are speaking to. Dealing with the painful emotions and evasive actions that interfere with the direct expression of these conflictual contents is the source of the most difficult obstacles to achieving far-reaching analytic goals. Paradoxically, this very struggle also provides the most advantageous circumstances to observe, influence, and master the chronically inhibiting pressures that constrict the fullness of psychic life.

In effect, a ubiquitous dilemma organizes the various tensions of the analytic situation: expressing oneself without inhibition is dangerous in the presence of a person who is becoming the focus of one's most intimate longings and archaic fears. Therapeutic momentum rests on the continued efforts of both parties in the encounter to resolve this dilemma in the direction of more consistent, less constricted freedom on the patient's part.

Expressive freedom, like any freedom, is both a burden and an opportunity. Generally, the burdensome aspects will come to the fore first as patients attempt one way or another to circumvent or circumscribe the radical implications of this invitation. It is the *ideal* of expressive freedom that is embodied in the technical requirement of free association; it serves to organize the direction of one's strivings, even as one inevitably fails to fulfill all its requirements. Kris (1982) argues that the most fruitful analytic events occur when the patient approximates this ideal of spontaneity, and that the importance and centrality of free association to the development of an analytic process cannot be overemphasized. He focuses on free association as a point of departure for the formulation of interpretations and as a powerful source of data on the contribution of both participants. While other methods may be usefully employed to serve various therapeutic ends, free association is unparalleled in its ability to deepen analytic exploration.

The potency of free association derives primarily from its ability to gain access to the fantasies, fears, wishes, and powerful, affect-laden derivatives of the unconscious. Facilitated by the analyst's general restraint and personal comfort with primary process modes of communication, free association enables previously unconscious contents to emerge and take center stage. Because of this access, the processes engendered by free association are very different from those generated by a more interactive model of therapeutic engagement where the patient's attention is repeatedly captured by the therapist's responses.

Creating a situation that permits repressed imagery to emerge makes possible linkages to the body and bodily sensations that are often bypassed in approaches that give exclusive priority to the patient's subjective representation of relational experience (Gill 1995). Kris (1982) expands upon the importance of this dimension:

> It is fundamental that the associations belong to the patient. They are derivatively a part of himself, especially of his body, as they come to express feelings, needs, and desires, and as they represent his self-image, symbolically. The analyst must take care not to dispossess the patient of them. They reflect not only the patient's investment in his body but his detachment from it as well. Where the patient can be helped to possess his associations more, by understanding more of his own meaning, he regains lost connections with his body and between constituent elements of his mind. [pp. 4–5]

This process was exemplified by a patient who repeatedly scanned the analyst's demeanor for reassuring indications of approval in face-to-face therapy. When she initially lay on the couch and free-associated, a fantasy of the analyst coming over and stabbing her in the gut erupted with a clarity and bodily immediacy that talking about fears of being judged never had in the more interactive mode of treatment. More importantly, it alerted analyst and patient to a largely unconscious, fantastical dimension to her subjective experience of being excessively concerned with other people's approval. The bodily sensation of anxiety and anticipated pain proved, upon further analysis (i.e., free-associative exploration), to be more than a metaphorical embodiment or concretization of the immediate interpersonal reality; it was a crucial linkage with an intrusive fantasy system characterized by sadomasochistic relationships full of terror and excited anticipation.

When free association is employed in conjunction with the couch, patients invariably encounter psychic contents hidden from normal conscious functioning. Equally important, however, this in-depth process takes place in the presence of another person. The relational aspects of free association have only been fully appreciated over time, but their contribution is now understood to parallel in importance the exceptional access to the dynamic unconscious made possible by free association. Free association structures into the analytic process a unique configuration that allows the patient to have an introspective encounter with his or her deepest emotional stirrings in the context of an interaction with another person. This integration of an in-depth focus on one person's inner world in relationship with another person has proven to be the most effective means of exploring dynamically structured personal experience. As the patient reports what comes to mind, issues on the edge of consciousness that have been warded off because of their painful nature are brought to the attention of both patient and analyst. The exclusive attention to an intrapsychic foreground alternates with an extrapsychic perspective as the interpersonal transference paradigm moves in and out of analytic focus.

The shared experience that develops from this asymmetrical focus on the patient's process in the context of analytic neutrality is, according to Pine (1993), a powerful therapeutic factor that is inherent in the structure of the analytic situation itself. It establishes a relationship with the patient that simultaneously destabilizes conflicting forces in the patient's mind while progressively enabling the patient to expose more vulnerable areas of self-experience. Most importantly, these relational features, which Pine sees as mutative, universal, and essential, are built into the structure of the analytic situation itself, and require no special action from the analyst.

One essential aspect of this interaction as structured by free association involves the way it evokes an early mother–child intimacy characterized by uncontrolled exposure and unconditional acceptance. In asking the patient to communicate whatever comes to mind, we tender an implicit promise to respect and treat with care whatever mental contents or emotional experience may emerge. In this framework, the guilty and shameful aspects of self, those aspects that the patient needs to disown, suppress, or dissociate are—from the beginning—potentials of an inclusive intimacy fostered by the analytic situation. The analyst, by resisting the easy preconscious temptation to engage in a superficial mutuality of conscious confidences, safeguards a potential asymmetrical intimacy of profound knowledge that comes of knowing oneself and being known by another (Freedman 1985, Freud 1915a, Loewald 1960).

Just as the opportunities for expressive freedom set in motion a broad defensive struggle, this implicit tender of emotional acceptance will be ambivalently greeted by the patient. Stone's (1961) classic monograph on the psychoanalytic situation reminds us that the patient's relative physical and emotional deprivation in analysis, bridged only by verbal bonds of speech, inevitably links the analyst to the "mother of separation." This "intimate separation" (p. 86)—implicit in the analytic situation—evokes a regressive longing for a return to the bodily gratifications of the earliest mother–child connection. When this temptation is too perilous, the patient may be forced to renounce or devalue the real and legitimate gratifications of verbally mediated analytic relatedness altogether, sealing off the affectively charged dimensions of the transference neurosis.

Though free association as a method is designed to evoke the most vulnerable areas of self—the fantasies, wishes, fears, and conflicts that have been vigorously disowned—it is an ideal that can only be approximated. More or less significant obstacles to the spontaneous verbalization of associations inevitably emerge. These impediments, however, can be turned to advantage, for they provide an ever-relevant point of departure for analytic inquiry. The point of derailment of free association, when it can be identified, offers analyst and patient an opportunistic encounter with the very attitudes, tactics, and emotional blockages that constitute the fabric of defensive structure. In effect, the process of free association provides the analyst with a map of the patient's resistances as they are mobilized in the context of an evocative object relationship (see Chapter 4). To the extent that the analyst succeeds in neutralizing the archaic fears and aversive affects that fuel such defensive efforts, a destabilizing process will gain momentum that permits progressive forces of personal integration and development to gather strength (Arlow and Brenner 1990). Increasingly open to disavowed internal experience, surprising and unexpected memories, feelings, and connections begin to be tolerated.

Employing free association thus helps patient and analyst to negotiate resistance, provides access to the dynamic unconscious, and structures an asymmetrical intimacy into the analytic situation that enables the patient to progressively trust exposing deeper levels of experience. But it accomplishes even more.

Asking patients to say what comes to mind without intentional censorship organizes the treatment situation around an ongoing confrontation with compulsive self-judging and self-punishing tendencies. Working with these punitive impulses is never easy, tied as they are to powerful, primitive affects and identifications that can erupt in unmanageable negative transferences or chronically simmer in covertly embedded negative therapeutic reactions. Free association, however, enables the patient to work on the intrapsychic dimension of these punitive trends through the continual action of struggling to say what comes to mind without censorship. Every time the patient is successful in bringing out an association that might have been inhibited, he or she is quietly but consistently working through a small piece of self-inhibitory functioning.

Part of the effectiveness of working in this manner involves the enhanced opportunity to become an observer as well as a participant in one's own internal process. The ability to achieve temporary distance from intense impulses and feelings is a crucial ego function pivotal in emotional maturation (Hartmann 1951, Nunberg 1931). As patients free-associate in the presence of an external auditor, they are forced to observe their own thoughts and feelings as they are being shaped into communicative language. This is very different from solitary introspection, where the stream of consciousness can flow uninterruptedly without having to be interpreted and made intelligible to another in words. It is also different from a more interactive mode of relating where the opportunity to observe one's own process is diminished. Through this effort to observe thoughts and feelings, patients gain an enhanced sense of personal agency, especially in regard to private areas of experience that might never be the subject of discourse in ordinary relationships. This sense of personal agency, which opposes passive trends, contributes gradually to a growing capacity to comprehend and reflect upon the impact of one's unique psychic organization.

It should be obvious that even in analytic therapy expressive license is not an unconditional privilege. Freedom of physical action is necessarily circumscribed, and even in the realm of speech, there may be times when a patient engages in verbal acts that violate the safety or dignity of the therapist. In the therapeutic situation self-expression is rarely an end in itself. Rather, it provides a text for a process of inquiry and interpretation that conventional manners would forbid. It is hard to overemphasize the analyst's dependence on the patient's uncensored spontaneity as a means of generating and validating relevant psychodynamic understanding. As an interpretive tool, free association ranks with intuitive empathy as a reliable source of information, outweighing even the resources of theoretical knowledge.

It must be borne in mind that expressive license is counterbalanced by a reciprocal loss of privacy that often proves onerous. The right to privacy, a core value in our society, is imbued with connotations of independence, autonomy, personal power, and self-control that patients are often reluctant to surrender. Yet one of the fundamental elements of the analytic situation is the implicit expectation that ordinary considerations of privacy will be waived and that the analyst will be granted privileged access to the patient's inner life as an auditor of private experience. Naturally, there are thresholds of trust to be crossed and tests of trustworthiness to be passed in this regard, which may be renewed at any phase of treatment when new psychodynamic territory is entered upon. There are many patients whose capacity to trust has been so compromised in early life that the analytic situation as commonly constructed proves altogether untenable. In these cases, personal autonomy and power are such tenuous achievements that we must fundamentally adapt the treatment situation around the vulnerability of the patient.

THE ANALYST'S ROLE

In an essential respect, the analyst's role in the psychoanalytic situation is complementary to the patient's role, in that it is organized around the prerequisites of listening and understanding in depth. These priorities, however, impose complex obligations upon the therapist, who must simultaneously absorb and integrate a host of competing pulls, tensions, and purposes in order to fulfill this demanding task. Analytic listening is a highly sophisticated and disciplined skill that prepares us to be attuned to and to monitor multiple levels of discourse simultaneously (what the patient intends to be saying, what the patient might be saying if less inhibited, what the patient is unconsciously saying, etc.) without ignoring our own emotionally charged stream of consciousness.

The advantages of free association that we highlighted from the patient's perspective have corresponding and related benefits to the analyst. Most significantly, our ability to listen to the patient is greatly amplified when the analytic situation is organized around free association. Furnishing the analyst with an instrument for micro-monitoring the patient's sequential experience enhances the analyst's proficiency in reading dynamic constellations more effectively (Gray 1973). In addition, it supplies the analyst with information about his or her own proclivities (personal and theoretical) that codetermine the analytic interaction (Kris 1982). Free association also provides us with a check on erroneous hypotheses and guards against inappropriate intrusion of our countertransference into the patient's process.

Staying with our patients as they free-associate is a complex task that employs the entire repertoire of an analyst's experience. We must draw upon our personal and professional development, our capacity for empathic identification, our visual and dramatic imagination, our emotional experience of the moment, our theories, as well as our sense of the current dynamics of the therapeutic interaction. Central to this capacity to stay with the patient in depth, however, is an ability to pick out the latent content of the patient's communication. Whether the patient is speaking manifestly about feelings, memories, relationships, or ideas, the analytically skilled listener attempts to discern the underlying thematic organization that motivates the sequence of associations. Getting to this latent level is fundamental in that it reflects the impact of unconscious determinants (i.e., conflicts, fantasies, or warded-off affects and impulses) on the patterns of relatedness and motivation that structure a person's subjectivity. Often the sequence of associations is revealing simply in its content, as when the associations are characterized by a central theme and can render the analyst's interpretations immediate, specific, and therefore real to the patient (Chused 1991). But the process of free association is particularly suited to expose this dimension because connections between associations not immediately observable to the patient can be apprehended by the analyst. Chused points out that in making the unconscious conscious, it is the determinants of the words and their sequence that we attend to. Thus, by literally reading between the lines, focusing on the implicit linkages between associations, the analyst gains access to a wealth and depth of meaning that the patient does not knowingly reveal.

The ability to stay with patients and recognize their issues clearly is a task subject to the development of false leads, especially when it is understood that behavior is multiply determined (Waelder 1936). While patient and analyst are both engaged in understanding the dynamics revealed in the analytic process, the nature of defense and the interaction between the analytic participants ensure that not all hypotheses will be of significant value to the patient at a particular time. Inevitably, some hypotheses, and some dynamics will be more salient than others in determining experience and directing decision making. A check on the interpretive process is vital to ensure that hypotheses that are not relevant can be set aside while those that illuminate the patient's psychic experience are emphasized. The ability to ascertain what, for the patient, is salient at the moment is enhanced by free association. Its data provide the analyst with just such a check, because as the associations are observed the analyst is afforded the opportunity to perceive not only the patient's conscious experience of an interpretation, but his or her unconscious response as well. Free association allows the analyst to stay on the patient's track.

Finally, in an era when analysts are increasingly encouraged to conceptualize the entire analytic process in here-and-now interactive terms (Gill 1982, Hoffmann 1991, Renik 1993), the restraint built into the free-associative process provides a judicious delay that can prevent impulsive, inappropriate countertransferential engagement of the patient by the analyst. From the perspective of free association, the meaning for the patient of any single psychic event, however moving or poignant, must be established in an associative context that can only be substantially revealed through the continued and uninterrupted introspective elaboration by the patient. The relevant context of meaning is often the immediate interactive elements of the analyst–patient relationship; but this cannot be assumed in the absence of specific associative confirmation.

NEUTRALITY

Neutrality is the technical name for a very complex attitude toward the patient's inner life and experience that imbues the analyst's listening in the analytic situation with a unique qualitative dimension. It permeates the surround into which the free associations of the patient expand expectantly, influencing how, when, and why an analyst responds. In this interactive sense it is better thought of as defining a specific quality of responsive presence, rather than as the "blank screen" or mirroring function some have described. Neutrality stands in counterpoint to free association, providing a means of framing and containing the intense processes generated by analytic work. Neutrality defines the boundaries, the edges of the interaction between patient and analyst where meaning takes shape.

The neutral analyst listens attentively, dispensing with a superficial social responsiveness that obligingly calls forth soothing indications of moral reassurance and sympathy. Instead, we hold ourselves out as a more ambiguous presence, emotionally evocative and receptive, though not fully personal or distinctive. This unique stance has been subject to considerable misunderstanding and is often caricatured—in the professional as well as the popular literature—as an inhumanly blank and emotionally wooden posture. Neutrality does not imply the eradication of the analyst as person from the interaction; to think in this way is to confuse the colloquial meaning of the word with the technical concept. It is a given that the analyst's personality contributes to the construction of the analytic situation, even as the stance of neutrality is aspired to. Part of the confusion lies in the sheer difficulty of conveying with more than broad strokes an attitude that embodies so many nuances of emotional and intellectual subtlety.

Fundamentally, the attitude of neutrality embodies an acknowledgment of what is true in the patient's psychic experience. A patient's feelings, fantasies, beliefs, wishes, and intentions are what they are, and the neutrality of the analytic listener

makes no demand that they be otherwise. We recognize in this
an ideal that elevates the love of truth above personal comfort.
It informs the analyst's functioning, in the same sense that
free association does for the patient, as something to be striven
for though not always fully attained. Some of the confusion
about neutrality in the contemporary psychoanalytic literature
arises from the failure to recognize that the concept embraces
several different dimensions. Traditionally, analytic neutrality
has referred to the analyst's attempt to remain equidistant from
the patient's conflicts without taking a moral position influenced
by personal values (Pine 1993). Neutrality relative to the patient's conflicts is rooted in Anna Freud's (1936) suggestion that
the analyst remain equidistant from id, ego, and superego,
although Fenichel's (1941) advice that there is value in starting
with what is closest to the ego is generally acknowledged today.
Inherent in this dimension of neutrality is an awareness that a
patient's conscious feelings, fantasies, wishes, and intentions,
however poignantly expressed or authentically experienced, are
seldom simply one way or another. In effect, that which is
currently manifest is not the whole story, and to fully acknowledge what is, means to leave room for what is yet to surface.
Perforce, the neutral listener is required to be a patient listener,
only reluctantly concluding that he or she has heard as much
as is likely to be learned about any particular topic at any
particular time. This caution, which is grounded in a hard-won
conviction of the ubiquitous influence of unconscious conflict on
conscious experience, mandates an instinctive reserve in the
analyst's responsiveness that serves as a counterweight to the
patient's natural eagerness for closure and certainty.

Early in an analysis, before they have come to appreciate the
reality of unconscious motivation, patients cannot possibly appreciate the virtue of this reserve. More often, it is experienced
as a failure of support or sympathy, rather than as a mature
respect for the patient's complex individuality. Initially, therefore, the analyst must walk a very narrow line between an
attitude that conveys acknowledgment of the subjective reality

of the patient's experience and one that may validate a tendentious version of reality. Our embrace of a neutral attitude protects us from prematurely committing the authority of the analysis to a one-sided and therefore limiting version of any aspect of the patient's current life or history, safeguarding the long-term potential for a more profound integration to emerge as defenses are progressively worked through. Of course, the whole story or the true story never does get told in its entirety; indeed, it is in our contemporary terms *a fiction*. What does emerge over time in an analysis are more complete, complex, consistent, and plausible versions of personal experience (Schafer 1992) that partake of both history and current experience.

Another dimension of analytic neutrality is neutrality as it relates to the sequence or timing of issues. One consequence of this attitude is a heightened respect for the autonomy of the patient, as well as a very considered awareness of the means of influence that we may legitimately bring to bear in an analytic encounter. Again, this arises from an appreciation of the inordinate complexity of human intention and motivation when it is apprehended in conscious and unconscious depth. The whole momentum of analytic work moves patients toward greater awareness and self-reflective deliberation in their choices, away from compulsive anxiety-driven and/or impulsive action (Hartmann 1951). However, the unique path that a patient in analysis takes in this regard is always a highly idiosyncratic matter. A neutral analyst accepts implicitly the inherent wisdom of the patient's process, and does not try to dictate the sequence or timing of issues. Themes and resistances are taken up as they come to the fore, either in the content, manner, or form of the patient's free associations, not in accord with some predetermined program or theory-driven plan. The procrustean couch is a relic of a time when analytic understanding and technique were in their infancy.

Perhaps the most demanding dimension of analytic neutrality is neutrality in relation to the patient's transference. Neutrality with regard to transference projections, displacements, and characterizations commits the analyst to a stance that acknowledges the subjective reality of the patient's experience as something to be explored and understood rather than suppressed or relinquished. It requires a remarkably high level of personal freedom (Poland 1988) and self-confidence for us to allow ourselves to be experienced transferentially in ways that are alien to our own self-experience, without protest or manipulation or withdrawal. Yet it is a fundamental premise of psychoanalytic treatment that only through a process of exploring and fully understanding the subjective reality of the patient's transference experience, including its unconscious determinants, that the most profound transformations of psychic equilibrium are made possible.

One of the most constructive means of managing the inevitable internal tensions that this role imposes is through the ongoing, often silent, exercise of the analyst's interpretive activity. This eventuates at moments of mounting emotional and psychic pressure in active interventions that take the form of personally framed transference interpretations (Adler 1991). When successful, the verbal formulation of the patient's inchoate impulses, affects, and archaic anxieties in the intimacy of the analytic relationship radically defuses the latent pressures on the analyst to make subtle and not so subtle role adjustments to accommodate or ameliorate the patient's wishes and fears. In effect, it is the skillful exercise of an interpretive art that allows us to maintain the essential neutrality with regard to transference upon which the very unfolding of the psychoanalytic process depends. Without this interpretive fluency, we would be forced to adopt more supportive therapeutic strategies, as much to protect our own emotional integrity as to help the patient.

One practical implication of this dimension of neutrality, therefore, is that we must conscientiously strive to avoid any attitude, posture, or technique that consistently predisposes patients to develop a particular kind of transference experience, either through undue frustration, gratification, support, persuasion, or moral pressure. We emphasize *strive to avoid* because we recognize that in the give and take of the analytic encounter, we are wittingly and unwittingly drawn into doing all of the above. Neutrality as a technical principle does not mandate a correct way of responding, nor does it commit the analyst to an emotionally vacant way of being; rather it guides us to avoid using feelings, attitudes, and postures in order to control the patient's transference experience. In a basic way it is not up to the analyst what transference the patient will develop.

We need to keep in mind that patients have transferences not only to our person, but to the structure of the analytic situation as well. This holds true no matter how the situation is organized. A therapeutic situation framed by very loose boundaries (e.g., around ending the session, paying bills, or the analyst's anonymity) will be just as subject to patient transference as one that is more structured. The attitude of analytic neutrality enables us to relate to these transferences as the patient's psychic experience; it directs us to use these transferences to the analytic situation as a way of exploring and understanding the patient's organization of the world. Analytic neutrality serves a function, that of protecting the patient's expressive freedom and enhancing the focus on understanding the patient.

It is of the utmost importance that we be "professionally ourselves" with our patients, for to do otherwise is to keep powerful resources out of our reach, to create an artificial barrier between patient and therapist, and to deaden the treatment. We must not lose sight, however, of the fact that having boundaries is part of being a "real" person, and that inhabiting professionally defined roles entails accepting the reality of prescribed boundaries. Analytic neutrality requires the ability to be a person with individual boundaries interacting with a patient in accordance with professionally defined boundaries in a singular way. Our personal comfort inhabiting and maintaining a psychoanalytically defined neutral attitude may vary considerably from analyst to analyst, or for a particular psychoanalyst from patient to patient, or with a given patient from time to time. This is one of the expectable tensions (of which there are many) that go with our work. However, when it is recognized that the analyst's intentional departures from neutrality explicitly redefine the boundaries of professional relatedness in that analytic dyad, it is incumbent upon us to be very considered in our choices. When a psychoanalyst's technical understanding of neutrality is a matter not of integrated personal conviction but of submissive identification with authoritative models, that analyst is prone to personify the role prescription with superego imagoes of implacable and inhuman expectation.

The roots of the persistent caricature, even in psychoanalytically sophisticated circles, of the coldly inhuman and rigidly demanding classical analyst is, we believe, to be found in the near-universal need to externalize unresolved superego tensions. It has, after all, been over thirty-five years since Stone's (1961) persuasive admonition to temper our technical framework with the moderation of "common sense and intuitive wisdom." His description of areas of legitimate gratification within the analytic setting—including the mature wish for sympathetic understanding as an acceptable form of analytic love—has, we believe, been widely integrated into the mainstream of psychoanalyis. Stone's compassionate vision was largely realized in Greenson's classic text *The Technique and Practice of Psychoanalysis* (1967), which informed the current generation of analytic opinion. The rigid observance of rules, even the most benign and cogently formulated, is understood as an unwelcome instigation to analytic resistance.

Situated on the margin between the inner and outer world, boundaries are distinctive aspects of our selves, especially well suited to represent issues involving separation and individuation. Psychologically speaking, the boundaries between people are veritable lightning rods for fantasy and conflict generated by explosive issues of merger, getting more than can be given, the unknowable uniqueness of the other, and unconditional parenting, to name just a few. The analyst's neutrality structures the therapeutic situation so that the analyst remains cognizant of the way boundaries between patient and analyst crystallize inherent relational and intrapsychic issues in order that their intensities can energize and find dramatic representation in the transference.

Boundary issues are not limited to the patient by any means. Indeed, boundary dilemmas are an inescapable part of being human. Throughout life the boundaries between the self and the other, as well as between the self and the forbidden, represent constant sources of temptation. Patient and analyst alike struggle with yearnings to merge and impulses to transgress taboos. It might be said that a great deal of psychopathology comes to focus at the interface of these conflicting wishes and the frame structuring the analytic situation (Gabbard and Lester 1995, Gray 1994, Langs 1973, Langs and Stone 1980). Given the powerful and largely unconscious impact both participants consistently have on each other, it becomes clear why the asymmetrical structure is a crucial frame that protects the participants. In the patient's analysis, it is the patient we are seeking to help and understand. Understanding the analyst's contribution to the therapeutic interaction is useful insofar as it furthers the understanding of the patient. Employing analytic neutrality encourages us to make use of the transference–countertransference experience as a tool to explore the patient's dynamics, rather than exploiting an opportunity to gratify the mutual longings. It is a one-neurosis, not a one-person, model of analytic treatment that is being elaborated here. This necessarily means structuring the situation so that the patient's unconscious issues will not be eclipsed, much as a pebble's effect is obscured when dropped into turbulent waters.

What are the possible consequences of not maintaining analytic neutrality? An example may be helpful in concretizing some of the issues involved. A male therapist has to take some time off to adopt a baby. He's happy and proud and although he suspects that analytic neutrality would counsel otherwise, he wonders if it wouldn't be better to "be a real person" with his patient by explaining why he needed to be absent. What could we expect if this analyst tells the patient that he needs to be away to adopt a baby? Even if he is aware that his statement will affect his patient on many levels and listens with that impact in mind, how likely is it that the patient will be able to experience, much less talk about, feelings of anger, envy, or abandonment just as his or her analyst is joyfully relating the achievement of a long-sought goal? Or is it more likely that the nature of the interaction established by the therapist's announcement will make it more difficult for the patient to talk about negative feelings—or about any of the specific feelings that he or she brings into the session? The goal of maximizing the patient's freedom of expression is compromised by this announcement, an action that interferes with the therapist's being neutral in regard to the sequence of the patient's process.

Above all, we never know when the patient comes to the session how he or she is needing to see the analyst intrapsychically. We perpetually seek to uncover what transference dynamics are currently central to the patient. For the patient to find the analyst of his or her creation in the interaction—a construction inevitably colored by aspects of the analyst as perceived by the patient (Boesky 1990, Brenner 1976)—the analytic work must consistently remain focused on the patient's intentions. Thus, for instance, to discern the often elusive, unconscious fantasies that pervade and organize the patient's transference experience, would it not have been more productive for the therapist to have analyzed rather than acted on his impulse to share his exciting news with his patient? Perhaps he might have discovered what unspoken wish or fantasy of his patient he was seeking to fulfill. Was he being drawn into an enactment or was he using his patient to fulfill his own needs? What gratifications fetter the patient or analyst to this particular mode of relating, and what fears prevent seeing other alternatives? We think that the apparent freedom of spontaneity that the analyst may believe he has gained through his revelation is more than offset by the diminution in opportunity for deeper analytic exploration.

Neutrality protects the integrity of the unfolding transference configuration.

Acting outside an analytically neutral stance raises the possibility of needlessly escalating an issue that could be more easily dealt with initially. By setting up a later confrontation when the intensity and psychological stakes are higher we only make exploration, discussion, and resolution of these issues more difficult. What happens, for example, when the therapist returns and the patient asks, "So how's the baby?" or "How is it being a father?" or even brings a gift for the baby? Perhaps the adoption founders and there is no baby. Does the therapist explain his difficulties to the patient? The therapist may now find himself in the awkward predicament of trying to rescind an intimacy he had previously offered. This hypothetical illustration raises the real problem of how far into our personal life it is advisable or even practical to involve the patient. More important, when do we stop? How do we decide what we communicate to the patient and what we do not? It is one thing to make use of the inevitable enactments we are drawn into, and quite another to structure the analytic situation around enactments. When these issues are left to the immediacy of the moment, the probability of our own needs and conflicts obscuring the patient's dynamics is increased. Furthermore, we put ourselves in the position of having to deal with these issues at a time when our ability to best manage them is compromised.

Ultimately, boundary issues will not be skirted. If initially avoided, they inevitably emerge later in the treatment. Acknowledging that both patient and therapist contribute to constructing a relationship with each other makes it even more imperative that stable boundaries be established and maintained from the beginning so that we can scrutinize the impact of our individuality. From this perspective, neutrality represents an established baseline that requires us to attend to the very dimension of relatedness, the specific edges of relationship, where intersubjective understandings are mutually negotiated. Do we want to leave these decisions to the pressures of the moment, when countertransferential impulses to act out our own issues will be at their zenith? We believe it is far preferable to have a built-in structure that focuses the treatment on the patient's issues with boundaries and therefore profitably directs these conflicts in the service of the patient's analysis.

Neutrality, we want to emphasize, does not apply to the analyst's attitude toward the patient's actions and adaptive solutions. Neutrality is defined by an attitude toward the patient's subjective experience, while adaptation and action necessarily entail consequential interactions with the external world. Thus, we are decidedly nonneutral in our attitude toward the patient's development and emotional growth. When it is unmistakably in evidence we welcome it and applaud it as a confirmation of our collaboration and our values. Nor can the analyst be nonjudgmental about actions aimed destructively toward the person of the analyst, the analytic situation, or more typically the patient's own best interests and needs. At times when we have good reason to believe that a patient is likely to act on such destructive intentions, we are obligated to express our opinions and use our influence. Obviously an analyst's personal values will inevitably enter into these judgments, and not everyone will agree on the criteria that call for intervention.

While it is the patient's process, it is the analyst's situation. In the organization of the analytic situation, it is always the analyst's obligation to safeguard the analytic dyad from potentially disruptive intrusions, whether they arise from mounting pressures within the analytic situation or from the needs of an outside party. One concrete manifestation of this entails providing a relatively quiet and private space with comfortable furnishings (chairs and/or couch), and regular periods of undisrupted time of sufficient length to make possible a meaningful unhurried exchange (by custom, 45–60 minutes). It is our role to monitor this "frame" and to see that moves to circumvent it are analyzed rather than enacted. In this sense the analyst defines the appropriate frame of analytic work, while the patient chooses to comply with or reject this definition (e.g., frequency of visits, use of couch, fee, etc.). Our authority may be challenged but it cannot be legitimately abrogated without severely compromising the integrity of the analytic situation (Bachant and Richards 1993, Kwawer 1995). An illusory "democracy" in which both parties negotiate the conditions of treatment from a position of equality is a collusive attempt to limit the depth of analytic exploration. When we go along with such a maneuver, unless it is clearly labeled as a temporary accommodation until the impasse can be resolved analytically, we understand that a specifically psychoanalytic alliance has been waived.

In a profound sense, therefore, neutrality requires that we have a firm intuitive grasp of the human boundaries of analytic engagement, and to unambiguously represent this understanding through verbal and nonverbal means, in all interactions with the patient. Secure boundaries are a prerequisite of working analytically, for patient and analyst alike cannot confront the irrational intensity of the archaic without a protective bulwark. At our best, perhaps, we could do without these protections, counting on spontaneous emotion and empathic sensitivity to ensure the appropriate scope of our actions and judgments. But analysis is a professional task, which we are not free to put down as the mood dictates. The emotional and irrational intensities generated by the analytic process are personally disruptive to ourselves as well as the patient. We firmly believe that it is a romantic idealization to expect any individual to have the emotional stability and stamina to be exposed to the buffeting of analytic practice hour after hour without a safety net.

The asymmetrical structure of the analytic situation, explicitly sanctioning different kinds of involvement and activity from each participant, is one of the most important factors that makes this high-wire act possible. While the patient is invited to reveal his or her inner life without restraint, the analyst brings a personally professional self into the relationship. The professional self is a gradually developed capacity for affective/cognitive integration that allows us to negotiate the twin demands of

emotional responsivity and reflective contemplation while interacting with the patient spontaneously in the immediacy of the
moment. It is a product of educational and emotional discipline
(i.e., of internalized standards, theoretical models, clinical rules,
a proper understanding of the limits of responsible analytic and
self-analytic activity, etc.), as well as innate gifts of psychological
imagination and creative empathy. The latter permit us to
construct vivid, complex, and multidimensional portraits of our
patient's moment-to-moment internal world. These portraits
simultaneously register the patient's subjective experience of
self and other (most importantly the analyst who is being
interacted with), as well as the unconscious impingements of the
forces of drive and defense in the patient's dynamically structured inner world. That such a daunting effort can be undertaken with reasonable hope of being successful is testimony to
the enormous potential of the human brain to accomplish
complex operations outside of consciousness. Indeed, when an
experienced analyst is working well, there is an almost effortless
sense that what one needs to know will be there at the appropriate time; understanding is immanent. This confidence frees
us to look inward and to cast at least one eye on our own
ever-shifting self-experience in relation to the patient.

The rigorous demands of participant-observership as described
by Arlow (1963), are particularly onerous to the beginner, who is
most likely to feel self-consciously wooden and mechanical
adapting to this role. This may inhibit personal qualities of
humor, liveliness, and empathic responsiveness. This awkwardness should pass with time. Increasingly able to integrate the
role requirements of psychoanalytic expertise with the more
familiar contours of ordinary personality (Sandler 1976), the
secure internalization of the proscriptive and prescriptive dimensions of analytic intimacy are ultimately liberating, allowing for creative and fearless engagement with irrational and
archaic levels of the patient's inner world.

SUMMARY

This discussion of the psychoanalytic situation is an attempt to clarify what we consider the fundamental elements of the psychoanalytic situation that make possible a radical exploration of human motivation in depth. At the heart of psychoanalytic technique is an interpersonal interaction defined by two extraordinary ways of relating. We have elaborated this in terms of differentiated role prescriptions emphasizing the synergistic power of free-association and analytic neutrality. Conceived as twin catalysts that systematically destabilize the neurotic equilibrium that constricts the patient's freedom, these reciprocal roles are unmanageable without carefully defined boundaries to absorb and contain the intensities of the analytic encounter. We have understood the invitation to the patient to search the limits of expressive freedom as a radical and frightening proposition that inevitably sets in motion a defensive process. This struggle offers a mutual starting point to explore and work through the specific strategies, attitudes, and motivations that inhibit the patient's emotional life. Our discussion of analytic neutrality has emphasized three essential dimensions as they bear upon the interactive process: neutrality with regard to conflict, neutrality with regard to sequence, and neutrality with regard to transference. We maintain that each of these components of the neutral stance makes a vital contribution to the integrity, depth, and tone of the analytic relationship that unfolds.

3

Dimensions of Transference: Adaptive and Archaic Transference Activity*

*An earlier version of this chapter was presented at the Scientific Meeting of the New York Psychoanalytic Society March 25, 1997, at Division 39 of the American Psychological Association.

Alongside resistance, unconscious fantasy, compromise forma- tion, and defense, transference stands as a nucleus of psycho- analytic thinking about technique. It is especially prized for its ability to crystallize the meaning of current patterns of interac- tion as well as its capacity to uncover the perpetually active unconscious wishes and fears from childhood that continue to organize experience. Acknowledged as a central dynamic force within the psychoanalytic situation since Freud's (1905a) post- script to the Dora case, this concept has generated an enormous and continually expanding literature. Burgeoning discussion among analysts of different theoretical persuasions is currently stimulating creative reformulations and innovative approaches to understanding the process of transference. Many of the most salient issues in this controversy converge upon the question of whether transference is better conceived as co-constructed in the analytic situation or brought to the analytic interaction by the patient.

One side of this debate advocates the idea that transference is co-constructed. Within this view the definition of transference is generally broadened to include the entire relationship between patient and analyst. Central to this formulation is the notion that transference involves adaptation to an interpersonal real- ity: both analyst–patient interaction and the transference itself are seen as mutually constituted. According to these conceptualizations, adaptation in the present, in particular to the actualities of the analyst's unique presence in the transference, becomes the focus of the psychoanalytic situation. In effect, the impetus of the analytic process is generated by how each participant reacts to, defends against, and fantasizes about the other's action. Change is attributed to a resumption of ego development contingent upon the relation with a new object, the analyst. Within this view, the unconscious is fully represented rather than disguised in the here-and-now interaction between patient and analyst, and the mutative aspects of this relationship—especially its greater authenticity—are emphasized over the interpretation of enduring unconscious conflicts.

The contrasting formulation understands transference as brought to the interaction by each participant. From this perspective, transference is an intrapsychic phenomenon, a compromise between all the components of psychic conflict: wishes and fears, values and moral dictums, affect, and defense. Transference serves to organize the relationship with the analyst on different levels of consciousness. Espousing a more circumscribed definition, transference is understood to be both expressed and disguised in the manifest interaction with the analyst. Transference, within this view, is an unconscious pattern of relating and structuring experience derived from our earliest efforts to pilot the forces of a unique history. Change comes about through the analysis of these largely unconscious dynamics in the context of the current relationship with the analyst, a relationship that serves to stimulate preformed transference wishes, fantasies, and emotions. According to this orientation, the interaction is mutually constituted; the transference is not.

How can we understand the divergence between these perspectives? One aspect of the problem is that transference is potentially manifest in any and every behavior. This multiplicity in presentation has created problems in defining and classifying transference phenomena. Initial thinking about transference explored whether transference should be understood according to its affective valence (i.e., positive and negative transference), its object of origin (maternal, paternal), its relationship to the treatment (objectionable or unobjectionable), or its primary drive (erotic, sadistic, etc.). These different emphases led to considerable definitional imprecision. Transference is a concept that condenses a complex array of psychological data gathered and observed over extended periods of time. Its usage, emphasis, and meaning have been subject to considerable variability even within groups of analysts who share common premises and technical commitments. While there is substantial overlap in the phenomena pointed to by these two perspectives, the distinctions between them are rooted in significant differences in conceptual focus and underlying theory. To understand the divergence between thinking of transference as mutually constituted or brought to the interaction, it is useful to differentiate two intertwined ideas of transference that have been prominent throughout its conceptual evolution.

EVOLUTION OF THE CONCEPT

The earliest, and until recently the dominant, idea of transference emphasized the inappropriate intrusion into a current relationship of fantasies, attitudes, wishes, and fears belonging to a person in the past. Transference was contrasted with the "realistic" component of object relations that enables a person to accurately assess the external world. Greenson (1967) illustrated this understanding of transference by considering a patient's annoyance at his analyst answering the telephone. Some degree of annoyance, Greenson maintains,

> seems realistic, in accordance with the circumstances, and appropriate to a mature level of functioning. This does not imply that the patient's reaction is to be ignored, but we handle such occurrences differently than we do transference phenomena. We might explore the patient's history and fantasies in regard to

anger reactions, but, despite our findings, we would remind the patient and ourselves that his overt reaction to the frustration was realistic. If the patient had become furious and not just annoyed, or if he had remained completely indifferent, then the inappropriate intensity of the reaction would indicate that we are probably dealing with a repetition or a reaction from childhood. The same would hold true if his annoyance lasted for hours or if he reacted to the interruption with laughter. [p. 156]

Though for contemporary analysts, assessing what is and is not "appropriate" to the situation poses thornier technical as well as philosophical difficulties than they once did, the idea that a simple human exchange may simultaneously engage multiple present and past object representations remains a radical perspective that is uniquely psychoanalytic. In large measure, this initial formulation of transference remains one of the most radical fruits of the breakthrough insights of *The Interpretation of Dreams* (Freud 1900). It contains the unsettling recognition that one of the most sacred phenomena of conscious psychic life, a human love relationship, can, like a dream or a pathological symptom, serve as a manifest prop for reliving the passionate desires and conflicts belonging to the formative experiences of earliest childhood. Within this perspective, developed by Freud (1905b), Fenichel (1941), Greenson (1967), and Loewald (1960), among many others, transference in the clinical situation is largely understood as a reenactment that can be identified by its lack of fit to the current situation. The patient's reaction, attitude, or conduct is inappropriate in that it is caused or augmented by feelings, wishes, meanings, and aims from the past. There is an overreaction (or underreaction) in intensity, duration, or tenacity, and frequently a sense that the person is relating more to a fantasy imago or internal expectation than to an actuality at hand.

Transference as inappropriate intrusion only becomes a pathological phenomenon periodically, as it erupts in response to particular constellations of internal and external events that trigger automatic repetitions of feeling, perceiving, and experiencing. The degree of pathology corresponds to its power to dominate our organization and interaction. Behavior in everyday life consists of a mixture of transference and appropriate reactions to reality. These two currents enable us to make use of what we have learned in the past in the service of relating in the present. This mixture is in a constant state of flux, manifesting a mutual interaction between the events of daily life and the persistent pressure of unconscious fantasy.

It was this aspect of transference, fueled by the "indestructibility" of childhood wishes and fears, that Freud (1900) portrayed in *The Interpretation of Dreams*. There he evoked Homer's haunting imagery of the Shades of the Underworld who "awoke to new life as soon as they tasted blood" (p. 553) in order to convey how these transferences feed off the actuality of the analytic relationship. Loewald (1960), with a somewhat different emphasis, eloquently elaborated upon this metaphor, explicating how the "blood" of conscious-preconscious life, the life of contemporary present-day objects, triggers transference activity:

> Transference is pathological insofar as the unconscious is a crowd of ghosts. . . . Ghosts of the unconscious, imprisoned by defenses but haunting the patient in the dark of his defenses and symptoms, are allowed to taste blood, are let loose. In the daylight of analysis the ghosts of the unconscious are laid and led to rest as ancestors whose power is taken over and transformed into the newer intensity of present life, of the secondary process and contemporary objects. [p. 29]

Treatment organized around the view of transference as inappropriate intrusion is focused on identifying and analyzing these "nightmares in the closet" (Mayer 1968) along with the wishes, fears, and fantasies that hold them in place.

Juxtaposed with this way of looking at transference is an

alternative conceptualization that follows an equally long, though perhaps less pronounced, line of development in psychoanalytic thinking. Loewenstein (1969) was one of the first to show that transference is ubiquitous. He reserved the term *object relations* for the realistic component of the transferences of everyday life. Building on the work of Freud (1915b), Loewenstein (1969), and Bird (1972), and on Arlow's (1969a,b) understanding of unconscious fantasy, Brenner (1982) describes transference as ubiquitous. Brenner contends that *every* object relation is a new edition of the first, definitive attachments of childhood, not just certain ones where there is an ill-fittingness with the current situation. Transference, according to Brenner, emerges in every psychoanalytic situation because it develops in every situation where another person is important in one's life. What is unique about psychoanalysis is not that transference is present, but that it is dealt with interpretively. According to Brenner, transference derives from the wishes and fears created by the interaction of experience and fantasy in the child's relations with mother, father, siblings, and similar figures.

This significant extension of classical theory holds that early experience gives rise to conflicts and compromise formations that determine the object relations of later life. All object relations are transferential in this sense, not just those that are characterized by manifestly pathological indications. The central aspect of this way of thinking about transference is that it exists in some fundamental amalgam, not, as it were, alongside a more realistic component of an object relationship, but as an irreducible dimension. Brenner challenges us to imagine an object relation without a transferential component. This view of transference understands it as a major determinant of how we function, affecting motivation, acts of will, indeed our every choice, from whom we love and hate or the vocation we pursue to the tiniest impulses and affectations that pepper our character. Pathology from this perspective is not a defining characteristic of transference. Transference, as both object relation and compromise formation, is pathological only when it meets the criteria of one or more of the following: too much restriction of drive derivatives, too much anxiety or depressive affect, too much inhibition of functional capacity, too great a tendency to injure or destroy oneself, or too much conflict with one's environment (Brenner 1982).

The essence of this vision of transference is the insistence that transference dynamics infuse our entire being. The early wishes, fears, and solutions to problems that faced us as children are now an inevitable part of us, coloring our actions, thoughts, and experience of the world. At times this influence will be less subject to conflict, operating rather silently, somewhat as sunglasses filter the light and enhance our vision. In contrast to the previously cited example of Greenson's (1967) patient who was disturbed by a telephone interruption, this understanding of transference as ubiquitous would have us listen even to "realistic" and "appropriate" reactions to an interruption for the particular manifestations of unconscious fantasy that clothe the patient's construction of the analyst or the analytic situation. Consider a similar incident from another treatment:

Elaine was only "realistically" irritated by the ring of her analyst's phone. Closer examination, however, revealed that the telephone calls stimulated fantasies of impatient rival "siblings" encroaching upon her time, unable to wait their turn. She assumed that her analyst was more interested in them than in herself and used these interruptions to reinforce her early idea that the best thing she could do when competing for her father's love was to "disappear," removing herself from the fray by cutting off feelings of desire to have her father to herself. Though it would be hard to characterize her reaction of irritation as inappropriate to the situation, this dynamic reveals the crucial influence of transference in structuring her ordinary interactions with others. Again and again Elaine would construct an idea of the other as not primarily interested in her and assume that what was needed in the situation was for her to retreat from any sustained involvement.

TRANSFERENCE AS PROCESS

While this formulation broadens our understanding, reminding us that transference is salient even when it is operating unobtrusively, it leaves us with a question about the specific nature of this dynamic action. Is transference properly understood as a result of conflict, a compromise formation, and/or an object relation, or is transference better understood as a function, an active process that characterizes mental life? To our way of thinking, this either/or formulation is unnecessary; transference is clearly both. We think of transference as ongoing activity, a constant feature of mental life, something the individual does to generate an expedient way of meeting the world. Yet this activity continues the influence of unconscious fantasizing—itself an expression of conflict—by contributing to the organization of the multiple forces that converge in every interaction. From this perspective, the question "What is the transference?" loses some of its theoretical and dialectical urgency. Considered as an activity or function, the salient question becomes, "How is the structure or quality of current experience organized transferentially?" This approach reminds us that transference activity is an ever-present dimension of all experience, imbuing it with a distinctive complexion. Interpretively we would be directed to consider how defensive, adaptive, and expressive action is being influenced by transference as an expression of unconscious fantasizing. Inevitably coloring the subjective experience of both analyst and analysand, transference, therefore, is simultaneously the result of early conflicting forces within the individual and an integrator of immediate subjective experience. Through its lens the person organizes the multiple forces that converge in every interaction with the external world—the intrapsychic, extrapsychic, and the interpersonal.

Stolorow and Lachmann (1984/1985), in an earlier formulation of transference as organizing activity, describe it as "an expression of the *continuing influence* of organizing principles and imagery that crystallized out of the patient's early formative experiences" (p. 26, authors' emphasis). Rangell's (1989, 1990) and Schafer's (1976) stress on the importance of action in psychoanalysis informs our emphasis on transference as process, and although there are differences, this understanding is related to Stone's (1967) distinction between the primordial and mature transference, Reed's (1990) process reconceptualization of the transference neurosis, and White's (1996) formulation of transference/resistance as a bridge from the intrapsychic world of the patient to the interpersonal world of the analytic situation.

Transference, in this light, is one manifestation of the broader synthetic (Nunberg 1931) and integrative (Hartmann 1964) functions. It is both a derivative of unconscious fantasy and an integrator of subjective experience. Human beings function in a way that synthesizes information from many sources. We don't develop static transferences; we transfer our responses to the world we apprehended as children onto an organization of the present. This transfer is a dynamic process of actualizaion whose various elements involve structuring, organizing, motivating and instigating experience in ways that render elements of the past alive in the present (Bachant et al. 1995b). From this perspective, transference, like compromise formation, is most usefully conceived as a process. Through this process of transfer, the deepest lessons of the heart continue to inform the mind. Stolorow and Lachmann (1984/1985) point out that understanding transference as an expression of organizing activity has the advantage of clarifying "both the patient's psychological structures and the input from the analyst that they assimilate (Wachtel 1980)" (p. 26) as well as encompassing the central importance of developmental transformations in the child's organizing activity. It is, as Bird (1972) reminds us, "a universal mental function that may be the emotional basis of all human relationships" (p. 267).

ADAPTIVE AND ARCHAIC
TRANSFERENCE ACTIVITY

This way of thinking allows us to understand transference both as a universal attribute of mental functioning that contributes to the construction of all experience and as a specific set of organizing principles that can be triggered by particular emotional and psychological constellations. Connecting these two understandings is the relationship between transference, the dynamic unconscious, and the process of repression.

Many analytic thinkers have noted a link between the repressed and the wishes and fears that fuel transference activity. Repeatedly emphasized in the contemporary clinical and theoretical literature is the idea that it is particularly those mental contents split off from the individual's developing psychic structure that generate the most intense and pernicious transferential reactions. Transference phenomena are clearly characterized by varying degrees of repression or defensive elaboration.

Transference as a universal function serving adaptation refers to the organizing activity of childhood wishes, emotions, and relational configurations that achieve higher levels of integration with the evolving self (less repression or defensive elaboration). On the other hand, transference in its clinically archaic sense centers on those modes of functioning infused with unintegrated longing and need that are a specific instigation to anxiety, depression, and guilt. Although for purposes of theoretical exposition we have presented them as discrete, it is important to emphasize that adaptive and archaic transference activity are not separate entities even though they may appear so to superficial view because of defensive isolation. We understand them as different aspects of the same synthetic process, interconnected by unconscious organization and mediated through fantasy. As Levine (1997) has commented, "even the most archaic of transference phenomena are also adaptive and . . . even the most adaptive of transferences are secretly hopeful of achieving disguised, archaic instinctual discharge" (p. 7). We can think of the archaic aspects of transference as providing an orienting framework while the adaptive dimension of transference supplies the flexibility essential for accommodating new experience. Every experience, then, will be characterized by a different balance of these components, manifesting aspects of both archaic and adaptive transference activity, much as Piaget (1952) speaks of cognition as characterized by the processes of assimilation and accommodation.[1] Clinically, some experience will be more influenced by archaic transference activity than others (e.g., the man who continually "finds" his expectations confirmed that women will be rejecting of him assimilates myriad possibilities into a rigidly held conviction that serves multiple functions). Other experience will be more open to accommodating the complexities of present-day living. Either dimension of transference activity can be used defensively against the recognition of the other in the service of resistance.

The adaptive aspect of transference, which can contribute to the co-construction of an interaction with another, operates within a relatively open system. It is receptive to maturation throughout development, and capable of being modified through interaction with the world. Kohut's (1971, 1977, 1984) concept of transmuting internalization as well as other constructions of analytic transformation that emphasize the impact of the analyst as a new object represent attempts to specify these processes as they apply to the analytic situation. The contemporary analytic spotlight on the intricacies of interactive involvement between patient and analyst has sharpened our awareness of the importance of this adaptive dimension of transference and

---

1. See Stolorow and Lachmann (1984/1985) for another application of Piaget's paradigm of assimilation to the concept of transference as organizing activity. Although this conceptualization bears some structural similarities to the present formulation, our understanding of archaic organizing principles is so different from theirs that the similarity is more in form than substance.

especially of the ways in which it can be used to develop analytic understandings that enhance development.

Transference in the sense of a general adaptive function contributes to an integration of conflicting forces within the person's psyche by enabling the person to seek out certain manifest or potential aspects of others that carry wished for, feared, or needed qualities. Reciprocal reparative fantasies in both patient and analyst may provide necessary gratifications that suppress or stabilize disruptive emotional intrusions within the dyad, and may afford opportunities to encourage maturational initiatives. It is in this sense that we can understand transference activity as a response to real aspects of the analyst in the psychoanalytic process. Specific features of the analyst are magnified or globalized to provide the patient with what is being looked for in the object. It is not that the patient has found the "reality" of the analyst but has constructed an object representation around some real element of the analyst's character or demeanor that he or she needs to find. The patient, for example, who finds it integrative to relate to the environment in terms of a power struggle will find some aspect of the analyst or the analytic situation (e.g., the analyst's policy to charge for cancellations) with which to engage that need. That aspect will then be used as a scaffolding around which an object representation of the analyst as dogmatically rigid is built. This aspect, which may be more than a grain of sand, is selectively attended to in a way that integrates intrapsychic needs with the realities of the external environment. Transference-infused organizing activity of the individual integrates many influences of the intersubjective field, significantly contributing to the selection of actions that maximize gratification and minimize pain. Transference, therefore, may be integrative on interpersonal as well as intrapsychic levels.

To assume, however, that transference itself is co-constructed is conceptually problematic. This theoretical move superordinates a broadened definition of transference, one that is virtually synonymous with the analytic relationship in its entirety. If taken as the only dimension of transference, the differentiated meanings—especially its original and most radical sense as a split-off organizer of subjective experience structured around defensively disguised archaic wishes and derivative fantasies—are abandoned in favor of a view that magnifies the nuanced surfaces of experience. Unconscious fantasies, dreams, and wishes become purely metaphorical or representational phenomena that derive their meaning from the structured reality of current and past interpersonal engagement or the conscious and unconscious cognitive schema distilled from that experience. The dynamic unconscious has virtually no motivational role in such a broadened approach to transference.

In the model of transference we are proposing, on the other hand, one can welcome the truly fascinating illumination of the intersubjective subtleties of transferential interaction—what might be thought of as the craggy surfaces of transference engagement, without neglecting the animating vision of depth psychology. Although it is indisputable that the external environment and the interpersonal field can stimulate transference activity, any understanding that fails to adequately account for the impact of unconscious fantasizing in the organization and construction of childhood and adult experience limits our clinical access to the irrational dimensions of object relations. We need be wary lest hypersensitivity replace fantasy as the psychological basis of transference. We recognize that an interaction must be mutually constituted (Odgen 1992a,b, 1994) and unconscious fantasies are inevitably mutually stimulated, but unconscious fantasy itself cannot be co-constructed.

In treatment, the adaptive aspect of transference comes to the fore immediately, expressed in mutual adjustments to the role requirements of the analytic situation. This ready availability provides access to dynamic forces that threaten to draw the analytic situation outside the preferred structure of neutrality and free association. Analyst and patient explore mutually constituted interactive patterns that encourage supportive, judgmental, or action-oriented modes of relating. This dimension of working with transference activity has been artfully elaborated by a number of contemporary clinicians from all points on the theoretical spectrum (Aron 1991, 1992, Bromberg 1995, Busch 1995, Chused 1991, Ehrenberg 1992, Greenberg 1991, Jacobs 1983, 1986, 1992, McLaughlin 1991, Mitchell 1988, 1993, Renik 1993, Roughton 1993, Sandler 1976, Stolorow and Atwood 1992, Stolorow and Lachmann 1984/85). Attention to the value of the adaptive transference in working with resistance and aspects of the analytic process that invoke anxiety has led Gray (1986, 1994), and Busch (1994, 1997) to advocate a careful monitoring of the free-associative process as a way of affectively engaging those ego processes that enable the analyst to access unconscious dynamics.

If we engage the patient only at the adaptive level, however, we will obscure the archaic dimensions of transference. Excessive interactivity can foster an analytic situation that effectively forecloses the possibility that archaic elements will emerge with sufficient definition to be recognized as such. Different aspects of a person's transferential mode of functioning may be highlighted by different analysts, or by the same analyst at different times, but as a stable and enduring mode of functioning established early in life, archaic transference activity is not subject to the degree of influence that characterizes relationships and interactions. The archaic transference, representing the deeper, repressed dimension of transferential activity, although less readily available for analytic exploration, is the most reliable pathway to the problematic and emotionally relevant experiences of childhood. Eliciting the wishes, fears, and fantasies of the archaic transference through defense and resistance analysis enables us to speak directly to the core motivational dynamics that infuse and structure psychic life. Working on the level of the archaic transference helps the patient to understand the pull of childhood solutions to early problems and the inevitable resistance to relinquishing them. It enables the patient to better cope with the disequilibria that result from maturational initiatives.

Transference in this more archaic sense is animated by the repressed dimensions of childhood experience that have been split off from the psychic evolution enjoyed by the maturing sectors of the personality. The repressed wishes, fears, and fantasies that reflect biopsychosocial imperatives that have been cut off from maturational development and integration are the facet of dynamic structure that analysts speak of as "instinctual" because of its resistance to change. Archaic transference activity is heavily weighted by the wishes and fears that anchor unconscious fantasy. The extent to which transference at any given moment may be serving as a resistance suggests the emergence of archaic, unconscious fantasy. Clinically, we observe the timelessness of these childhood imperatives in the repetition of patterns of relating to self and others that directs the person's choices with an automatic and peremptory quality. This dimension of transference is triggered by aspects of our current lives that echo repressed and conflicted opportunities. Transference as an expression of immutable, archaic wishes and fears related to specific developmental epochs made manifest in unconscious fantasy involves a projection onto the outside world as well as onto the world of internal representations. What is transferred are the fantasies based on these unconscious wishes and fears. Both the way we seek to live out these fantasies and the meaning we attribute to them change as a result of analysis.

In his Monday session, Henry expressed mortification about a game of charades he played that weekend at a social gathering of friends from the office. He did well enough, he explained, until the very end, when his last performance was to determine the winning team. Unnerved by the stress of heightened competitive tension, Henry crumbled. "Will I ever get it?" he asked plaintively, referring obliquely to the fact that after five years of treatment, much of his conflictual behavior in competitive situations had been understood but not necessarily overcome. He proceeded to single out Larry, a member of the opposing team, who he thought had been particularly aggressive in the "friendly" teasing and taunting that accompanied the game that evening. He anticipated that Larry would not let it go, that if they met in the cafeteria later in the day that Larry would gloat triumphantly and rub it in how Henry had "clutched." He proceeded to condemn himself, mercilessly, for "giving the game away" and "never learning." Writhing on the couch theatrically, he moaned that he was nothing but a "wimpy baby." His analyst intervened for the first time in the session, "Why a wimpy baby?" At first, Henry was puzzled by the inquiry, and in a characteristically defensive way, complained impatiently that he "just wasn't good at this free-association game."

Analyst: Perhaps you want to give this game away, just the way you did the other night.

Henry: You're some help! You just sit there and kick me when I'm down. I come in here and tell you how shitty I feel, and you say, "Yes indeed, what a piece of shit you are!"

Analyst: That's odd, I had the impression that *you* were the one asking me to treat you like a worthless piece of shit, and that *I* was trying to tell you that you are more capable than you think!

Henry: You certainly have a funny way of expressing yourself. Next, you're going to tell me that I made it up about Larry putting me down all night! . . . I can't get over that schmuck! He's such a macho piece of shit. You know, when he was dating Amy [a girl in the office who was at the party], he used to brag about his sexual exploits. Can you believe it? He claims to have had her right on the couch in his office. I couldn't stop thinking about that scene. She's quite a babe!

Analyst: So Amy is a babe and Larry had her on his couch!

Henry: Right! A "*whimpering* babe," to hear Larry tell it. . . . Actually . . . could there be a connection? It's hard to believe, but the charade I was trying unsuccessfully to act out had to do with O. J. Simpson. All I could think of was Simpy

Son. So I tried to play that I was a little boy and I waived my wrist in an effeminate way. Get it? Simpy/Son? . . . Well, no one else did, either. I really should have played dumb rather than feminine—the simple son.

Analyst: Perhaps you should have played it as a lady killer! But then, this lifelong charade of yours, this special way of dealing with male competition . . .

Henry (interrupting): Yes, yes . . . passive, dumb, and helpless. Come fuck me over cause I'm one big asshole!

At this juncture in his analysis Henry was already familiar with many of the psychodynamic elements condensed in this brief vignette. After an interpretation that he was playing out his passive surrender in the analysis ("Perhaps you want to give this game away"), Henry quickly resumed an active position with regard to an analytic dialogue that was infused with macho repartee and homoerotic struggle. Though he couldn't have framed his insight in technical terms, he had come to "understand" his defensive tendency to project fantasies of castration onto his self-representation as a strategic solution to competitive conflicts, a solution having its origins in a number of specific childhood temptations, dangers, and dilemmas. These included an identification with his father's aggression toward women (O.J. Simpson's son); a desire to regress to an earlier, less conflicted time (the "wimpy baby"); a wish to be "passive, dumb, and helpless" as a defensive strategy to avoid competing with his father ("I'm one big asshole"); a genital identification with his degraded mother as an object of father's love (a "whimpering babe"); and an attempt to position himself as helpless in order to be rescued/punished (the hopeless patient). Understanding the multiple sources of these feelings and ideas about himself had substantially changed their meaning. Henry was freer to relate to himself and his analyst in new ways. In effect, they were no longer simply undesirable elements of his self experience, but alien states that possessed him in specific, usually competitive, situations that could now be clearly identified. Instead of portraying himself as an inadequate male in treatment with a powerful male, the patient had begun to see how he represented himself as inadequate as a means of resolving many conflicting wishes, needs, and fears, including the wish to be related to in a certain way by his analyst. This shift of attention to the dynamic meanings of this representation and experience of self was a link to his disowned agency, which now manifested itself more forcefully in his interactions with his analyst and others in his life. He now usually knew when he was choosing to maintain a position of inferiority and low self-esteem. Analyzing both the adaptive transference activity (the myriad ways Henry presented himself as helpless and inadequate to the analyst and invited or provoked the analyst into treating him in just that way) and the archaic dimensions of transference (the underlying wishes, fantasies, and fears that propelled this particular integration of his experiential world) was essential for a comprehensive understanding of this person's psychodynamics. Transference activity thus has a central role in both ego functioning and unconscious fantasizing.

Given the complexity of transference, it is understandable that issues concerning its fundamental nature have generated debate. Each perspective has elaborated different processes and dimensions of transference, while contributing essential understandings to an overall picture of its operation. Those who theorize a co-construction of transference focus primarily on transference as a general adaptive principle, a mutual process of assimilation and accommodation within a context of ingrained adaptive patterns, cognitive sets, and thematic sensitivities. This view emphasizes elements of past experience with others that have already been integrated into the person's ego functioning in conjunction with the adaptive compliance or stimulation of the immediate environment. On the other hand, those who emphasize the timeless and unwavering contribution of the dynamic unconscious to a relatively fixed mode of organizing activity that is highly resistant to change have concentrated primarily on the impact of the more repressed, archaic dimension of transference. They recognize the complex infantile compromise formations that are condensed in the details of Henry's "adaptive" passivity, determining both his choice to behave helplessly and his wishful efforts to resurrect the father of childhood as a current object of dependency and desire.

Our own understanding of this controversy attempts to draw inspiration from the considerable virtues of both perspectives. To the extent that the analyst is looking at the patient from the perspective of the adaptive elements of transference activity, the analyst's own contribution to the patient's organization of experience—in terms of either countertransferential pressures, unique qualities of subjectivity, or theoretical and methodological bias—may be at the foreground of interpretive attention. To the extent that the focus shifts to the archaic dimensions of transference activity, exploration of the unconscious roots of the patient's subjectivity will take precedence. Both dimensions are aspects of the same phenomena, present in every person's engagement with the world. Sometimes the archaic transference is palpable either in the patient's associations or resistance, but can only be accessed through the adaptive transference, as in Henry's case. At other times the adaptive transference dominates the interaction but operates defensively, concealing unconscious wishes and fears that organize the patient's experience:

Mary's analyst gradually realized that over a period of years she had never heard any direct references to herself as a person who existed outside the psychoanalytic situation. Indeed, when she reflected upon her ideas, intuitions, and images of this patient, she could retrieve no developed representation of Mary's idea of her (the analyst's) personal life. Did Mary believe that she was married, single, celibate, rich, poor, or cultured? Did she imagine the analyst summered in the Hamptons, safaried in Africa, or trekked in Nepal? As this awareness crystallized, the analyst considered how it was possible that she had not noticed this avoidance before. The patient was an otherwise emotionally related and lively analysand, who over the course of time had expressed many transferential reactions to the analyst's way of being and working within the consulting room. She simply had no idea of how Mary thought/felt/fantasied about her private life.

As so often happens when an analyst finally registers an unrecognized resistance, a fortuitous therapeutic opportunity quickly came to the fore. By chance, the analyst's telephone (connected to an answering machine) rang repeatedly in a brief period of her session. Mary, who was engrossed in recounting a story about a recent date, tried hard to ignore the insistent and piercing rings, until finally she couldn't bear it any longer. "God, that's an annoying sound!" she exclaimed forcefully. Then, after a pause, she added with considerable sarcasm: "*Somebody* certainly is eager to speak to you!"

When she tried to return to her interrupted narrative without further elaborating on her outburst, the analyst interposed an observation: "Apparently you don't want to share with me your thoughts about that somebody. Perhaps you would prefer that you never had to be disturbed by thoughts about the people in my life outside this room."

Mary's response was surprising, considering the depth of her involvement in the analytic process: "Why should I have thoughts about that stuff?" she argued. "You're not going to tell me about your private life or your other patients, are you?" This argument would have been more plausible if she were only referring to expressing thoughts about the analyst's private life.

With genuine puzzlement, her analyst inquired: "Why would that prevent you from having thoughts about my private life?"

Mary (somewhat tentatively): Perhaps I think it's too nosy, like I'd be sniffing around in your personal things. . . . (more heatedly) And it seems unfair! You get to see everything, I expose all my shit to you and you get to sit back there as if your life were a bed of roses.

Analyst: I end up smelling like roses, and you stink like shit! Perhaps you are holding back your thoughts about my life to keep from befouling some idyllic picture you want to have of me! (After a pause) Does anything come to mind about this "sniffing around in my personal things"?

Mary (laughing): Nothing to do with the toilet, if that's what you're getting at. Actually, before, when you said that about the bed of roses, I flashed on an image of my mother's old bedspread. It had a floral pattern . . . I'm not sure if it had roses, though. . . . I'm now remembering a time . . . I must have been 12, 13 or so . . . when I began baby-sitting for my brother. After he fell asleep, I'd sort of go into my parents' bedroom and look around. You know how kids do. I went looking in my mother's drawers.

Analyst: Only your mother's drawers?

Mary: I heard that! "Mother's drawers!" Very good. I don't think I ever found anything really, no dirty stuff or anything. But I do remember I liked the smell of my mother's things, her nightgowns and stuff smelled like perfume.

Analyst: Her "drawers" smelled floral, yours . . .

Mary: Ugh! That's around the time I got my period, you realize.

In this interpretive dialogue, Mary's annoyance at the telephone interruption became an analytic opportunity to explore a resistance that had recently come to her analyst's attention. The analyst's first intervention goes too far ("Perhaps you would prefer that you never had to be disturbed . . . "); it is an interpretive leap inspired by speculative evidence that had not been sufficiently substantiated in the material at hand. Mary's defensive retort, however, points to an adaptive transference— she resentfully withheld her curiosity in reaction to the role inequality of the analytic situation—in the service of resistance. When Mary introduces an olfactory metaphor to represent the injustice of asymmetrical exposure (sniffing around/ bed of roses, etc.), her analyst takes it to be a figurative expression of a narcissistic transference paradigm: the patient protecting an unsullied image (idealization) of the analyst by suppressing her curiosity. Again, her analyst is a bit too eager for closure. Mary, however, misunderstands her analyst's encouragement to free-associate in connection with the "sniffing image" as a symbolic anal interpretation ("Nothing to do with the toilet . . . "). She proceeds to correct her analyst's purported implication by producing associations of a genital nature. Indeed, it is not clear, even at the end of the vignette, whether her analyst has caught up to the patient who is consistently attributing a symbolic resonance to her analyst's interventions that probably is unintended.

Following the associative path with the luxury of hindsight (the jealous avoidance of "somebody"—some bodies—in the analyst's life, the adolescent envy and curiosity about her mother's underwear and erotic activity—the mother's "bed of roses" in contrast to her own repugnant anal and genital discharges) clearly suggests that an archaic transference paradigm of envious and jealous comparisons with an erotically sophisticated rival lies concealed behind the oppositional resistance. Mary's refusal to allow thoughts about the analyst's private life to intrude into their relationship expresses a wish not to be confronted with the evidence of other "bodies" who share her analyst's bed. We could well imagine another time in this patient's treatment or in another patient's treatment where the adaptive transference would have been a more important strategic agenda. However, at this time in Mary's treatment, issues of equality and demands for mutuality were not a prominent dimension of the analytic relationship, nor of her living outside the analysis.

All successful sublimations involve transference displacements that connect our conscious commitments to unconscious sources of primitive vitality, heightened intensity, and wish fulfillment. Perhaps the ultimate distinction is that transference activity stemming from the repressed operates with less boundary permeability—"the elemental contents of core conflicts and repressed experience resist the transformational influence of ongoing experience" (Adler 1993, p. 585)—while transference activity that has not been subject to repression is more open to influence through current experience. Unconscious fantasy, manifest through adaptive and archaic transference activity, is an organizing function of the present, integrating current developmental needs with archaic wishes and fears. Within this framework we can understand the idea of transference as distortion (Arlow 1985, Greenson 1967, Loewald 1960). Archaic transference processes, the representation of the repressed, loads our organizing activity with phenomena that have not grown up with the rest of us. Transference in this respect distorts the integrative functioning of the individual as higher-order, synthetic processes are replaced by more automatic, rigidly fixed modes of perception and response that fail to register the subtle but crucial distinctions that mediate our apprehension of social reality. Distortions of self and object experience are inevitable. To maintain analytic neutrality with regard to transference, the analyst must empathize with the integrative elements of the patient's subjective experience *and* the more archaic, repressed dimensions of functioning. The analyst's task might be described as one of constructing a bridge—the transference neurosis—from passively experienced repetitions[2] to what Loewald (1971) described as active re-creations.

Although once the dominant paradigm of therapeutic action in psychoanalysis—a virtual litmus test of the genuine article—the concept of the transference neurosis has gradually been eclipsed in contemporary psychoanalytic thinking. Built upon Freud's (1914) remarkable insight that repetition phenomena are an incomplete form of remembering, the model conceives a

---

2. Passively experienced repetitions are the manifestations of transference in the more archaic sense of repressed forces of the dynamic unconscious not yet brought under the integrating influence of the synthetic functions (Freedman 1985, Hartmann 1950, Loewald 1960, 1971, Nunberg 1931).

discrete constellation of libidinal/aggressive wishes and defenses organized around the conflictual, object-related striving
of a specific phase of development (the oedipal stage and/or anal
and oral regressions therefrom) evolving spontaneously within
the psychoanalytic situation. Archaic wishfulness gives impetus
to a dramatization whose illusory structure of enduring infantile
experience is created out of the actual events and interactions
of the psychoanalytic relationship. By safeguarding an interpretive stance outside this dramatic space, the analyst is in
position to identify the real infantile action behind this manifest
facade, thereby guiding the patient to recall a vivid, forgotten
past, while discovering new solutions to psychically formative
conflicts. Today, this formulation, despite its theoretical ele-
gance and unity, is widely regarded as too narrow a view of
processes that are diverse in their pathways and possibilities.

Too few treatments were ever adequately described—though
a good number were probably inadequately described—within
this procrustean format. Instead, concepts like the therapeutic
alliance (Zetzel 1956), the real relationship, and the working
alliance (Greenson 1965) developed to answer a need to incor-
porate alternative therapeutic processes while preserving this
primary model of therapeutic action. Representing the course of
an entire psychoanalysis in terms of the evolution and interpretive resolution of a transference neurosis became, in effect,
a reductive exercise that highlighted certain events and processes to the exclusion of others whose contributions to the
eventual therapeutic outcome were correspondingly downplayed.
Sometimes these dimensions were acknowledged less formally,
regarded as a species of clinical wisdom or tact, rather than as a
part of clinical theory.

This special status of the transference neurosis was embedded
in a mode of interpretation that emphasized the archaic to the
exclusion of the adaptive elements of transferential experience.
By isolating an infantile past transposed onto the present,
adaptive phenomena that have since come to the fore in our
thinking were marginalized as peripheral interpersonal trans-

actions. Our contemporary perspective emphasizes the importance of maintaining a balance between adaptive and archaic dimensions of experience. It leads us to first establish how the patient strives to both transform and represent our person (or the analytic situation) as a version of an acceptable/ unacceptable past, present, and future. It might be said that this interpretive focus lingers at the intersection of reality and fantasy in the analytic encounter, before determining a particular direction. This enables us to exploit a richness in the texture and structure of this analytic surface that had been previously neglected in the eagerness to find the "royal road" to an archaic core of experience. Accordingly, dream interpretation, the analyst's most refined tool for excavating dynamic tensions, meanings, and connections originating in the arcane wishful depths, has been supplemented by an interpretive emphasis that acknowledges the complexity of enactments at the intersubjective surface of analytic engagement. Unconscious fantasizing, archaic wishing, proactive or reactive defensive maneuvering, and dramatized repetition phenomena are viewed primarily from the perspective of their impact on an ambiguous current reality, rather than as means of reconstructing an unknowable past.

In emphasizing the patient's effort to create a wishful and/or fearful representation of the analyst in the face of clinical ambiguity, we carefully explore and elaborate the specific strategies employed to accomplish these effects: the categorical thinking; the affective selectivity; the representational evasions, generalizations, and symbolic condensations. This exploration precedes the attempt to consign the entire effort to a specific context of genetic antecedents, systematic unconscious fantasizing, or adaptive imperatives. In this light, adaptive constructions of experience stand revealed in their transferential aspect as functional activity, preparing the way for more persistent wishful and fearful distortions through channels of projection and displacement. This fluid attention to dynamic, cognitive, defensive, and transactional aspects of transference neurotic activity gives contemporary transference analysis a playful aspect. Mutually contradictory temporal perspectives may be elaborated with some irony, underscoring paradoxical tensions that crystallize in the patient's relationship to the analyst and the collaborative work. Thus, for example, one might interpret how the patient constructs an image of the analyst as a benevolent omniscient guide out of ambiguous fragments of experience, only to turn and flee fearfully in the next moment from an unwanted psychological dependence on such an awesome figure whose power cannot be contained. The very act of creating a wished-for protector to help regulate the tensions of living generates the specific psychic danger that necessitates an avoidant flight (either in deed or in fantasy). This dependency conflict, may in turn need to be elaborated from the perspective of omnipotent control: the patient's insistence on making him benevolent juxtaposed with a fear of being controlled by an ominous and potentially malevolent analyst. And, yet again, the entire situation may evoke erotic fantasies that take a form repugnant to the patient's sensibility: sadomasochistic enslavement.

Working with transference neurotic activity at the surfaces of the analytic encounter in this way yields abundant material, provided that both analyst and patient are capable of entertaining shifting perspectives within the actuality of the analytic relationship. We cannot assume that our reality is self-evident, one-dimensional, or unambiguous to the patient. Of course, we encounter patients who also insist upon a simple, rigidly defined, representation of the reality of the analyst in their lives. Such reality-bound transferences are appropriately considered a form of tendentious functional activity whose purposes must be explored assiduously if the analysis of transference is to be a meaningful bridge to archaic dimensions of subjective construction. Often, the structure of such unshakable attributions is established by ascribing a defined set of motivational dispositions to the analyst that are then inflexibly asserted in order to negate all contradictory evidence. For example, when the analyst directly tries to explore the possibility of loss or abandonment associated with an anticipated summer break, such patients will insist that this is a "silly" idea in light of the fact that the analyst is a professional and that all professionals take time off. If, in the course of the ensuing interpretive dialogue, we impatiently challenge such premises, these patients will disclaim any untoward reaction, asserting that they know the analyst meant well, since he or she is there to help. Though the pseudo-logic involved in such attitudes is transparent, we generally aren't successful in inviting patients to adopt a self-reflective stance. Yet we need not be stymied. By shifting the plane of our interpretive approach, we quickly recognize that patients' stubborn effort to create an analyst toward whom they can have unshakable confidence is itself an important piece of transference neurotic activity worthy of exploration and analysis. We must consider what needs, wishes, and fantasies this action serves: Is it, perhaps, a species of primitive trust based on constricted imagination, which provides, albeit rigidly, a viable structure of safety from which to explore nontransferential dimensions of the patient's life? Does it permit authentic maturational initiatives that have therapeutic benefit, even while avoiding deeper transferential insight or paranoidal fears? (This is not identical with what is known as a "transference cure," in which an unconscious fantasy about the analyst is stimulated that permits a number of new actions to be carried out in the external world only as long as the fantasy is undisturbed.) Will these therapeutic steps lead to a consolidation of strengths that subsequently permits a more penetrating analysis of this fixed transference situation? When our paradigm of analytic process allows for these variations, we are freer to entertain such hypotheses and to suspend judgment long enough to explore their consequences.

On the other hand, this flexibility is only empowering when it is employed within a framework that informs us where things stand with regard to the deeper dynamic structure of the patient's psyche. Adaptive transference activity serves multiple functions, all of which are of interest to us. We believe, however,

that often enough if the analysis of the analytic surface is
followed through systematically in terms of both transference
and resistance, an archaic substructure composed of genetic
antecedents and derivative unconscious fantasies will begin to
emerge with compelling focus: A transference neurosis is constituted that has an altogether different texture and ambience
than the transference neurotic activity that has previously been
explicated.

Although this cannot be said to occur spontaneously without
considerable interpretive preparation, the form and content of
the transference neurosis is always unpredictable and puzzling.
In some treatments this state emerges and remains consistent
for a substantial stretch of time. In others, it may appear
intermittently, interspersed with long periods in which alternative modes of analytic relatedness hold sway. The pace and
playfulness of interpretive activity may slow to a sluggish,
hypnotic pace, as if thought and action were no longer bound by
ordinary temporal considerations. Both patient and/or analyst
may experience drowsiness and modes of reverie that border on
dream states. The patients' emotional reactivity is alternately
lethargic or explosive, though we have much less success in
anchoring these responses to plausible events or actions in the
analytic interaction. Indeed, we may have the disorienting sense
that we are no longer the person we had assumed ourselves to
be to the patient. In all, the psychic ambience is more sleep-like
than fully awake, and the analyst is increasingly required to
employ principles of dream interpretation to make sense of
manifest events (Kern 1987, Lewin 1955) (Chapter 6). The
patient's immersion in this state of being may continue for a
prolonged period, but one gradually gains the impression that
a particular scene, time, and place is being staged with painstaking concern for detail and nuance of meaning. Intermittently,
there will be moments or entire sessions marked by greater
clarity, in which the patient and analyst will gain unobstructed
glimpses into an actual historical event or situation being
psychically worked over.

To refer to this dimension of transference as "functional activity" is less apt than descriptions that emphasize the passive experience of emotions, impulses, or fantasy contents, as one would speak of a dream or hallucination or seizure. This transference neurosis is generally confined to the analytic situation, a transitional phenomenon integrating the genetic imperatives of unconscious neurotic structure with the adaptive prerequisites of analytic relatedness. Core components of characterological compromise formations seem to break up, becoming animate in a mobile synthesis that creatively transforms the manifest events of the analytic situation into a symbolically charged alternate reality. In this time and space, the most profound wishes and fears that once were centered upon primary figures of childhood are actually transferred onto the analyst and into the analytic situation. Bird's (1972) aphoristic definition of the transference neurosis as "a new edition of the patient's original neurosis but with me in it" (p. 281) seems to capture this quality of experience. Although a real relationship and a therapeutic alliance may be presumed to exist as a necessary ground upon which this process can unfold, they are rarely in evidence at this time. Therefore, it is no longer accurate to say that the patient experiences the analyst "as if" he was her mother, or a part of her mother, or the entire parental unit—he simply has become the symbolic embodiment of these things. Interpretation in the realm of the transference neurosis is correspondingly concrete. "You want to suck milk from my breast and fall asleep," which could only be heard as a metaphorical interpretation at the level of adaptive transference activity ("You want to find in me a nurturing and restful refuge"), takes on a concrete specificity that engages archaic desire in terms of body parts, substances, and interactions. Such interventions evoke neither surprise, shock, nor incomprehension from the patient at this level of experience.

The resolution of a transference neurosis is admittedly mysterious. Indeed, the fact that the patient steps into and out of it at the beginning and end of each session suggests that it

involves an altered state of consciousness—a regression in the
service of the ego—carrying some measure of autonomous
choice. On the other hand, interpretation of the underlying
events, fantasies, and fears, often in archaic bodily terms,
frequently has the effect of raising the patient's consciousness to
a more alert or wakeful state. Over the course of time, the
frequency and depth of these states seem to decrease markedly.
It is not altogether clear whether the process itself, without the
benefit of the analyst's interpretive constructions and integrations, might run a natural course that has substantial therapeutic impact above or beyond the analyst's effort. Ultimately,
the transference neurosis seems to run out of steam. Because
the intensity of the involvement is consistently interpreted and
worked through, an indefinite maintenance of the transference
neurosis opposes the primary thrust of analytic involvement in
depth—using understanding to more fully engage self and
others. We often observe, for instance, that the diminishing of
the transference neurosis coincides with a transition in which
patients report a subjective sense of enhanced energy, power,
and self-awareness in their daily living. Paradoxically, working
with the transference neurosis immerses the participants in the
most fertile levels of fantasy even as it prepares the way for a
broader appreciation of reality. We believe that an analysis that
engages and addresses both the adaptive and archaic dimensions of transference is most likely to reach the deepest levels of
understanding and attain the highest order of personal integration.

SUMMARY

Contemporary understandings of transference diverge around
the issue of whether transference is co-constructed by both
parties of the analytic interaction or brought to it by each
participant. Examining the evolution of the concept of transference distills some of the issues inherent in this controversy.
We suggest that each of these conceptualizations contributes

something essential to the development of a broader picture of the way transference functions in the clinical setting. If we view transference as a process operating along a continuum of repression, both co-construction of the interaction and the primitive wishes, fears, and fantasies brought to the interaction can be parsimoniously accounted for. The distinction between adaptive and archaic transference activity is developed and we assert our belief that both dimensions of transference, dynamically interconnected, are essential aspects of analytic understanding. We concluded with a reconceptualization of the transference neurosis that stresses the importance of balancing archaic and adaptive dimensions of transference activity.

4

Intrapsychic and Interactive Dimensions of Resistance*

*Portions of this chapter were presented at the 21st Annual Scientific Conference "What's Love Got to Do with It" on February 2, 1997, at the Washington Square Institute, New York.

The observation that all patients devote considerable time and energy to activities that impede their analytic progress has impressed psychoanalysts of every persuasion. Freud's trenchant definition of resistance—elegant in its simplicity—as "whatever interrupts the progress of analytic work" (Freud 1900, p. 517) focused exclusively on the psychoanalytic situation. Early analysts, in keeping with an as yet rudimentary conception of psychic structure, tended to locate this resistance in the rebellious willfulness of a difficult patient—a rebellion directed against the analyst's authority to structure the psychoanalytic situation. Technical discussion was limited to specific behaviors and attitudes that avoided or obstructed the scheduling of appointments, use of the couch, payment of fees, or, more problematically, the fundamental pillars of the psychoanalytic process itself: free-association and analytic neutrality (Adler and Bachant 1996). This circumscribed and inadequate understanding of resistance bolstered a deteriorating, largely antagonistic view of the relationship between patient and therapist, wherein the patient's passivity and the analyst's uncontested authority became defining elements of a "productive" working alliance.

The first and probably most significant breakthrough in this adversarial understanding of resistance came about through a clarification and classification of the modes of defense. Freud (1895) had noted early on that patients typically struggle to maintain the defenses they have developed, viewing the treatment—and the analyst—in the context of an attack upon their established ways of feeling safe. However, with the growing recognition that defense was itself a phenomenon shaped by complex unconscious processes, clinicians were finally in a conceptual position to begin to extricate themselves from an increasingly frustrating technical impasse. Resistance could now be addressed analytically through exploration and understanding rather than through force of personal persuasiveness. This new understanding of defense emphasized two divergent yet overlapping concepts: character style, primarily articulated by Wilhelm Reich (1949), and the mechanisms of defense elaborated by Freud (1894, 1895, 1896, 1915a,b, 1925/1926) and Anna Freud (1936). Each of these ideas opened somewhat different technical and theoretical paths that subsequently proved invaluable in the evolution of psychoanalysis. Character as defense was elaborated as the primary conceptual framework for a neo-Freudian or culturalist's approach to resistive phenomena. Their work with resistance was rooted in the recognition that the patient rebelled against the analytic situation because it presented a fundamental challenge to a basic pathological orientation to life. Confronting and undermining these fundamental premises so that the patient might approach the therapy with emotional authenticity became central to this technical approach. Developments within mainstream ego psychology took another direction, emphasizing the analytic clarification and working through of intrapsychic defense mechanisms. Working individually or in concert, these defense mechanisms were seen as generating the foundation for a host of elusive obstacles to the uncovering of unconscious contents.

In time, other major theoretical advances in psychodynamic understanding eventually translated into more sophisticated appreciations of resistance analysis. As the role of aggression in intrapsychic conflict received expanded theoretical emphasis

(Freud 1919, 1923, Strachey 1934), psychoanalysts came to appreciate that reorienting a patient's values with regard to previously unacceptable desires was a naive formulation of their task. The largely unconscious contribution to resistance of systematically structured self-punitive and self-sabotaging action and attitude had been thrown into sharp relief. The pivotal role of guilt, both as an obstacle to self-awareness and as a motivation for clinging to constricted and compromised forms of relating, came to the fore in this heyday of superego analysis. Similarly, as theoretical explications of guilt began to identify the dynamic role of internalized object representations embedded in psychodynamic structure (Klein 1957), an unforeseen malleability in the structure of analytic experience came into view. From this perspective, projectively externalized representations and stimulated reenactments could subvert the analyst's liberating intentions. Analysts became sensitized to the way their benign interpretive activity could be perniciously corrupted by projected and introjected imagoes of a menacing or overstimulating nature. Correspondingly, advances in our understanding of narcissism—both in its grossly pathological and more normative vicissitudes (Kernberg 1975, Kohut 1971, 1977, 1984)—led to renewed interest in shame and self-shaming attitudes as a motivational force underlying many obstinate forms of resistance in the clinical encounter. An empathic grasp of this crucial vulnerability with regard to an experience of cohesive selfhood dictated a more refined timing and articulation of interventions. Calling a spade a spade might not always be the best approach. Interpretations, it became evident, had to be finely tuned with an ear for the subjective echo in the patient's mind or its reverberation would drown out every other awareness.

Informed by these multiple perspectives, contemporary psychoanalysts have come to feel increasingly uneasy about considering resistance exclusively within any one of the traditional theoretical frameworks. Formulations that emphasize characterological defense strike us as too broadly pathologizing large areas of adaptive and healthy personal functioning. On the other hand, formulations that isolate discrete mechanisms of defense within an ego apparatus organized to integrate drive derivatives and environmental demands seem too narrow and mechanistically conceived. A reluctance to be hemmed in by traditional analytic conventions has played a significant role in shaping our contemporary handling of resistance in the clinical encounter. In this context, a growing appreciation of Waelder's (1930) principle that mental processes serve multiple functions has emerged as a specific conceptual pivot, propelling theoretical integrations that encourage greater technical flexibility in many areas of analytic practice. Accordingly, our conception of resistance, like our concepts of transference (Sandler 1983) and defense (Brenner 1982), has evolved from a rather discrete process that points to limited and particular mental activity, toward one that encompasses aspects of all mental activities (Levy 1984, White 1996).

Today we recognize more clearly that resistance is a dimension of every analytic experience and that as one gains an increasingly synoptic perspective on the complex unity of any patient's inner world, neat conceptual distinctions between resistance, defense, transference, or character lose their clear boundaries. Such hybrid technical terms as *transference resistance* and *defense transference* represent conceptual condensations that attest to this ambiguity.

While contemporary thinking about resistance analysis is marked by evolving complexity, at its core is the hard-won appreciation that whatever we come to identify as the resistant attitudes and behaviors of a given clinical encounter are never simply resistant. "To some extent, we no longer speak of resistances per se, but rather attempt to identify the resistance inherent in all the patient's activities" (Levy 1984, p. 71). Resistances serve multiple purposes, as do all the psychological phenomena we observe, only one of which is to subvert the analyst's goals and procedures. Resistant attitudes and behaviors simultaneously defend against the painful affects of anxiety and depression, express or enact unconscious fantasies, repeat or protect genetically significant relational patterns, as well as preserve psychically vital states of autonomy, identity, and self-cohesion from potentially destabilizing impingements. As such, resistances embody desperate psychological imperatives imbued with unconscious infantile misconceptions. From a clinical perspective, an important implication of this understanding is that any behavior or attitude can serve the purposes of resistance only until an analyst finds the technical resources to exploit its other relevant meanings. If this occurs, rather than impede the analyst's efforts, resistive phenomena further our intentions by announcing and defining crucial areas of meaning that must receive specific elaboration.

The basic technical strategy is to establish a context of meaning in which the attitudes, fantasies, and/or behaviors that we have identified and described as resistant will be recognized as having an imperative emotional investment for that person in that place. Our goal is to fully appreciate this contingent meaning, rather than to change the patient's behavior. This can be realized only by carefully detailing the psychodynamic structure of the patient's subjective perspective within the analytic situation. What painful affect is the person warding off? What threat to psychic equilibrium is anticipated? What wishful or reparative fantasy is being advanced? What relational pattern is being conserved? Equally important, how are the analyst's behavior, attitudes, and expectations being construed in regard to these intentions? Do they articulate these anticipations in ways that intensify or ameliorate them? In principle, therefore, whether it takes an hour or an entire analysis, one approaches all varieties of resistance with the same patient and persistently inquisitive attitude. We try to observe with precision and describe in detail the attitudes, behaviors, or fantasies in question, to identify the immanent concerns within the context of the analytic relationship, and to explore the manifest and latent fantasy structure of the motivations involved, including their genetic foundation.

RESISTANCE AND DEFENSE AS GUARDIANS
OF PSYCHIC EQUILIBRIUM

An early and still fundamental orienting perspective on the problem of resistance is anchored in our conception of psychodynamic equilibrium. Rangell (1983), following Freud (1937), Fenichel (1941), and Greenson (1967), is the contemporary analyst who most clearly articulates the view of resistance as a universal motivational force mobilized against the undoing of a defensive system calibrated to maintain intrapsychic equilibrium. Children, adapting to internal and external pressures within a familial environment, develop stable modes of functioning that ameliorate the inevitable conflicts of early childhood. The evolution of this unique organization, represented by an unfolding of unconscious fantasy in response to a predictable sequence of maturational challenge, can be counted one of the most significant achievements of childhood. Satisfying multiple considerations, these early "solutions" endow us with powerful protective functions that persevere into adulthood. In this sense, the force of resistance can be said to be concentrated upon—but not created in—the psychoanalytic situation. Bypassing resistance, either through ill-considered maturational initiatives in life or by premature interpretation in analysis, overloads the adaptive and interactive capacities of an individual, evoking a desperation born of helplessness. This, in turn, becomes the impetus for an immediate counterpressure toward establishing a new, or reestablishing the old, homeostatic balance. Resistance, therefore, is an inevitable and even healthy phenomenon. It guards psychic equilibrium in dangerous— though archaically conceived—circumstance, until an improved solution can be subsituted. It is only from an external vantage point that it will seem unnecessary, contrary, or constrictive. The motivational force of resistance, mobilized by any anticipated change, will express itself in the variety and persistence of a person's actions, thoughts, and attitudes that ward off emotional novelty. In Greenson's (1967) words, resistance "defends the status quo of the patient's neurosis" (p. 36).

In this context, it is relevant to draw a distinction between defense (or more narrowly, defense mechanism) as a discrete attribute of mental functioning and resistance as a ubiquitous dimension of the psychoanalytic situation. From the perspective of psychoanalysis as a clinical process, resistance is by far the more embracing concept. When psychoanalysts refer to defense analysis, they are thinking of treatment conducted within a conceptual framework that appreciates the role of certain habitual patterns of mental and emotional action closely allied with homeostatic adaptation. Broadly speaking, this refers to the balance of pleasurable and painful affects that are tolerable to a person in a particular psychodynamic context, and the automatic strategies or habits of mind that are initiated to avoid traumatic overstimulation. We do not, strictly speaking, observe defenses in action (Fenichel 1941); rather, we observe the mental and affective consequences of a defensive process. Indeed, when defenses work effectively we can only infer their existence by the absence of something expected or the presence of something unexpected. Like a default setting on a word-processing program, though its effects appear at the surface of awareness, its ordinary operation takes place in some hidden recess of the mind. Defensive action basically attempts to reestablish homeostatic equilibrium in response to disruptive tensions clinically identifiable as anxiety, depression, shame, and guilt, emotional states that give warning of potentially traumatic psychic threat. Just what this ultimate traumatic danger consists of is hard to grasp phenomenologically, as patients who approach such states often have difficulty articulating their experience coherently. It seems to be rooted in the losses, real and fantasized, that evolve in earliest childhood experience of self and others. Intense dread and helplessness are its most accessible psychic contents.

Each theorist tends to infer some content of traumatic states that accords with his or her own premises. Thus, object relations theorists tend to emphasize a state of isolation or abandonment, while self psychologists characterize the traumatic state as dissolution of the self, and ego psychologists define trauma in terms of a state of unmanageable excitation. Important as this understanding may be theoretically, within the analytic situation one rarely draws attention to defensive patterns of mental action without reference to their impact on the immediate psychoanalytic process or transference configuration. We don't tell patients that they forget important feelings and thoughts (i.e., employ repression) without anchoring it in a specific context that suggests *motivated* action with regard to the analytic process (i.e., resistant action or a transferentially meaningful action). Though it may be conceptually cogent, it has limited technical impact to simply point out defense mechanisms as such. To do so is to shift our interpretive perspective from the motivations of a person who is living a life, to the operations and patterns of that person's mind as an instrument of psychobiological adaptation. Clinical effectiveness generally resides in the meaning of the defensive action in the context of the psychic processes that have been or are about to be mobilized within the psychoanalytic situation: "You didn't want to remember that you had an erotic fantasy about me in our last session, perhaps because it would suggest I was becoming too important in your life." Psychoanalysis undermines habitual defensive modes of thought and action by identifying and ameliorating the essential dangers that make them imperative.

SUSTAINING THE WORK WITH RESISTANCE

The psychoanalytic situation is specifically designed to set in motion processes that challenge existing psychic equilibria while clarifying the preconditions of safety immanent in a person's ongoing adaptation (Chapter 2). Its open-ended structure thwarts comfortable consolidations, as each new equilibrium is progressively examined and undermined in turn. This confronts us with the inescapable dilemma inherent in radical change: *it doesn't feel good.* Indeed, we often hear patients complain: "I feel like I've left myself behind," "I'm profoundly alienated . . . as if stepping out into a terrifying void." This lament is to be expected as patients confront their apprehension of surrendering familiar ways. Not infrequently, a central aspect of this distress revolves around the way in which early defenses and compromises have become imbued with parental functions, representing sustained contact with parental care in the present (Schafer 1960). Patients speak poignantly of the way in which growth involves separating from the experience of "appealing to" or "connecting with" a parental figure, a fantasy most clearly expressed in the transference. As one patient said in describing her struggle to stay with new ways of relating to herself and others, "It just doesn't sit easily. It doesn't do something for me. Maybe because there's nothing, no one to appeal to." Inevitably, the process will be painful. For some people, it will be psychologically unacceptable.

This understanding puts us in a better position to respect the enormous personal courage patients must find to challenge, struggle against, and renounce resistive tendencies. It is important to remind ourselves of this frequently, for our awareness of resistance in the clinical encounter is of something that frustrates our intentions or wishes. Resistance quite literally puts us off, creating emotional distance and intellectual confusion. It disrupts the satisfying rhythms of analytic engagement that assure us things are going well. The friction of resistant attitudes, behaviors, and constructions strains our resources of patience and hopefulness. Yet our availability as a sustaining source of emotional connectedness, containment, and support to patients during their efforts to change is often crucial. This availability, ultimately an expression of our own capacity for love and commitment over time, is communicated in countless ways: It is palpable in our attention to developing a partnership with the patient, a joint process that is continually informed by the goal of fostering the patient's autonomy (Busch 1995, Gray 1982, Greenson 1967, Renik 1995). It is evident in our persistent effort to stay in touch with the intersubjective underpinnings of analytic process, so that when we approach patients' conflicts, they can stand with us and accept a truly self-reflective perspective. It is represented in the recognition we extend to emergent maturational initiatives, in our acknowledgment of genuine advances (Chapter 8), and in our ability to mediate a more integrated and articulate vision of the patient's core process (Loewald 1960). As Schafer (1960) has made clear, "Normal courage, endurance, and ability to withstand intense stimulation or deprivation, all depend on the feeling of being recognized and attended to by the superego" (p. 175). That the analyst serves in the psychoanalytic situation as auxiliary—and one hopes more benign—superego (Strachey 1934) underscores his or her importance in the analysis of resistance. In effect, resistance is most likely to become a truly pernicious obstacle to progress when we do not fully accept the necessity of analyzing and empathizing with the patient's unconscious sense of danger. Wishing to make the resistant attitudes and behavior stop or disappear so that something we consider more productive can take place is human and understandable, but it is not a helpful analytic attitude (Brenner 1976, Friedman 1997, Schafer 1983). Inevitably, it intensifies the very behavior or motivation one wishes to resolve.

An impetus to slow down or flee the momentum of psychoanalytic processes points emphatically to the enduring dynamic relevance of a more fundamental psychic framework that preserves a person's earliest relational configurations while containing the conflicts and unconscious fantasies that mediate an archaic apprehension of the experiential world (Bachant and Adler 1997). Resistance can be observed even when a person endeavors to engage in self-analysis outside the orbit of the psychoanalytic situation. Since Freud encountered violent resistance to his self-analytic efforts, he was naturally reluctant to view it exclusively as a creation of the analytic interaction.

The establishment of such a stable psychic framework serves powerful adaptive functions that are essential to psychic survival. Early structuralization eliminates the need to sort through infinite decision-making possibilities by preordering a complex array of mental imagery (Damasio 1994). This aids immeasurably in the difficult task of negotiating the risks and opportunities of an uncertain world, enabling us to increase our predictive abilities in space and time. No parent, however nurturing and competent, can adequately prepare a child for the emotionally intense, frequently overwhelming dilemmas of childhood. Here the child is inevitably alone in a landscape ambiguously defined by external and internal desire, intention, and fantasy. It is important to remember, however, that the resulting resolutions, however limiting in the life of the adult, are true testament to eros; they express an enduring determination to nurture the self. Although constructed around compromise formations arrived at by a cognitively immature and psychically vulnerable child, the efforts to preserve this framework is a force with which every true analysis must contend. Modification of fundamental structure is the highest aspiration of the psychoanalytic enterprise.

Freud's (1905b) initial formulation of the self-preservative drive, Kohut's (1971, 1977, 1984) focus on the development of the self (including his principle of the primacy of preserving the self), and Winnicott's (1960) description of the protective function of the false self each represents an important contribution to our understanding of the ways in which the individual actively strives to preserve the cohesive dynamic and representational structures that anchor a sense of secure identity. An appreciation of this profound psychic investment must always inform our effort to articulate, explore, and analyze resistances. When encountering frustrating and recalcitrant defensive efforts to protect the self from pain, we are mindful that these solutions embody a dedication to caring for oneself, a self-concern that must be validated, nurtured, and won over as an ally of any thoroughgoing therapeutic process. Nowhere is it more consequential to align oneself with a patient's potential for growth and integration than when dealing with resistance and the emotions that generate it. Working to strengthen these areas of vulnerability, what might be described as the growth plates of therapeutic engagement, inevitably intensifies resistance. Patients reinstitute automatic modes of dealing with anticipated injury (Arlow and Brenner 1990, Busch 1995, Gray 1994), as the analytic process threatens adaptations structured during childhood. Emphasizing the adaptive functions of resistant behaviors and attitudes is crucial. It mitigates the person's dread of being helplessly exposed to overwhelming danger. Without a strategy for mastering the depression, guilt, shame, and anxiety that accompany a serious challenge to old ways, few persons would find the courage to change. As patients come to appreciate how and why particular self-protective ways of perceiving and organizing the world developed, their insight serves to guide them through turbulent currents of emotional distress that surge upon each new tide of change. By aligning ourselves with patients' yearning to escape confinement, we support their taking maturational risks, which in turn place them once again in harm's way. Added to the terror of functioning in an uncertain world without familiar defensive structures is a confounding sense of loss as one surrenders key elements of early organization, elements that may feel like the foundation of personal identity.

We begin to better appreciate the tenacity of resistance; at bottom it speaks of the desperate effort to hold onto a fundamental orientation that makes sense of and stabilizes one's experience of the world. This orientation feels both desperately needed and painful to discard. When the patient identifies and begins to reorganize these earlier configurations of meaning, desire, and avoidance, the relationship with the analyst in both its adaptive and archaic dimensions becomes pivotal to the process of working through. Analysis of resistance immerses us in powerful issues of attachment and separation, loss and integration, safety and avoidance. The need for the analyst as a supportive ally during this process is palpable, even though patients may struggle to ward us off as an unwelcome disturber of their peace.

CASE ILLUSTRATION

Harriet came to her session wrestling with what she called "crazy thoughts." Her adult daughter had called to inform her that she was meeting her cousin for lunch later that day. Although Harriet could identify no rational grounds for her apprehension, she could not rid herself of the disturbing idea that the true purpose of this get together was only to give the two of them an opportunity to unite in their criticism of her. With considerable reluctance and shame, she haltingly acknowledged the details of the scene she envisioned, a scenario essentially constructed around a derisive, conspiratorial accounting of her inadequacies as mother, aunt, and human being. While Harriet "knew" that all this was "paranoid and neurotic," vivid images of an imagined alliance plagued her relentlessly, accompanied by familiar feelings of being, once again, ostracized and alone.

Harriet went on to express surprise that she was "torturing" herself this way, because until she had spoken with her daughter she had been having a particularly fine morning. She had accomplished a lot of what she had set out to do, and was feeling a sense of contentment about her productivity that she hadn't experienced for some time.

Following the logic of these associations, her analyst asked if there might be a connection between her experience of contentment and the "crazy" fantasies she had described.

Harriet: I think there may be. I've come to see how compelling the fantasy of being the outsider is for me. I mean, I know that Jennie and Sally aren't getting together to make fun of me. I see how I undermine my sense of well-being so much of the time. It's almost as if the fantasy serves to justify an impulse to take something away from myself.

Therapist: To take something away from yourself? What occurs to you about that?

Harriet (reflective pause): Actually, I'm thinking about my favorite doll, in childhood, Eloise. When my mother was in the hospital that week that Carole was born, I was farmed out to my Aunt Flora. My cousin Nina—Sally's mother— was a year younger than I and during the time we were together (and my memory tells me it was a very long time) she grew attached to my Eloise. For some reason, when my father came to bring me home to meet my baby sister, I gave Eloise to Nina as a present. I don't know what possessed me! Everyone thought it was so sweet of me, but as soon as I left, I began to feel horrible regret. I knew that I had done something terrible and irrevocable. I remember that for a long time afterward . . . every night I would cry myself to sleep thinking miserably how much I missed Eloise.

Therapist: You gave your baby away just when your mother was bringing her new baby home. Perhaps this was not coincidence. We've come to appreciate just how traumatic your sister's birth was for you. How profoundly abandoned you must have felt. Taking charge of the situation by cutting off must have helped you to feel safer.

Harriet: What are you getting at? That I abandoned Eloise? But I suffered terribly.

Therapist: As you do in your fantasy about Jennie and Sally. But at least you are in control, not waiting helplessly for the worst to happen again.

Harriet: It's hard to believe I could do something like that to myself. . . . I'm remembering something else about that week. Nina and I had an elaborate fantasy game that we played out around Eloise. Eloise was a sick child . . . a baby . . . and we . . . I mean *I* had to take her to the hospital and Nina was the nurse who took care of her. I think that must have been how she got so attached to her. Taking care of her in our imaginary hospital.

Therapist: You mean Nina got attached to Eloise as your mother got attached to your sister—in the hospital.

Harriet: And I cut them both off, Eloise and my mother.

In Harriet's treatment, abundant analytic evidence supported the idea that she had experienced the birth of her first sibling as a catastrophic abandonment. Abandonment, in one form or another, had emerged as a central theme of her adult living and was a ubiquitous stimulus to transference reactivity in the analysis. However, as the above piece of analysis suggests, already in place at a very early age was a tendency to turn passive into active by making happen what she feared most. This was apparent in the remembered struggle to master a sense of impending loss, and to redirect destructive wishes away from her anticipated new rival. She exercised control through fantasy (the play with Nina) and enactment (giving her doll/baby away) over the tensions (the fear, guilt, and depressive anxiety) of passive waiting. Through this proactive step, she succeeded in mitigating the traumatic helplessness of unexpected loss, experienced at the birth of her first sibling. She became the agent of loss and anguish (vis-à-vis Eloise) in her own life. As this memory also suggests, derivatives of oedipal and sibling rivalry were already implicated in this complex "solution" to a profound childhood dilemma.

As an adult, Harriet's undermining herself by taking away any contentment that she might enjoy at her own capacity to produce, both as a parent and as an artist (i.e., the children of her creativity), was a ubiquitous strategy for gaining control of potential threat. Analytically observed, this undermining action could be seen as a repetitive effort to reestablish psychic equilibrium in the face of threatened abandonment or loss. Feeling left out or not good enough was a price she willingly paid to manage a dread so overwhelming that she could articulate only the edges of it. Predictably throughout a period of years, Harriet had desperately resisted the terror of surrendering herself to the uncertainties of spontaneous expression in the presence of her analyst, unless she was articulating a punishing state of loss or worthlessness. This circumscribed range of transference affect, which was initally represented as a reworking of early traumatic experiences of disappointment with her mother, was eventually revealed as an unconsciously initiated resistant strategy. Its purpose was to forestall a risky transferential encounter that might put her analyst's capacity for devotion and reliability to a more searching test. Treating her analyst like her once beloved Eloise, Harriet repeatedly "gave her away" to avoid discovering that she was not the real thing, but only an inadequate surrogate.

Understanding resistance as a fundamental aspect of how the mind works has value for both analyst and analysand. It provides a context within which the inevitable vacillations that characterize analytic work become comprehensible. This can be immeasurably helpful in assessing the feelings, thoughts, and actions that emerge in the course of treatment. In Harriet's case, for example, a growing understanding of the complex reasons for her dread of uncertainty enabled her to gradually stay with this feeling long enough to allow a deeper exploration of its triggers in the psychoanalytic situation. This understanding also provided her with a tool with which she began to assess the endless repetitions of self-initiated loss in her daily life, empowering her to establish, bit by bit, a new relationship to her fears.

Working primarily in the transference, Harriet's analyst gave attention to the flow of her associations, stimulating a developing capacity to observe her own mind at work. This sustained collaboration enabled analyst and patient to identify multiple meanings of her transference dynamics. These included but were not limited to the following: positioning herself as a child needing adult help and validation; containing, denying, and expressing rage at usurping rivals; punishing herself for the greedy and rivalrous wishes that she believed had caused her early abandonments; and enacting a relationship with the analyst in which she would be passively penetrated and impregnated by a powerful analyst/father. As she understood more fully this unconscious transferential context within which her dread of uncertainty had taken root, she began to strive to establish new foundational principles of psychic equilibrium based on adult productivity and well-being rather than on the avoidance or acting out of sibling and oedipal rivalries. Although Harriet still confronted wishes that were frightening in their intensity, her experience of these urges underwent change. She began to be able to differentiate aspects of experience originally fused in an overwhelming explosion of terror. Yet even after she had come to recognize and integrate many of the essential elements of this dynamic configuration, the resistive pull of her childhood solution—here expressed once again as the impulse to give away her (now adult) baby and to restore a fantasy of abandonment—was easily evoked.

Resistance, as a manifestation of the patient's need to control the pace and extent of progress, is a dimension of the analytic situation that can never be fully resolved. We no longer expect, as the psychoanalytic pioneers apparently did, that resistant behaviors and attitudes will disappear when they are observed and described. We ask no more of the patient's willpower than a temporary brake on impulsive or compulsive dispositions. We hope to render them less consuming so that analytic exploration of the traumatic fantasies, overstimulating wishes, and unbearable conflicts that make these adaptive strategies seem imperative can be excavated. Analysis of the resistance provides us with a map of the boundaries of the archaic psychic organization, identifying the territories that need to be explored.

THE CLINICAL ENCOUNTER WITH RESISTANCE

A problem with some early clinical theorizing was that intrapsychic and interactional dimensions of resistance had been dichotomized. We were asked to ally ourselves with either one understanding or the other. Yet to focus solely on the intrapsychic dimension of psychic organizing neglects the human hallmark of experiential adaptation, a special flexibility that allows us to assimilate and accommodate novel experience. Counterbalancing the rigidities of a relatively fixed psychic framework in human functioning, we also must recognize a genetically programmed adaptive flexibility that enables human beings to

continually construct ongoing experience (Damasio 1994, Kriegman and Slavin 1989, Langs 1996, Ogden 1986, 1989). Adult
living continues to influence those elements of prestructured
psychic activity as long as a vital connection with the experiential dimension of adaptive functioning is maintained. Clinically,
this directs us to stress the importance of the personal meanings, feelings, and thinking that mediate the actions and interactions that constitute a therapeutic process. It is here that
our descriptive understanding of resistance takes center stage
as analyst and analysand work together to explicate the entrenched obstacles to increased awareness that arise in any
working relationship. Both the fundamental psychic organization—the framework—and the capacity to fully engage the
physical and social environment—the flexibility—influence our
constructions of all experience. The checks and balances delineated by these two contributors has significant implications for
the analysis of resistance. Specifically, given the tenacity with
which we cling to early psychic organization, it directs us to
consider that working with resistance may require both analysis
(Busch 1995, Freud 1914, Gray 1994) and active efforts to
overcome it (Freud 1919).

Although the foundation of persistent resistive structures will
always be firmly anchored in the emotional, conceptual, behavioral, and even physiological bedrock of very early childhood
experience, our immediate awareness of the ongoing dynamic
interplay of intrapsychic and extrapsychic expressions of resistance informs our technique in the clinical encounter. In this
arena, depth of interpretive focus is not easily equated with
impact; we need to address salient points of disjunction if we
want to keep our forward momentum. Boesky (1990) contends
that disjunctions are integral and informative aspects of any
analytic encounter. Starting with the observation that patient
and analyst inevitably fail in their respective goals of free
associating and maintaining analytic neutrality, he maintains
that the relationship between these failures provides us with a

potent source of information. The mutual construction of resistance becomes an essential focus for analytic interaction.

Every resistance, no matter how trifling, is a resistance to something, and its exploration—in the moment—provides us with a bridge to dissociated experience. Inevitably, an expression of the patient's most problematic love relations shades and shapes these resistant surfaces. Engaging a patient's interest in exploring precise moments of interaction is a critical aspect of working with resistance that has been incisively elaborated by Busch (1993, 1994, 1995, 1997), Gray (1982, 1986, 1994), Schwaber (1983, 1986, 1994), and others. Central to this endeavor is the importance of addressing experience that is consciously available to both parties, what Renik (1995) has described as "facts of observation that are available [to] and have been agreed upon by both analyst and analysand" (p. 88). Technically, this may involve helping the patient oscillate between spontaneously verbalized thoughts and feelings regarding the analyst and taking this subjective mental content as a point of departure for further analytic inquiry. Early in treatment, patients often have difficulty sustaining this open-ended, associative momentum. Typically they regard their thoughts and feelings exclusively as reflections of external reality, demonstrating an intolerance of inferential ambiguity largely shaped by the categorical pressures of archaic conscience and calamity. As analysis deepens, thinking about thinking and being able to observe the process of creating meaning itself (Busch 1995, 1997, Gray 1973, 1994) enable the patient to construct "definitive" realities from the potential realm of plausible possibilities. In this sense, transference, defense, and resistance analysis are synergistic dimensions in the process of expanding the subjective perspectives that can be tolerated within the analytic encounter. As patients come to understand that they are acting, fantasizing, or thinking in order to protect themselves, the analyst can, with appropriate tact and timing, use these targeted resistances to uncover buried or disowned wishes and fears, as well as to define the ideas, emotions, and unconscious fantasies that give rise to signals of danger. Giving specific form to these dissociated elements plays a crucial role in developing the therapeutic relationship.

It is important to emphasize that it is not a behavior or attitude in itself but only its functional or motivational role in thwarting analytic goals that identifies something as resistance (see Brenner 1982 for a functional understanding of defense). Potentially fruitful analytic efforts turn barren when dimensions of resistance are neglected. Virtually any aspect of the analytic situation, even essential analytic processes intimately associated with progressive momentum, can become infused with resistant purpose. When patients relentlessly elaborate insights or fearlessly undertake daring maturational initiatives, we may legitimately begin to wonder whether avoidant intention is in ascendance: Preconscious thoughts, such as, "Until I fully and finally understand this, I never have to give this up or change my behavior" and "If I change my behavior, control this feeling, or adjust my attitude, I'll never have to come to terms with what it means to me" form the core of familiar strategies to curtail the most profound reach of psychoanalytic therapy.

In the psychoanalytic situation, resistance is what patients do to curtail the momentum of analytic change. Our attention is alternately drawn towards disruptions of intrapsychic equilibrium and to disguised meanings in the patient's relatedness to us, those intra- and extrapsychic poles that define the elusive field of resistant activity. In the course of a treatment, the phenomena embraced may be more or less circumscribed, strategically significant, and/or recalcitrant. Entire areas of psychoanalytic exploration may be blocked, as is the case when a patient avoids all fantasy expression, hides erotic impulse, or chronically forgets dreams and affectively loaded memories in the analyst's presence. Yet it is a commonplace of clinical wisdom that patients who fill multiple sessions with obscure and thematically disorganized dreams overwhelm the analysis with an embarrassment of riches that are intended, in actuality, to impoverish the process. Although flooding the analysis with undigestible fantasy is not an impediment of the same magnitude as the inability to recall any fantasy derivatives or affectively loaded memories in the analyst's presence, its resistive meanings must be addressed on multiple levels and various locales. Our copious and unproductive dreamer, for example, may, upon further analysis, be seen to be expressing wishes with regard to the analyst: to go on sleeping in his protective presence, to be his incontinent infant, to confront him with menstrual outpourings of her pubescent body. She may, as well, be enacting a scenario of defiance and rebellion: "You asked for my uncensored, uncontrolled self; here, take it, make something of it!" She may, on the other hand, be warding off the anxiety aroused by the phallic thrust of the analyst's incisive understanding, flooding him with images, words, and meanings so that he will remain passive and silent.

Psychodynamically "successful" solutions that satisfy archaic needs and fears are, as we have seen, among the most significant sources of resistance, cherished like the tattered blanket of childhood. Yet like the child's need for his transitional object, the manifestations of resistance point us directly to the underlying object of desire. Resistance occurs at the cutting edge of the patient's development; it points us unfailingly to the place where crucial analytic work awaits our attention, to the specific attitude and/or behavior that is blocking a more profound evocation, exploration, or integration of psychic life. Exploring these junctures offers patient and analyst a first-hand opportunity to approach dissociated experience. Understanding the essence of these split off, unconscious desires and fears is a crucial aspect of deepening the therapeutic process, for an expression of the patient's archaic love relations lies hidden beneath its surface.

Jonathan, an attractive, articulate 42-year-old man, came into treatment because his marriage of twelve years was in trouble. He wondered whether he should continue to work on it or "call it a day." As his relationship with his wife was explored, it became evident that behind Jonathan's marital difficulties was an even more disturbing set of internal experiences: Jonathan lived with almost constant suicidal thoughts and feelings. For as long as he could remember, these thoughts were present soon after he woke up and stayed with him unless he intentionally distracted himself. This preoccupation was an ever-powerful undercurrent of daily experience, always threatening to drag him under. As this dramatic internal reality was brought into focus and clarified, he could easily recognize that years of heroin addiction (he described himself as "an addict in recovery") and endless struggles with sexual compulsions had essentially been his attempt to deal with the perpetual torment of these suicidal thoughts and feelings.

Analysis gradually revealed that Jonathan's suicidal preoccupation embodied a powerful compromise formation, a mode of relating to himself that satisfied many internal and external demands. These included, most prominently, a need to punish himself for childhood transgressions as well as a desire to ward off involvements with potentially rejecting others. But suicidal feelings also embodied the disguised object of Jonathan's dissociated desire, for it maintained a conflictual relationship with a disapproving maternal imago who relentlessly offered the same damning judgment of his worth—Jonathan's "life was not worth living."

Although he had struggled valiantly to manage these impulses, there was an intractable quality to this tormenting obsession; it had become pivotal to an intrapsychic balance that contained his despair, rage, and thwarted longing toward the primary objects of his love. In this sense, the tormenting idea of suicide had become a trusted companion as well as an object of allure, and he strenuously resisted giving it up. It had accompanied him for years, despite attempts to banish, suppress, or narcotize its painful aspects. This struggle now came to the fore in his transferential constructions within the analysis. Jonathan ingeniously developed endless scenarios in which his analyst would have to say no to him, in fact as well as in fantasy. For example, by confusing the time of his appointments he would arrive an hour or a day ahead of schedule so that she would have to turn him away.

A crucial insight was emerging: Jonathan was very comfortable with rejection, whether it was rejection of his own desire or rejection at the hands of someone else. He rejected both his desire to be loved as well as any gratification in being loved. Jonathan's violent impulse to cut off any desire to love or be loved was concretized in the fantasy of cutting off his life, even as this desire preserved a punitive attachment to a cruelly ungiving maternal imago—the grave beckoned to him with its cold eternal embrace. Working with Jonathan's resistance to moving away from suicidal thoughts and feelings pointed directly to this archaic desire. A more deeply buried longing to elicit a loving response only became evident through the analysis of unconscious transference fantasies carefully disguised in his self-destructive and provocative acting out. Not surprisingly, as the resistant elements of his obsession with self-rejection were worked through, profound feelings of sadness, loneliness, and longing began to emerge and take center stage in his conscious experience.

As this case material illustrates, analyzing resistance steers us to the wishful longings and fears that are most problematic for the patient. Working through these obstacles unveils an elaborate unconscious organization of fantasy and motive that introduces a conflicted and consequently tendentious bias to the construction of current experience. We observe this influence most clearly in a reductive filtering of potential meaning in the analytic interaction through which the therapeutic scope of our intentions, words, and deeds are severely circumscribed. Here we are encountering a dimension of transference as resistance, one of its original and still relevant meanings. Jonathan seemed insistent on finding in his analyst a cold, ungiving, rejecting maternal presence; his actions, his attitudes, as well as his constructions of her expressive action all conspired toward the same end. Only as Jonathan's resistance to seeking new forms of relatedness with his analyst was confronted and worked through did these archaic dimensions of experience lose their preemptive authority (Busch 1995, Gray 1994, Loewald 1960).

To make it possible for a patient to begin to encounter life in its fullness, we must nurture an alliance in the present that bridges the losses that occur as patients relinquish the past. Our awareness that this transition is a perilous one can help us to approach the analysis of resistance with both tact and tenderness. We must bear in mind that the nature of this bridge is not exempt from analytic investigation. Inevitably, there are inducements to confusing the caretaking functions of the analytic process with the fantasy of being the patient's caretaker. We must be wary of what Levine (1993) has formulated as conceptual drift, a tendency to imbue our concepts, interactions, and the analytic process itself with unconscious fantasies that carry parental representations often experienced as soothing and permissive. Unanalyzed, these fantasies can distort technique by impeding efforts to recognize and understand unconscious conflict. Understanding the patient's experience requires that we maintain our analytic attitude even when a more facile explanation is at hand.

Surrendering the safety of childhood solutions is never easy, even when the analyst meets these emotional and technical challenges. The patient faces an ever-present temptation to strive for the excitement and/or constriction that psychoanalytic exploration has revealed to be one more variant of the familiar excitement or constriction of the past. Often enough, excitements of this sort are mistaken for the genuine passion of life, and the constrictions are viewed as its necessary conditions of safety. As in a fairy tale, the allure of living out ancient fantasies of blissful engagement calls with siren serenade, promising the fulfillment of our heart's desire. But surrendering to these illusions condemns us to imprisonment in the past, imposing upon a more innocent and welcoming reality a sentence of blind repetition. Thus drugs, perverse erotic scenarios, and the endless pursuit of exquisitely desirable, unavailable women lured

Jonathan endlessly on, only to leave him empty and forlorn as these excitements repeatedly betrayed their exotic promise. Working through resistance, however, opened the gate to complex and sustainable passions. It facilitated an opportunity to find and preserve the love of a real person in the real world. It unveiled the illusory ties that bound him to an archaic past with its fantastical pleasures and dangers. Through work with the resistance, especially its manifestations in the transference, patients can come to learn, in Winnicott's (1974) words, that the trauma they anticipate is, in part, a trauma that has already happened.

THE INTERACTIVE RHYTHMS OF RESISTANCE

Interactive elements of the analytic relationship have become a primary focus of contemporary advances in resistance analysis. Until recently, the analyst's contributions to the creation of therapeutic impasses have been conceptualized mainly within a framework of countertransference (Chapter 5). It was seen as an expression of unconscious conflictual responses to the patient or to the patient's material, a problem of the analyst's transferences or defensive organization. This recognition had been the inspiration for Freud's prescription that every psychoanalyst should have an analysis before doing analysis, to eliminate "blind spots" that might lead to collusive avoidance and to master irrational intensities that might be expressed through surreptitious reenactments. Our contemporary approach acknowledges that entrenched resistances may also form around the appropriate and non-conflictual exercise of the analyst's particular mode of analyzing. The way we embody neutrality, establish boundaries, interpret symbolism, or are guided in our formulations by particular theoretical models or educational influence are unavoidable expressions of a unique professional subjectivity—a subjectivity that has numerous edges to snag the momentum of an analytic process.

Eliminating these blind spots is difficult, if not impossible, since they are built into the lens of an analyzing instrument that we are not prepared to abandon. The analogy is apt, however. To scrutinize an object through an instrument such as a microscope reveals detailed phenomena that escape the attention of the naked eye, making things seem in some sense larger than life. The analyzing instrument through which our vision of clinical phenomena is brought into focus—by observing precisely the associative linkages in patients' narratives, clarifying the transference–countertransference interaction, discerning the symbolic allusions in their denotative language, or empathizing with an unspoken affective posture—reveals unconscious concerns and motives that otherwise elude attention. It is our means of making the unconscious conscious. Yet it also renders these phenomena disproportionate to the person who is living that life. When patients accuse us of "making a big deal out of nothing," they may be objecting not so much to the content of our observation as to the focal length of the lens through which we clarify it. We are not suggesting that there is one appropriate distance or perspective for observing an analytic patient. Many perspectives are useful in developing the depth of vision that we strive for. Rather, we are saying that the analyst will be more effective in addressing certain resistances when he or she is prepared to observe the impact of the multiple observational perspectives brought to bear, as well as shifts between convergent perspectives. In effect, part of analyzing resistance involves attending to these various facets of our analytic lens.

Whenever her analyst made an interpretation that touched upon any aspect of Leslie's envious animosity toward a rival, she would be thrown into a state of enormous turmoil and despair. Regardless of how inconsequential the thought, feeling, or action in question appeared to be to her analyst, Leslie would protest vehemently: "How could you think such a thing of me? I feel completely misunderstood by you! You accuse me of being such a destructive and hateful person. I can't stand it!"

An extended silence would ensue. Initially, Leslie's analyst had read these reactions of distress followed by silence as both indicative of the magnitude of her resistance as well as confirmatory of the interpretive content. She considered it an instance of severe intrapsychic disequilibrium induced by a challenge to the defensive isolation that warded off the destructiveness of her envy. Leslie couldn't bear thinking of herself as envious. Her interventions, following this understanding, emphasized the defensive projection of Leslie's accusatory conscience onto herself. "You prefer to see *me* as condemning *you* in order to keep yourself blameless." However, as her patient's recalcitrance and despondency persisted with inexhaustible fury—expressed in virtually the same form and wording whenever or wherever it was triggered—she gradually came to doubt the adequacy of this understanding. It seemed that any approach to the subject was completely taboo, no matter how incrementally or tactfully broached.

Her analyst's doubts did not concern the accuracy of the interpretation, as far as it went. These eruptions of despair occurred in contexts that left little question as to the nature of Leslie's underlying impulses or the cast of her feelings. Rather, she focused instead on the meaning of Leslie's disproportionate despair and resentment at having the interpretation made to her. She was particularly impressed by the vehemence of Leslie's attribution that she had completely misunderstood her. It seemed unfair on a number of grounds. She could, upon serious introspection, detect nothing accusatory in her attitude toward Leslie. What she had attempted to point out wasn't something that she personally considered hateful. Indeed, she had gone to great lengths to try to convey through wording, tone, and intonation her belief that such feelings were simply a part—albeit a rather disagreeable part—of everyone's human nature.

Internally occupied with reflections such as these, she chose to interrupt Leslie's aggrieved silence: "Why do you say 'completely'? That I completely misunderstand you?" she wondered out loud.

Leslie (appearing to be slightly mollified by her analyst's query and with a note of beseeching appeal softening the accusatory pointedness of her anger): You only tell me when I'm bad, you never say anything positive about me. It's as if you're listening to prove that I'm in the wrong and that I'm unworthy!

Analyst: I think I understand what you're getting at. You feel that my listening is biased toward the unsavory things you think and feel.

Leslie: Isn't it?

Analyst: I would have said that I'm simply listening carefully to what you don't say as well as what you say, what is implicit but not stated directly.

Leslie: That may be how you view it, but it doesn't feel like that. Yeah, I might have been a little jealous of Nancy's engagement, maybe you're right, but I love her, she's my best friend in the world! I need to feel that you're on my side.

The way each partner organized this analytic exchange can be charted along a mutually determined continuum. We can describe this process as moving from an unproductively integrated adaptation characterized by pathological relatedness (dominated by archaic fears and fantasies) to an accommodation of enhanced communication. Leslie was embroiled in a struggle to both ward off and reenact an anticipated traumatic repetition, while her analyst was understanding her as engaged in a specific defensive effort to deny a set of wishes, impulses, and fantasies. Each found in the other's behavior sufficient evidence to support their construction of events. Their mutual understanding within this context, however frustrating and disturbing, was more incomplete than distorted. Contemporary approaches to the analysis of resistance have increasingly focused on mapping the specific, subtle, intersubjective elements of such dynamic interplay. We follow elements, which might best be described as recurrent rhythmic patterns of interrelatedness, and attend to the stylistic nuances that characterize each individual's participation. By carefully coordinating these observations, tracing the elaborate interface of resistance-intensifying interactions, shifts from productive to disjunctive momentum can be isolated. Although the elements of this vignette are undoubtedly interpretable within a broader framework of transference—the patient believed that her mother had favored her younger sister throughout childhood and that "the little angel" could do no wrong—resistance became most salient as Leslie distended those dimensions of the analyst's vision that could serve to close off an encounter with this more ambiguous reality. It could be said that Leslie's despair was triggered not so much by a confrontation with her own destructive envy as by the belief that once again she would have no hope of fulfilling a long-deferred wish to be seen as "the most worthy one." Resistance permeates this belief. To allow herself to openly acknowledge her wish for something different in the present involves moving away from the defenses and ideas that protected her from anguish in the past. Leslie anticipates that she will be seen as bad, organizing her interaction with her analyst along familiar lines, rather than confronting the uncertainty of wanting something she fears she can't have.

Resistance at this descriptive level is a manifestation of the patient's adaptation to the psychoanalytic relationship, in this instance to the analyst's function of exploring manifestations of the patient's unconscious. Although subject to a number of relevant interpretive contexts, this patient's despair could be most productively worked with when recognized as a reaction to structured aspects of the analytic situation embodied in the person of the analyst, that is, the analyst as interpreter of the patient's disowned desires. This dimension of the analyst's role could plausibly be construed in terms of specific interpersonal configurations of childhood (Gill 1994): "My analyst will never love me. She will always magnify my faults and find my rivals blameless!" These aspects may be inaccessible within our immediate field of attention, not because they are subject to defensive distortion, as in countertransference, but because they are the structuring elements that determine our field of vision. If we are viewing our patient's experience through a particular lens, we must catch our reflected image in the mirroring eye in order to properly observe the impact of our analyzing instrument.

From our contemporary perspective, it is not only our professional subjectivity that may snag the momentum of analytic progress. There are incalculable ways in which the analyst's personal subjectivity contributes to the development of resistance as well. The analyst inescapably views the analysand through tinted lenses that are colored by certain preferences influenced by deeply rooted conflicts, childhood solutions, and fantasies. We know that this perspective is communicated in every decision the analyst makes, from how to intervene and when to be silent as well as in the tone, tension, and timbre of every utterance. Inevitably, the interaction between the participants plays a significant role in the choice of what will become the focus of the analytic process and what will be resisted. As Kupferstein (1997) has phrased it, "Resistance is an avoidance or interference in the here and now by the there and then" (p. 6), expressed concretely in the analytic interaction. This view, incorporating the necessity to understand both past and present, has led some contemporary thinkers to propose that it is resistance, not transference, that is co-constructed.

According to this perspective, the analyst inadvertently but decisively contributes to the formation of resistance through an emotional interaction with the patient (Boesky 1990). Engagement at this level is essential if analysis is to reach the deepest levels of experience and avoid becoming an intellectual exercise. However, while the depth of this emotional involvement is mandated, it comes at a price. Not infrequently, it triggers a potential in the analyst corresponding to that of the patient: to act out rather than to analyze the resistant activity they have jointly created. As with many of the processes we make use of in analysis, this potential can either bolster resistance or be turned into a powerful therapeutic incentive for working it through (Boesky 1982, Chused 1991, Jacobs 1986, McLaughlin 1987). On occasion, the lure to resist analyzing jointly created enactments that further resistance can be compelling enough to derail an entire treatment. If, however, we frame our engagement through an oscillating perspective that moves between participatory immersion and participant observation (Arlow 1963), we bring an observing ego to bear on the analytic interaction that is often inaccessible to the patient and crucial to working through resistance.

Does the idea of co-construction of the resistance imply that a patient's analysis will be different depending on the analyst? Yes and no. Certainly we recognize that because every analyst makes a unique contribution to the interaction, no two analyses can be alike. Inescapably, some issues or conflicts will be more salient depending on the analyst's personality, and unavoidably some will be given short shrift. Yet if the analyst maintains a focus on the patient and is able to structure a psychoanalytic situation around neutrality and free association, the patient's core conflicts and the resistances that accompany them will inevitably emerge. Balancing an ability to exploit the interaction for those manifestations of resistance triggered by the distinctive analytic couple, while simultaneously maintaining a focus on the patient in an analytic situation, gives us access to the broadest array of analytic possibilities.

CHARACTER PATHOLOGY AND RESISTANCE ANALYSIS

There are many classifications of character pathology in the psychoanalytic literature. Virtually any dimension of human motivation or behavior can serve as a basis for such a classification, from libidinal type, level of psychopathology, cognitive or defensive style, to preferred modes of social and interpersonal adaptation. It is always enlightening to compare and contrast patients along these or similar dimensions, but such diagnostic assessments prove too coarse a filter to sift the finer clinical detail that determines treatment outcome. Just about every prognostic generalization we might posit would have to be qualified and coordinated with the technical resources and experience of the particular therapist to render it clinically useful. Indeed, the idea of character as a consistent, integral structure, though necessary for broad diagnostic generalization and professional communication, involves a degree of reductive fiction that ongoing psychoanalytic experience inevitably calls into question.

Therefore, it is not generally helpful to draw too sharp a clinical distinction between circumscribed resistances and those that seem to stem from the broad characterological dispositions of the patient. The crucial technical considerations revolve instead around two fundamental questions. First, to what degree does a particular constellation of traits or predispositions compromise the integrity of the psychoanalytic situation? Second, can these aspects of the patient's functioning be turned into a meaningful object of analytic inquiry? Psychoanalysis is, first and foremost, a relationship based on some capacity for spontaneous communication and self-reflection. Patient and analyst must be prepared, however ambivalently and/or anxiously, to both let it happen and to look at what is happening. There are human beings presenting themselves for treatment who are so essentially withdrawn, affectively constricted, and emotionally isolated as to be virtually inaccessible to a therapy based on the expressive elaboration of feelings and meanings. There are also people so inclined to precipitous action and unbridled affective discharge that they are all but lost to any process that calls upon them to reflect upon their experience or motivation. In our experience, people of such extreme disposition rarely remain engaged in analytic treatment long enough to seriously try the analyst's skills. Less easily identified are those whose initial presentation, however promising on the surface, conceals a concatenation of resistant and defensive processes that ultimately draws the entire treatment into a problematic impasse. In these instances, the question of analyzability may only be definitively established by a lengthy trial.

Alex consulted a psychoanalyst because of growing frustration and rage at his wife and a global dissatisfaction with his family life. Over time it became apparent to his analyst that the limited emotional pallet with which Alex painted this vision of domestic life colored his entire experience of the world, including his relationship with his analyst. When this last observation was described explicitly, Alex freely conceded the point, manifesting an almost defiant pride in his bold assertion of his "right" to feel his own feelings. A determination to defend emotional autonomy—and to fight what he experienced as the intrusive expectations of others—was a psychodynamic pivot around which many of his most characteristic traits, attitudes, and problematic actions were lining up. Over a series of subsequent sessions, Alex went out of his way to make it clear that he wasn't about to "clean up" his act for anyone. Attempts to explore his vulnerability, his need to protect himself against the perceived sadistic intrusions of others, or even simply to elaborate and examine his feelings in these situations were invariably dismissed on logical grounds.

Over time, Alex's analyst felt increasingly stymied by the dull, pedantic force of Alex's irrefutable logic and iron-clad control as repeated attempts to turn this controlled and controlling behavior into a subject of the analysis ran aground. The treatment was being inexorably drawn into fixed roles, and any attempt to analyze the implications of this process from the perspectives of transference–countertransference enactment met with little comprehension, as if Alex could only think in highly abstract or, alternatively, extremely concrete categories. All playful, fictive discourse as a means of reaching underlying truths or psychic tensions animating the resistance fell on uncomprehending ears. In sum, the resistant and tendentious motive organizing Alex's adaptation to the psychoanalytic situation went effectively unchallenged; all his behaviors and associations continued to be shaped by the constraining objective of holding the analyst at bay.

Although the patient's desire for treatment expresses both pain and an interest in changing, it is impossible to know at the beginning of an analysis how rigidly the forces that hold a neurotic equilibrium in place are balanced or how good a match any particular analyst will be for a given analysand. However, given that limitations of style, personality, orientation, and unconscious need pervade every analysis, a tolerance of inferential ambiguity, however transitory, is essential for collaborative exploration and understanding in depth. It enables the analyst and analysand to work together on understanding fundamental aspects of the process that can obstruct change while avoiding an iatrogenically induced adversarial dimension marked by the analyst's assertion of privileged access to "the Truth." Patient and analyst work at fundamental cross-purposes and ultimately may not be able to engage an analytic process unless mutually agreed upon goals can be negotiated. We are not suggesting that analyzing the adversarial aspects of relating will not be important and at times essential aspects of an analysis, but only that the structure of the analytic situation should not be adversarial in itself. It is understood that the analyst will be transferentially imbued with aspects of adversarial as well as benign authority.

The fact that resistance is not a monolithic phenomenon can help us through some impasses. Certain aspects of functioning may be rigidly defended against, while others may be more amenable to exploration.

Some patients are characterologically incapable of sustaining the profound psychological processes that psychoanalysis may engender even if they agree to frequent sessions on the couch, and in this sense a psychoanalytic situation isn't necessarily viable. With certain patients, what could be called character "pathology" pushes the limits of neutrality and analyzability. Often this takes the form of the patient attempting to structure the analytic situation in a very narrow manner in an effort to extract from the analyst fantasized fulfillment of functions seen as vitally needed. The man who needs to sadistically control the analytic situation as his father once controlled him, the woman who resists taking her medication so that she can re-create a terrifying, conflict-ridden involvement with her mother, and the man who refuses to engage his analyst on any but logical grounds are structuring interactions with the analyst that they desperately want to hold onto, not analyze. Inevitably, we lose some of these patients. It is often possible, however, to discover, or create with the patient a small clearing in what may seem like a forest of opposition, in which there is some openness to the analytic process. Sometimes this is just enough room for genuine analytic work to be tentatively engaged. At other times, fate, in the form of powerful external events such as illness, death, the birth of a child, or a traumatic divorce, can shift the balance of forces just enough for the patient to tackle resistances that were previously impenetrable. There is considerable agreement that the task demands enormous resources of analytic skill and patience. As with all prognostic generalizations, however, the outcome depends on such intangible personal qualities in each participant that only a course of treatment will reveal whether significant success can be achieved. In undertaking such an arduous task, the analyst must take solace in the knowledge that small psychological gains can have a large impact on the overall scope and dimension of a patient's living.

THE LIMITS OF RESISTANCE ANALYSIS

Operating on all levels of development and serving multiple functions, resistance is never completely resolved in analyst or analysand. In this sense, resistance analysis is truly "interminable" (Freud 1937). The wishing, fantasizing, and compromising that are manifest in resistant activity serve vital and varied functions that will be obscured by a conceptualization of the process that emphasizes only its detrimental effects. Finding the aspect of resistance that faciliates development and understanding is an indispensable aspect of deepening analytic experience. Resistance asserts a fundamental framework that organizes experience. How, then, do we know what the limits are of resistance analysis? How do we know where to stop?

Freud (1937) suggested that there are some wishes that give the analyst an unusual amount of trouble, yielding to analytic influence reluctantly, if at all. Here we have the oft-cited psychological bedrock of conflicts around the distinction between the sexes, manifest in girls as penis envy and in boys as a struggle against passive or feminine wishes toward another male. Freud maintained that Ferenczi (1928) was "asking a great deal" in requiring that a successful analysis demonstrate mastery of these two complexes. Some limitations, Freud seems to be saying, need to be acknowledged. Limitations can be seen as emanating from biological givens, such as components of gender, maturational timetables, ability to tolerate frustration, and the constitutional strength of libidinal and aggressive drives, as well as deriving from the wishes, fears, and fantasies constructed in earliest relations with others. Some issues will be more central and more deeply rooted than others.

Less often noted is Freud's description of these bedrock resistances as anchored in a repudiation of femininity common to both sexes. While it remained for future generations to elaborate and correct Freud's understanding of female development, his emphasis on repudiation of femininity as a core issue in working with resistance points to recent clarification of the centrality of the early mother–child interaction in organizing psychological functioning. It places lifelong, fundamental struggles around attachment and separation, dependence and independence, and the losses associated with the calamities of childhood at the heart of analyzing resistance. A regressive pull to the "golden fantasy" (Smith 1977) of early bliss seduces analyst and analysand alike, with its illusions of protection actualized through omnipotent ideas of perfection. We need to acknowledge that bedrock modes of functioning will continue to trigger impulses to organize experience in habitual ways even after they have been essentially analyzed. In these instances, we can rely upon changes in patients' more integrated understanding of these experiences to alter their meaning. In this way their relationship to the original solution is fundamentally transformed. A familiar aroma that once made us salivate may now only evoke nostalgic memories of childhood experiences long gone.

Although the ideal of neutrality directs us not to impose a particular way of being upon patients, it does not follow that we have no ideas or even wishes about the sort of changes patients should make, particularly with regard to their resistant attitudes and behavior in the analytic situation. Our wishes for our patients are inevitably colored by our history and our own transferences, but within broad and flexible guidelines psychoanalysts are committed to certain normative values of psychological health that we cannot disown entirely in good faith. We seek to help patients to identify and resolve pathological resistances: those that cause pain (Brenner 1982, Freud 1895) stand in the way of higher integrations (Bachant and Adler 1997, Freedman 1985, Loewald 1960) and necessarily, those that undermine the analytic process itself. By clarifying the resistances to change, we help patients to understand more fully and direct more successfully the forces continually converging in their construction of experience. An ability to acknowledge our own limitations is essential here, because even the most intense or empathic treatment can never fully comprehend the complexities of another's unique experience. Ultimately, the choice of what to accept and what to struggle against must reside with the patient.

SUMMARY

An integration of contemporary perspectives on resistance analysis is presented that emphasizes the salience of both intrapsychic and interactive dimensions of this phenomenon. Viewed as embodying desperate psychological imperatives imbued with unconscious infantile misconceptions, resistance is presented as serving multiple functions and encompassing aspects of all mental action within the psychoanalytic situation. Within this broadened understanding, resistance arises at the cutting edge of the patient's development; it points us unfailingly to the place where crucial analytic work awaits our attention, to the specific attitude and/or behavior that is blocking a more profound evocation, exploration, or integration of psychic life. The thoughts, actions, and attitudes that come to be identified as resistance in a given clinical encounter are never simply resistant. Finding the analytic resources to exploit its relevant meanings is described as a central and indispensable aspect of working in depth. Several basic strategies for working with these phenomena are delineated in this chapter and the continued usefulness of understanding the role of resistance as guardian of psychic equilibrium is highlighted. Emphasis is given to safeguarding an analytic relationship which both sustains the patient and provides a vehicle for the exploration and modification of resistant activity. A functional definition of resistance in which any aspect of the analytic situation can become infused with resistant purpose is offered, and some technical considerations relating to the limits of resistance analysis are described.

5

The Analysis of Countertransference

Countertransference is a general term that subsumes a very complex array of psychic phenomena. An orientation to the overall topography of this psychic territory is necessary in order to clarify one's position, for within this landscape one encounters experiences that may be extremely subtle or dramatically florid, of momentary or lasting duration, and of fateful or merely tangential significance. Countertransference can take us through emotional peaks and valleys that exhaust our stamina and bewilder our senses. At other times, it may seem little more than a gentle breeze that stirs the undulating grasses of an even plain. It creates the Janus-faced illusion that has become familiar in our work with transference, alternately opening up paths of progress or rising up as daunting impediment. It is simply a given that in every therapy we conduct, our interpretive activity, emotional expressiveness, and private fantasizing are profoundly stimulated in ways that influence the unfolding course of treatment. The precise forms and specific nature of this impact often eludes conscious awareness for extended periods, and, as with other ubiquitous dimensions of analytic relatedness, perhaps can never be fully articulated. From outside the analytic dyad, complex patterns of our responsiveness—autonomous acts and intentions within a boundaried analytic field—will be seen to be molded to conform with repressed actualities

of the patient's unconscious life. It is this receptivity of unconscious fantasy to be influenced, stimulated, or shaped outside
our awareness that accounts for the prefix *counter* in the term
countertransference.

Although the constructive potential of transference was recognized early in the evolution of psychoanalytic technique
(Freud 1905a), the acceptance of countertransference phenomena as a useful dimension of psychoanalytic relatedness has
aroused considerably more ambivalence and controversy. Many
explanations of a psychological, cultural, and philosophical
nature have been put forth to explain this delayed acknowledgment. Recent attention to the uses and meanings of countertransference has certainly gained momentum in a broad shift
away from a view of analytic authority anchored in an unobstructed objectivity. As a consequence of this undermining of
positivist assumptions, contemporary analysts are more welcoming of a wide range of personal affect and fantasy, seeing it
as a sign of emotional engagement in the analytic process.
Indisputably this has had a liberating effect upon a generation
of analysts who were trained to view irrational responses to
their patients as a troubling failure of emotional maturity
betokening further personal treatment.

While its status as a foundational clinical construct is now
nearly universal among contemporary analysts, debates over
the most appropriate means of integrating countertransference
into our technical practice still generate heat. Indeed, there are
psychoanalysts who give central priority to their countertransferential responses, both in formulating and articulating their
interpretive activity. They consider the revelation of intimate
feelings and fantasies about the patient to be one of the most
authentic and powerful means of initiating an interpretive
dialogue or of inducing a mutative exchange. Others view this as
an undisciplined approach that potentially compromises the
treatment for what is dismissed as a passing and uncertain
clinical advantage. Between these dialectical extremes are analysts who are more likely to consider countertransference one of

several important sources of deeper knowledge about the patient or the process. The polarization of published opinion may obscure a larger continuity between practitioners in which some flexibility of response in regard to unique clinical circumstance is the reigning pragmatic principle. Rather than phobic avoidance or reactive idealization, these analysts meet countertransference as a challenge—an opportunity to constructively direct and transform the inevitable psychic tensions that accompany psychoanalytic work in the service of progressive momentum.

Our own perspective on the analysis of countertransference follows from our understanding of psychoanalysis as an emotional engagement that stimulates and provokes both partners of the relationship but maintains the explication of the internal world and adaptive struggle of the patient as the primary goal of interpretive activity. An essential function of therapeutic engagement is to help patients experience and understand the many ways in which they actively contribute to their misery and unhappiness, so that they can find less destructive ways to deal with their conflicts. Recognizing that the boundaries between ourselves and our patients are psychologically permeable, we expect to be buffeted by projective, introjective, or identificatory forces in the intimate currents of a psychoanalytic encounter yet still seek to navigate this essential course. Restoring this analytic stance is made considerably more difficult when regressive pressures and unconscious conflicts pull the analyst off course (Freedman and Lavender 1997).

A prerequisite for maintaining our balance is a highly sophisticated self-analytic consciousness. We regularly monitor our moods, affects, fantasies, and intentions, as well as the direct and implicit attributions of the patient with regard to our subjective states. The analyst's consciousness of self in the analytic situation demands a complex emotional/cognitive integration. To achieve this we must generate multiple and multidimensioned representational schema of self-and-object and self-as-object. Committed to putting our emotional lives at the service of our work, we cultivate unconventional candor through rigorous supervision and personal analysis in which we consistently expose our spontaneous feelings and thoughts about every aspect of our work. Self-analytic consciousness presumes access to the full spectrum of countertransferential experience, a receptive openness that differentiates it from compulsive and inhibitory forms of self-scrutiny that stand guard against painful intrusions of mortification or guilt.

Our continued willingness to confront, contain, and work over our emotions, impulses, and fantasies is constantly tested by encounters with a wide variety of patients. Some patients get more deeply under our skin than others. Some patients get more deeply into our hearts. Each analyst has areas and periods of heightened vulnerability, if not blindness. When the analysis of countertransference approaches archaic strata of our psyche, we will be reluctant to endure and work through moods of anxiety, guilt, and despair. We will also be slow to renounce gratifying illusions of harmonious union or the narcissistic allure of therapeutic omnipotence. The sheer effortfulness of this undertaking over time puts our higher purpose to a searching trial. Although the self-analytic function acts as a general restraint against impulsive action under the press of immediate transference provocation, it is no guarantor. The analyst's transferences to the patient, both in their adaptive and archaic dimension (Chapter 3), are always stimulated, and enactment of transference–countertransference paradigms is inevitable.

It is in our assessment of the risks and potential rewards of such enticements and enactments that contemporary psychoanalytic attitudes toward countertransference have changed most significantly. While the threat of disruptive countertransference derailing a treatment must be acknowledged, our interest has shifted to the ways that enactments productively contain (or dissipate) complex dyadic tensions and fabricate elaborate intersubjective patterning that are both illuminating and potentially reparative. In the ordinary course of things, swelling countertransference tensions are discharged through interpretive dialogues without engaging the patient directly in our internal process. There are, however, transference–counter-transference entanglements that cannot be adequately resolved without a more explicit exposition of the analyst's emotional position and/or psychodynamic contribution. We believe this is useful technique only to the extent that an analyst has re-strained and explored the spontaneous intensities of his or her countertransference.

Reports in the literature of impulsive countertransference responses having profoundly ameliorative impacts upon pro-tracted transference–countertransference impasses have to be evaluated cautiously. They tend to be presented in a selective manner that may not acknowledge deeper unconscious dynamic meanings or long-term process implications. Has depth been sacrificed to an impatient demand for momentum? While not inherently unbelievable, such accounts may be organized by narrative conventions that arouse appropriate analytic skepti-cism: the analyst despairs of reaching the recalcitrant patient by ordinary interpretive means and only an inspired act of sponta-neous emotional risk saves the analytic endeavor by provoking a cathartic breakthrough or crucial turning point. Our reserve in the face of these accounts is rooted in an awareness of how often core transference wishes are situated in demands and covert attempts to pressure the analyst into departures from an interpretive stance. The idea expressed in the longing "for me, an exception must be made," or "this one time, an exception," must often be a focal point of prolonged transference and resistance analysis involving core narcissistic and object libidi-nal desires. Of more relevance, such accounts offer very little generalizable guidance or technical direction outside the context of the specific episode reported, unless we subscribe to the principle of analytic spontaneity and authenticity as a primary curative agent. In our view, this inclination encourages one to ignore more fundamental analytic principles.

When self-analytic consciousness encompasses both interac-tive and intrapsychic dimensions of response, our approach need not be inherently exhibitionistic, emotionally manipulative, or confessional. Introducing the self as a subjective presence into an interpretive dialogue we employ does not necessitate confronting a patient with raw emotion, uncensored fantasy, or unanalyzed dreams about the patient in order to break through a transference–countertransference impasse. This would be an attempt to enlist our patient in mutual analysis (Ferenczi 1932). However, with tact and considerable discretion, an analyst can represent his or her self as an emotionally involved and interpersonally active agent in the analytic field.

Dr. Bender found his sessions with Eric increasingly unpleasant as his patient's transference intensified. Almost from the moment he began using the couch, a consistently dismissive and contemptuous attitude had surfaced with a vigor that had not been evident when they were face to face. Just about every remark or observation he offered was greeted by a derisive or witty rejoinder, as if Eric's whole purpose in coming to his sessions had turned to proving that his analyst couldn't understand a thing about him. Attempts to direct his attention to this apparent transformation of his character by interpreting the anxieties and concerns that his new attitude were masking fell on uncomprehending ears. Eric's thinking, which had initially struck Dr. Bender as capable of subtle psychological discriminations, became increasingly obtuse. He relentlessly attacked both the process and Dr. Bender's person, insisting that his time and money were being wasted needlessly on a process that was "old-fashioned" and ineffectual. Besides, he doubted that Dr. Bender was competent enough to do the job as well as his friend's analyst, who, he made plain, provided effective advice and support "about the real world."

Initially, Dr. Bender was confident that he understood the winds that were fanning the flames of this assault, and he patiently tried to explore Eric's anxieties around his exposed and vulnerable position. But understanding the general nature and context of this conflagration was not sufficient. As long as there was no alliance to analyze this content in depth, he could not identify the spark that had—and would continue to—set it afire. Eric seemed unwilling to give him a clue. Instead he hurled back each explorative inquiry or interpretation with sarcastic bravado. "Which textbook did that one come from?" "Is that the best you can do?" At first, it was as if Eric was taunting him, challenging him to come up with an interpretation that would have an impact—hit me with your best shot, so to speak. Gradually, however, the animosity of his attacks seemed to take on a more ominous, belligerent tone. "That's stupid!" "What malarkey!" "I'm supposed to listen to this shit!" Dr. Bender emerged from these sessions feeling as if he had been beaten with a blunt instrument. He felt bruised and increasingly resentful and struggled to suppress a powerful retaliatory impulse to throw Eric out of his office.

In thinking about his struggle, Dr. Bender realized that he had lost patience with Eric in a manner that undermined his analytic attitude toward his own countertransference and the meanings of Eric's transference. Increasingly, his interventions carried a sarcastic and antagonistic edge. Replaying their recent sessions in his mind, he heard himself prefacing interventions with provocative statements such as, "I suppose you'll say I sound like a textbook, but it seems to me . . ." in an argumentative tone that directly challenged Eric's defensiveness. He understood that behind this proactive attitude, he was feeling increasingly wounded, abused, and dismissed.

After many efforts to get Eric to reflect upon the process and to see what was happening to the relationship, Dr. Bender formulated an interpretation that vividly incorporated his emotional experience: "I feel increasingly hesitant to say what is on my mind, as if you're waiting with a bludgeon to crush anything I might say or do. It's as if you were a bully trying to hurt me, and I want to shout something at you and run away." To his surprise, Eric didn't immediately dismiss or ridicule this statement, which in other less dramatically and personally evocative forms had been said many times before. "You know," he said reflectively, "it's very strange that you should say that, but when I was a boy, I once hit another boy in the head with a baseball bat. He was really hurt and I was terrified. I felt so guilty but it really was an accident! Well, maybe not an accident exactly. He was threatening me. We were arguing about a disputed call. Perhaps you don't know how boys argue in Brooklyn. Neither listens to the other. It's not about who's right, its about who's the top dog and who backs down. I picked up the bat without thinking . . . just to scare him I guess . . . I was scared. I immediately realized by his gestures that I had done something drastic, gone too far, crossed a line. I gave him a good smack on the head and ran away. For months I lived in almost continual fear that his friends were going to come and beat me up or that his father would report me to the principal and that I'd be sent to reform school! I was sure that I was going to be sent away from home, which terrified me."

Following this intervention and Eric's associative responses, Dr. Bender was able to regain an analytic stance. His empathy was restored through conscious, as opposed to unconscious, identification with Eric's boyhood self, now that he was feeling analytically empowered, rather than bloodied and bullied. He easily brought to mind analogous situations of escalating competitive tension and schoolyard struggle over dominance and submission in experiences from his own childhood. He also empathized with Eric's anxiety and guilt about anticipated punishment for his unpremeditated aggression. He was in a position to help Eric begin to understand the specific connection between the couch (a passive submission) and his escalating attacks upon the analysis and the analyst (defensive preemptive strikes against unconsciously fantasized anticipations of blame and reproach). He and Eric had been reliving a dramatized version of this early episode of macho competitive argument, preemptive attack, and retaliatory dread restaged around the use of the couch and interpretation as instruments (i.e., weapons) of analysis (i.e., submission to the analyst's domination). His impulse to throw Eric out of treatment was the denouement of this drama, simultaneously the most dreaded punishment (being sent away from home) and the means of escape from the analytic (playing) field of danger. He also recognized but had no alliance to bring into the analysis at this point, the symbolic equations: interpretation = bat = phallus and battering = buggering = homoerotic domination.

The deeper substrata of countertransferential reactivity necessarily lie in the conflicting and cooperating psychic tendencies at work in the mind of the analyst. Conflictual resolutions of childhood yearnings and fears are operative in the analyst as well as the analysand, organizing perception and influencing choices in every aspect of the analytic process (Brenner 1976, 1982). They are implicated in the pursuit of a career in a helping profession, and especially, in the election of long-term, intensive modes of therapeutic engagement as a preferred way of working. This means that there are emotional preconditions that bolster an analyst's working equilibrium, permitting each of us to abide by the stringent psychic demands of the psychoanalytic situation (Chapter 9). While many of these needs are filled through our relationships to colleagues, supervisors, students, or institutions, to a greater or lesser degree, we cannot avoid depending on our patients as well. In effect, each of us needs some things from the relationship with our patients to sustain our optimal effectiveness—perhaps to be allowed to be helpful, or to be close, or to have our efforts appreciated or to be loved and admired, or to be emotionally stimulated and intellectually challenged. In the ordinary course of analytic work, when such needs are not overtly obstreperous, they can be accommodated within our communally sanctioned standards of role and conduct. There are many legitimate gratifications that our work and relationships with patients afford. Inevitably, each analyst interprets the analytic role in accord with the particularity of these personal needs.

Yet our understanding of psychodynamic structure informs us that an analyst's specific emotional preconditions are closely entwined with tumultuous developmental struggles and conflictual vulnerabilities. An analytic identity, like any identity, is both a constructive achievement of professional individuation and a defensive mask of personal protection. Our particular gifts germinate in the same soil as our most profound vulnerabilities. It is not surprising, therefore, that alterations in the analyst's emotional balance, whether intrapsychically or dyadically induced, can lead to pathological disruptions (or regressions) in which the analyst's analyzing capacity is seriously inhibited. At such times, emotional needs, fantastical fears, and archaic wishes assume a peremptory disruptive intensity that cannot be ignored. It is important to remember that patients do not cause or create these regressions in the analyst, though they may well stimulate and provoke them unconsciously. Not every analyst would be provoked, seduced, or stimulated in the same way or to the same degree.

Dr. Hertz became aware of recurrent feelings of sorrow that would emerge unexpectedly during therapeutic hours over a period of months. In its initial manifestation, she was only conscious of a diffuse, nonspecific sense of gloom, pessimism, and helplessness. She had trouble connecting this state of mind with any particular patient or dynamic situation. A sophisticated therapist, she was alerted to the possibility of a countertransference reaction and she paid increasing attention to the vicissitudes of her moods in the context of work with specific patients. Eventually she succeeded in discerning a recurrent precipitant: whenever any of her patients spoke directly or indirectly of leaving treatment, out of either dissatisfaction or accomplishment, she would experience an aching sense of loss deep within. Sometimes the mood could be contained by refocusing her attention on her patient's needs and conflicts, only to find it reemerging after working hours, leaching into every recess of her waking day. Dr. Hertz had never before been aware of her vulnerability in this area, and she was frankly disconcerted by her response. "After all," she reasoned with herself unsuccessfully, "patients speak of leaving often, much more frequently than they actually do. Why am I feeling so insecure?"

Her confusion and vulnerability continued until the following incident occurred: She was in session with an older female patient who was speaking with acute remorse about a college boyfriend who had once loved her. The woman recalled how casually and thoughtlessly she had broken off the relationship with this devoted suitor, an action that she now regretted, imagining retrospectively that the union might have led to great and lasting fulfillment. Dr. Hertz could barely suppress the tears that came into her eyes while listening to this reminiscence. However, she realized that her imagination had been engaged not by her patient's remorse, but by the poignant image of her rejected suitor.

Almost immediately a corresponding situation in her own life flashed in her mind. Shortly before the disruptive period of work under consideration, a man whom she had been dating rather briefly precipitously terminated their intimacy. At the time, she had felt angered and hurt, but had soon gotten over the injury—or so she thought—immersing herself in the busy demands of her professional schedule. "Why should this have such a hold on my emotions?" she wondered. This reflection led to the recollection of a scene, a passing moment really, after an evening out with Richard. Standing in her kitchen drinking a glass of milk, she had momentarily thought, This is a man I could really love! It now became apparent to her that after the breakup she had short-circuited a mourning process. Without fully realizing it, her heart had already become engaged. By shifting her emotional investment to her patients she avoided the grief, only to reencounter "countertransferentially" the very rejection and loss she was seeking to escape.

This last piece of self-analysis was liberating, soothing the disruptive vulnerability she was experiencing at work and allowing her to begin to work over the emotions and the multiple meanings connected with the long-standing disappointment in her love life. As we would imagine, the meaning Richard had assumed in her emotional life had a history of antecedents in other emotionally significant relationships, both recent and long past.

The restoration of neutrality, empathy, and a balanced interpretive perspective becomes the primary function of the analysis of countertransference at such times. Making effective use of countertransferentially derived information depends on maintaining an analytic attitude. It is our responsibility to negotiate this difficult pass, without blaming or resenting the patient for the psychic pain we may endure. Working with disruptive countertransference is inherently difficult, requiring emotional honesty, tolerance, and maturity. It unfailingly engages vulnerable areas that our entire psychic organization is engineered to protect. Constructs like the frame, an analytic attitude, or the ideal of analytic neutrality are the substance of a framework that serves to contain these emotional reverberations. The urge to depart from these guidelines often signals our reluctance to undertake an uncomfortable piece of self-analytic effort by taking refuge in a mutually constructed resistance against clarifying an underlying transference–countertransference configuration (Boesky 1990).

Although it is necessary to acknowledge that the dynamics of a patient's transferences and an analyst's countertransference are homologous, they are adapted to quite different purposes in the psychoanalytic situation. The asymmetrical structure of the analytic situation, bolstered by proscriptions on the analyst's expressive freedom and a vast disparity in mutual dependence, mandates crucial differences (Chapter 3). By design, this asymmetry stimulates and expands the emotional sources of the patient's transference love while simultaneously restraining and moderating the analyst's emotional involvement. When transference takes hold in this controlled environment, situated within an object relationship of carefully nurtured evocative potential, its roots are free to draw nutriment from latent tributaries of buried childhood emotion. This engorgement of unbound transference love resuscitates the most archaic dimensions of transference. In this atmosphere, unconstrained countertransference expression carelessly violates a climate of safety that has been cultivated with meticulous care. It puts a withering chill to that fragile "hot-house specimen," transference love (Bergmann 1987).

This understanding directs us to give priority to countertransference analysis before the analysis of transference. It is the primary means of sublimating loving and destructive potentials into professionally restrained forms of concern and caregiving (Loewald 1975). When the analyst can restore a balanced analytic attitude in the face of disruptive countertransference, the understanding wrested from such encounters stimulates both empathic responsiveness and acute insight into immanent dynamic actualities. Unless mastery is secure, however, disruptive countertransference threatens to undermine an otherwise productive analytic situation. The ideal that one should succeed in preventing all enactments from taking place has been superseded in contemporary practice by an attempt to employ the analysis of countertransference to facilitate the transformation of enactments into therapeutically constructive events. In effect, we analyze countertransference to free ourselves to analyze transference, and in analyzing transference we come to understand the precise nature of our countertransference.

After several years of productive collaboration, Dr. Emile noticed increasing tension in his work with Tamara. An anger in his analysand had begun to surface that differed in quality and intensity from anything he had experienced with her before. Dr. Emile also sensed in Tamara a level of exasperation with the treatment that he didn't understand. Indeed, he began to feel that the very treatment itself was in jeopardy, as Tamara focused increasingly on the angry agitation she now felt upon leaving almost every session. Dr. Emile was aware of feeling blamed and intimidated by her rage and thinly veiled threats to terminate. "If this is making me feel worse instead of better, it doesn't make any sense to continue" became a plaintive refrain that carried an unmistakable message of warning. It generated an uneasiness in him that he recognized contained elements of anger and concern, as well as a profound desire to rescue.

Although he experienced an increasingly intense pressure to salvage the treatment, he was at a loss to explain what had produced so radical a change in their interaction or how to address it. He found himself reminiscing about what a rewarding patient Tamara had been to work with. Nevertheless, he couldn't forget a long-standing and unresolved issue between them. It revolved around his tone of voice. It was rarely right for Tamara. No matter what inflection he gave his voice, Tamara frequently discerned a critical edge in it. Dr. Emile had not experienced himself as feeling critical toward Tamara at these times, although he did recall feeling frustrated with her touchiness. He had learned to be especially careful to relate to her in a way that was sensitive to her needs, exercising considerable caution to frame his interventions with elaborate tact.

Dr. Emile noted a defensive ring to his current reflections, almost, it now seemed to him, as if he were trying to prove to himself that he hadn't been critical in the way she had maintained. It suddenly dawned on him that he must have bought into her transference representation of himself as the ceaselessly critical analyst. Hadn't he started to think of himself as not good enough and to enact with this patient the idea that if he could just find the right way to relate to her, everything would be all right?

He was somewhat taken aback when he asked himself if he had analyzed Tamara's experience of his critical attitude toward her. Of course he had! They had addressed this issue over and over again in the treatment. But had they ever really gotten to the bottom of it? He had to think for some time about the question before discerning that, at least in part, he had begun responding to her criticism rather than analyzing it. In fact, now that he thought about it, he realized that there were many ways that he had been reacting to Tamara instead of consistently exploring and understanding her experience of him. The "reality" of their interaction had taken precedence over the analysis of the transference. This recognition helped him acknowledge that he had lost an analytic attitude with regard to the transference–countertransference implications of their interaction.

Dr. Emile returned to the analysis in a less anxious and guilty frame of mind. In this mood it was easier for him to identify the essential unreasonableness of her spiraling demands and accusations of injury (e.g., that he should have steered her to a more suitable profession, challenged her choice of lover, and related to her in a way that didn't invoke anxiety). He was now quite aware that he and Tamara had been caught up in an unconscious enactment, constructing an interaction in which it was he, the analyst, who had all the power as well as the responsibility to make everything come out right. It was an enactment that had escalated in intensity as the omnipotent fantasies that both had subscribed to became increasingly untenable.

But before Dr. Emile could regain his analytic attitude entirely, a significant piece of self-analysis still had to be accomplished. Why had he been susceptible to her invitation to engage in a masochistic manner? After considerable internal resistance, he eventually succeeded in establishing a compelling link between his feelings and thoughts about Tamara and a pattern of guilt-ridden masochistic submission to his own father. Not surprisingly, this psychodynamic history had been a prominent theme in his personal analysis, though he had avoided thinking of Tamara in this context until this moment. His wish to be Dad's good boy by making him proud had often meant protecting his father from the many disappointments he experienced in Dr. Emile's more rebellious siblings. This striving to fulfill his father's expectations had become the focal point of a lifelong inhibition against his own freedom to feel and act with self-assertive independence. He realized that all of this had little to do specifically with Tamara. He saw that struggling not to feel controlled by Tamara's/Father's expectations had been stirring rebellious tensions. His struggle to suppress these tensions were read by Tamara as "criticalness" and when his repeated efforts to analyze her transference attributions had been thwarted, a regressive process had ensued.

Dr. Emile was now fully prepared to use this understanding to refocus his attention on the meaning of Tamara's sadistic and masochistic provocations. These were brought to the surface by confronting the fears and fantasies involved in Tamara's experience of his criticalness, which, rather than deflect guiltily, he now was capable of analyzing. Most importantly, they began to understand together Tamara's investment in giving him control over her life. He could directly acknowledge his contribution to her expectations through working too hard to find answers for her. This, in turn, led to their uncovering what was being avoided in the manifest enactment—her gratification in constructing their interaction within an omnipotent, sadomasochistic framework. Dr. Emile found that his countertransferential involvement was now useful as a way of generating hypotheses about his patient's process, including the types of transferential dynamics and erotic fantasies that were indirectly expressed through this interaction. He also could allow himself more freedom to accept his angry feelings toward his patient, as he disentangled *his* frustrations from *her* transference projections. He accepted the fact that he often had reason to be irritated with Tamara's resistant or provocative behavior quite apart from his displaced resentment toward his own father. Being able to

THE ANALYSIS OF COUNTERTRANSFERENCE

balance these realities of the interaction with the unconscious transference–countertransference fantasies that were pressing for actualization enabled him to openly explore areas of her inner life that had previously been forbidden.

In this extended example, Dr. Emile's annoyance, as well as his resonance with Tamara's persecutory fantasy, established an obstacle to the full emergence of the transference. This contributed to what can be described as a mutually constructed resistance to clarifying the underlying transference–countertransference paradigm (Boesky 1990). As we see, differentiating an analyst's countertransference from the patient's transference projections can be a struggle. Yet it is an essential step in resolving transference–countertransference impasses and refining our interpretive efforts. We explore transference projections by pursuing their meanings to the patient; countertransference eruptions have to be addressed—initially at least—within ourselves. Through self-analysis we distinguish adaptive and archaic elements in our countertransference, clarifying the extent to which our reactions are properly understood as a response to the patient's transference or simply a trigger to externalize our own issues.

Tamara's attempt to live out a fantasy of omnipotent protection increasingly turned persecutory as her analyst failed to live up to her escalating expectations. Could this enactment have been avoided if Dr. Emile had analyzed it in a more timely fashion as an initial resistance embedded in regressive wishfulness? Did his responding to her transference overtures with an adaptive counterwish (i.e., his attempt to embody her omnipotent fantasy) simply prepare the ground for a later crisis, or was it also a necessary reparative element that potentiated an inevitable interpretive dialogue? If his own countertransference dynamics had not become entwined in the process, would it have unfolded smoothly and with less disruption? We raise these questions not to provide definitive answers, but only to suggest the kinds of ambiguities and possibilities contemporary analysts must consider as they reflect upon their work. Increasingly, we are becoming accustomed to recognizing that maintaining rigid models of correct procedure or outcome is of less value than acknowledging the achievement and limitations in what has transpired in a particular analytic couple.

A CONTINUUM OF INTERPRETIVE EFFICACY

How to employ the knowledge gained through the analysis and sublimation of our countertransference—specifically in what forms we communicate this knowledge to the patient—is at the crux of the the technical challenge posed by countertransference analysis. In principle, we try to interpret only what counter-transference analysis has revealed about the patient's dynamics rather than what it may say about our own (Levy 1984). Yet this knowledge is closely grafted to our personal neediness, vulner-ability, and wishfulness. It may inadvertently betray a dimen-sion of our being that is burdening to our patient, however exciting and provocative in the moment. Patients have varied reactions to both intentional and inadvertent departures from our ordinary disciplined presentation of self—predictably some ambivalent amalgam of privilege and distress. The unforetellable and untraceable reverberations of these highly charged ex-changes in the unconscious recesses of the patient's mind give cause for concern. To the patient, transference is the foundation of emotional reality made immanent in the analytic situation. For the analyst, countertransference is a work inhibition, even when deeply entangled in archaic psychic struggles. Transference–countertransference dynamics are therefore never reciprocal; what feels like a moderately intense or even mild emotional exchange to the analyst may arouse the most profound rever-berations and reservations in the patient. A brief expression of spontaneous exasperation may portend a paralyzing threat of abandonment or imminent attack. Interpretive activity is nec-essarily constrained by the recognition of long-term objectives within the press of immediate therapeutic opportunity.

While our aspiration is to use the entire countertransference experience, including disruptive, archaic, or split-off elements, our ability to be optimally responsive falls along a continuum of interpretive efficacy largely determined by self-awareness and mastery. Unraveling our emotions, fantasies, and attitudes is an important aspect of understanding any patient. Revealing or acting hastily upon these predispositions, however, without adequate grounding in an analytic framework, is likely to obscure rather than illuminate a patient's dynamics. An analyst, like any other human being, is subject to moods and conflicts that compromise one's professional effectiveness. Thus, even when we've clearly identified the trigger of a specific response in the patient's behavior, there may be extraneous pressures that influence our reactivity. Attempting to interpret on the basis of countertransference alone, without balancing a host of other corroborating sources of information, can mask a covert wish to engage the patient as our psychotherapist. General interpretive principles and safeguards prevail here, as they do in any other area of analytic exploration (Chapter 7). Is the patient in a place that enables him to comprehend an interpretation? Is it premature? Too deep? Are we "stealing the patient's thunder," usurping an emergent realization to feed our sense of interpretive pride? Does the intervention set up a power struggle that could obscure rather than facilitate the analytic process? Would revealing countertransferentially derived information compromise the analysis by suppressing the emergence of other wishes and fantasies that may be more important and difficult to reach? Clearly, such questions can only be answered within a given context, after the therapist has synthesized a bewildering array of information that defies easy summary. That countertransference is operative is never sufficient justification to introduce it into the analytic process.

As long as countertransference reactivity is containable, it retains a signal function, directing our attention to emerging phenomena or initiating lines of interpretive speculation that might otherwise be overlooked. Our understandings can be productively broached with the patient in an interpretive (rather than confessional) mode. Many—some might argue all—interventions carry an implicit countertransference allusion. "You want me to struggle with you and force you to submit to my will, so that you won't have any responsibility for getting on the couch" is qualitatively different from "I'm tired of arguing about this. Unless you take the couch this analysis cannot proceed!" Yet some patients will react as if we had said the latter, submissively agreeing (or rebelliously refusing) to go along with what they take to be an impatient command. If we inquire further, the patient might say, with some plausibility, "I know I'm being a pain in the ass and it's understandable that you would be frustrated!" Despite the plausibility of the inference, it is a projective attribution. We can either explore the manifest transference implication—"You have thoughts about my frustration?"—or proceed with our initial line of interpretation—"I guess if you believe that I've lost all patience and that now you have to appease me, you will avoid having to acknowledge that you are making a free choice here." In effect, we must engage in an interpretive dialogue about our frustration (or about our selves as frustrated participants of an interpretive dialogue) without confirming or disconfirming the patient's experience directly if we are to remain on the plane of psychic reality. "You're right, I'm frustrated with you" is largely irrelevant, as long as we are confident that we are having an exchange about the patient's subjective experience within the transference.

At either end of a continuum defined by two extremes, situations where the analyst is too bewildered and emotionally helpless to use countertransference material or, on the contrary, situations where we have comfortable mastery of our emotions, the technical recommendations are pretty clear cut. The former calls for continued self-analytic integration; the latter directs us to attend to the relevant transference–countertransference issue. These two poles serve as a rough guideline for orienting our thinking about how and when to intervene. Some situations are clearly best handled through consultation with a third party.

Included here are many reactions and interactions observed in the work of inexperienced analysts. Some instances may present in the form of intensely disruptive countertransference, but are, upon investigation, more accurately looked at as issues arising from an incomplete technical understanding. Before one has become adept at managing the unexpected complications that regularly confront us in analysis, we are simply more vulnerable to states of acute anxiety and misjudgment. Fear may stimulate antipathy and ill-considered action. Libidinal bonds will be exaggerated to ward off antagonistic confrontations. Without a thorough appreciation of the parameters of the analytic situation and accumulated resources of interpretive or therapeutic flexibility (Chapter 2), we are likely to exacerbate situations of therapeutic distress through awkwardness, avoidance, and/or untimely confrontation. Although expressed as countertransference disruptions, these are fundamentally by-products of our relative helplessness. Indeed the first valuable lessons that one can learn regarding the analysis of countertransference is how to use affective cues to forestall crises and to understand how our characterological dispositions typically impact upon our work.

Ms. Albright was aware of a special feeling of pleasure accompanying her thoughts and feelings about Adrienne, a relatively new patient. She looked forward to sessions with eager anticipation and in her company experienced a level of attunement and interpretive timing that, in her own experience, was exceptional. Despite her patient's presentation of a problematic personal history with evidence of multiple traumatization at an early age, Ms. Albright was optimistic about Adrienne's prognosis, especially in light of her remarkable adaptation to the requirements of the analytic situation. She was capable of being expressive, self-reflective, and tolerated the tensions of exploring her feelings and fantasies about the analyst without much apparent anxiety. As is so often the case with pleasurable feelings, Ms. Albright's motivation for questioning the basis of this special rapport was not compelling. Indeed, as a candidate in training, she had powerful motives for wishing to believe that this fortuitous situation was a reflection of personal gifts and talent. She certainly never thought of her relaxed and gratifying state of mind in terms of countertransference. Rather, she simply attributed it to a good fit and, understandably, viewed it pridefully as evidence of her emerging skills and sensitivity as an analyst. Overall, the transference–countertransference situation could have been epitomized in one word: *lucky*. Adrienne was terrifically fortunate to have emerged from her background with such remarkable resilience, and to have hooked up with a therapist who had the sensitivity to appreciate her.

This extended analytic honeymoon proved stable for quite some time. It was accompanied by dramatic changes in the patient's life circumstances, which only seemed to confirm Ms. Albright's optimistic attitude. Adrienne took a new job, entered into a relationship that seemed quite promising, and gave every evidence of transforming her understandings and experiences in the analytic situation into constructive, life-changing action. Therefore, her analyst was completely flabbergasted when Adrienne began a session with the casual announcement that she didn't think that therapy was working, and that she was thinking of taking a leave of absence, beginning today. Indeed, Ms. Albright barely had the presence of mind to ask why. Adrienne explained her thinking by pointing out that she simply didn't expect "this talk therapy to get us very far!"

"I don't understand," her analyst virtually stammered in reply. "Things are going so well!"

"Really? But I still get sad at times, and I'm just as socially awkward as ever. How can you say that?"

As the session progressed, Ms. Albright felt more and more confused, anxious, and helpless. She could think of almost no way to intervene except in the end to exhort Adrienne to return for one final session. Reflecting upon this experience in her supervision, she began to reconstruct the sequence of events and contents that had so disarmed her. Her supervisor was able to help her see that the crux of the issue rested in Adrienne's expectations of her therapy. It was apparent that this patient, who had seemed so responsive to every analytic effort, harbored a fantasy of transformation well beyond anything that was possible under the best of circumstances. Her extreme cooperativeness concealed this impatience. Reflecting upon this understanding with her supervisor, Ms. Albright came to realize that Adrienne's exorbitant expectations of her therapy were not as unusual as the fact that she hadn't heard any echo of them in the material. It also became clear that her own feeling of luck at having such an exceptional patient to work with had itself been a countertransferential echo of the patient's preconscious fantasy of being miraculously capable of rising above the numbing impact of brutal circumstance. In short, Adrienne secretly considered herself to be one of destiny's darlings, and Ms. Albright—weighed down by the rigors of her own analytic training—had taken comfort in seeing herself reflected in the warm glow of this magic light.

After catching on to this, Ms. Albright, who was indeed a talented candidate, was in a position to successfully address these issues with Adrienne in what was to be their final session. She succeeded in helping Adrienne overcome her disappointment and renew her commitment to treatment. After this crisis was resolved, Ms. Albright could attend to the clever ways in which Adrienne consistently constructed her experience in line with ideas and images of transcendence. She easily identified Adrienne's subtle blandishments which previously had seduced her into sharing in this experience of unique destiny. Her new awareness ushered in a period of analytic work that proved less balmy but ultimately more constructive. Although the special feeling about this treatment did not return, Ms. Albright was now prepared to meet the increasingly frequent expressions of doubt, frustration, and mistrust that accompanied their work together with a more sophisticated appreciation of the inevitable complexities and resistances of analytic work.

In this example, Ms. Albright's optimism, a decided element in her character, did not prevent her from coming to terms with the dynamic basis of her countertransference, or of using it to advance this patient's treatment. The clinical dilemma was resolved through an educational process in which she learned about some of the adaptive pitfalls of transcendent fantasies (one form of denial). Her own optimism (and its component of denial) was not called into question, for she spontaneously recognized its influence in the form of a willingness to suspend disbelief in Adrienne's miraculous story of good fortune. To the extent that this aspect of Ms. Albright's individuality can be integrated with an appropriate analytic attitude, it does not pose a problem. Undoubtedly, further experience will either temper or confirm her optimism. In all likelihood, for some treatments it will prove an asset, in others, perhaps, a liability.

When characterological rigidities seriously impede the internalization of an appropriate analytic attitude, they have to be addressed in supervisory consultation. These countertransferences are more likely to be evident in chronic attitudes rather than discreet reactions, attitudes that distort the technical approach of all—or a significant subset of—that individual's clinical work. Here we would include specifically moralistic, sexist, or homophobic attitudes and agendas. Generally, such dispositions do not reflect the analyst's individuality as much as an attempt to use one's work in the service of resolving or regulating persistent intrapsychic tensions. Attempts to escape self-scrutiny, while subtly infusing significant dimensions of clinical perspective and thinking, can be pernicious. It is more likely to be called to attention by a supervisor who views one's work from outside, rather than through personal introspective effort. Usually, little can be learned with regard to the specific dimensions of the patient's transference from an exploration and understanding of these phenomena inasmuch as the patient is subject to an adaptive challenge imposed by the analyst rather than by the analytic situation itself. Because the exploration of these attitudes and technical biases threaten the analyst's unconscious defensive balance, they may be elaborately rationalized and difficult to broach directly. Resolution often requires psychoanalytic, in addition to supervisory, intervention.

Dr. Kiener presented his patient in supervision with deliberate care, compassion, and sensitivity. He was especially eager to convey to his supervisor how well he understood Linda's sense of injury at her father's hard heartedness, the callousness he continually displayed in the face of her longing for recognition and validation of the worthiness of her creative aspirations. How could a father fail to support this daughter's idealistic ambitions with fiscal and emotional sustenance, when he so generously poured his resources into her brother's professional education? Although his supervisor was initially impressed with his student's grasp of the nuances of Linda's sensitivities, over time he became mindful that a picture of her life circumstances was being consistently drawn in somewhat two-dimensional, almost melodramatic form. That Linda viewed her life as a heroic struggle with a series of rather malevolent adversaries, and that she viewed the object world in terms of cartoonish fictions of good against evil, was one thing, but that her analyst gave no indication that he held a differentiated or tentative view of these attributions was another. Dr. Kiener's clinical interventions were characterized by an unquestioning acceptance of Linda's representation of events—without further inquiry into the circumstances. He displayed a tendency to frame interventions in an absolute manner that left no room for ambiguity concerning the objective factualness of those events or ambivalence toward her inner objects. He would declare, "Your father is cruel. How could he say that!" rather than "His saying that must have hurt you!" or "As you describe your father's actions, he sounds so cruel!" When the supervisor pointed out that the phrasing of his intervention made it seem as if he were endorsing her construction of her father's motivations, Dr. Kiener retorted righteously, "But we must validate our patient's experience or we'd be committing the same emotional injuries that they sustained in childhood!" His tone conveyed unmistakably that he took what he had just said as self-evident, and that to his way of thinking there was nothing more that could be meaningfully said about the matter.

This supervisory impasse was inadvertently helped out by the patient herself. Shortly after the discussion just described, Linda began to escalate in frequency her requests that Dr. Kiener make scheduling adjustments for an increasingly erratic work situation. He had always been accommodating, and had fallen into a routine of granting such requests without further question. However, when Linda asked that he change an appointment time so that she could have her nails done for an upcoming family gathering, he found himself "going along with some misgivings." He had quieted his misgivings in the moment with the thought that this family gathering was so important to her. His reservations, however, proved more powerful than he realized. He completely forgot about the appointment change and was unaware that he had missed her rescheduled session until he found himself sitting alone waiting for her to appear at her regular hour.

Exploring the incident in supervision, he acknowledged that when he arranged to reschedule the session with Linda, he had felt "slightly demeaned" by her giving priority to her manicurist, but was "uncomfortable" raising the issue directly. Yet he really didn't feel he ought to experience it that way, that this was being "touchy." He hadn't thought much more about this reaction until he realized that he had forgotten her appointment entirely. He "guessed" that he was angry at her and that "it looked like" he had retaliated against her, but he was still uncertain as to how he could have handled the situation without injuring her feelings. His supervisor observed that while he was the one worried about hurting her feelings, the evidence suggested that it was *she* who had succeeded in hurting *his* feelings. "But I shouldn't respond so narcissistically, I'm the therapist," he protested. From his supervisor's perspective, Dr. Kiener seemed to be nurturing an illusion about the kind of superior human being he as a therapist ought to be. Apparently he believed that only by being "good," "selfless," and "loving" could he provide his patients with the kind of therapeutic experience which would be curative. As Dr. Kiener was in analytic therapy as part of his training experience, his supervisor was able to suggest that some of these issues could be profitably and appropriately brought into his personal analysis. He offered his opinion that perhaps the analyst's "goodness" might reside in how he handles the feelings that are elicited within him, rather than in having only the "right" kind of feelings in the first place. Clinically, he recommended that Dr. Kiener ground himself more by attending to impulsive actions in the relationship that violate the frame, and that he also focus on the patient's personal agency in addition to her sense of injury.

Countertransference often foreshadows impending therapeutic events. An experience may tug at the periphery of awareness long before we can clarify its implications. Like an early-warning system, a lingering mood of unease, a restless state of erotic arousal, or a vivid personal fantasy or bodily preoccupation having no apparent connection to what is going on in the room can be the only perceptible indication of a dynamic drama about to explode the tranquil surface of therapeutic events. The analyst's emotions are purposefully stimulated in order to unconsciously stage a highly charged (often exquisitely detailed) dynamic scenario. The underlying scene may be structured with all the symbolic and metaphorical density of a dream, before undergoing an extrapsychic transformation that enlists the analyst's moods, actions, and fantasy (Kern 1987). As in a dream, the impetus to expression serves to animate and work over—in various levels of disguise—primal issues of longing, trauma, dread, and mastery. Since the analyst has only fragmentary awareness, there is little real alternative except to participate in such dramatizations. We trust that they will be turned to considerable therapeutic advantage once they have played out far enough for us to begin to understand them.

Dr. Slufay began to experience a recurrent state of drowsiness that descended upon him whenever he was in session with Janie. Soon after she entered his consulting room, his eyes would begin to glaze over. Although he would drink black coffee or surreptitiously pinch himself, he could not hold his attention on what Janie was so earnestly confiding in him. Face to face, she held him intently in a fixed gaze. Although her facial expression was impassive, her eyes spoke eloquently with an urgent fragility. Her hurried speech condensed many experiences within a single densely packed hour. However, she rarely came to a definitive conclusion or drew a strong connection between disparate episodes. The themes of her narrative loosely revolved around relationships of disappointment, misunderstanding, and deprivation punctuated by a desperate search for refuge in the solitary purity of artistic pursuit.

Although Dr. Slufay knew how vital it was in her case to maintain a nonverbal connection, to meet her desperation with a responsive soothing presence, he couldn't summon the appropriate reciprocal feeling. This was puzzling to him, because he considered her a profoundly sympathetic person and was aware of very much wishing to help her. He began to feel, however, as if he were locked in struggle with a diabolical hypnotist intent on inducing a soporific state. Every effort and trick of will proved insufficient. His only recourse was to break free of her searching gaze and to turn his face away. Attempting to mask his discomfort with a feigned nonchalance, he stared casually at a tree in the garden outside his office window. Janie gave no apparent indication that she noticed his drowsiness, nor that she experienced anything wanting in his responsiveness. Her speech persisted in its rapid, urgent intonation, as if she were filling her mouth with words to ward off a demand for something more sustaining. Did she not see? Was she afraid to confront him?

As this situation persisted, Dr. Slufay felt himself to be very much an empty vessel, devoid of wisdom, understanding, or tender human comfort. Yet he also sensed that to raise the question of her frustration and disappointment with his responsiveness directly would be met with incomprehension. At whatever level she might be taking in his state of mind, she gave no outward sign.

Dr. Slufay spent time outside of Janie's sessions trying to make sense of his countertransference. He wondered if his sleepiness was a form of withdrawal, an escape from the latent intensity of her devouring need or the implicit demand in her unexpressed longing for connection. Consciously he was aware of compassion for this woman and he could not convince himself that her neediness represented an intolerable emotional threat to him. Nor could he discern any suppressed erotic or aggressive tensions that might account for this clouding of consciousness. His associations provided no indications that he had linked her to any emotionally important figures in his personal history. He considered the manner and style of her communication, studying the rhythm of her speech, the thematic sequence of her narrative with its latent disjunction of content and emotion, eagerly seeking clues that might help dispel the enervating malaise. Yet each time he reentered the room with Janie, his eyes would begin to glaze and he would seek escape once again by looking out the window.

Janie missed a week's sessions in order to go home to visit her family. One of five children, she had grown up on a midwestern farm. Although the life was a spartan one, Janie recalled a relatively happy childhood brought to a tragic and chilling end when her mother was killed in an automobile accident. She was 10 years old at the time and she grew up with the feeling that all warmth and tenderness had left her home that dismal winter day. In response to an inquiry by her therapist, it had become apparent that Janie really didn't have a clear idea about the accident. Exactly when, how, or where had it happened? None of those details were available to her. But she also realized that no one back home had ever wanted to talk about "the tragedy," least of all her father, who presumably knew the most.

In her first session after the break she came into the office in a mood of unusual excitement. She immediately announced proudly that she had gotten up the courage to break "the taboo of silence." She had asked her stoical father to tell her what he knew about her mother's death. Janie and her father had just finished dinner and were still sitting at the kitchen table across from one another. When she asked him, she had become immediately frightened by her boldness, especially as she recognized the twisted and frigid expression that came over his face. Nevertheless, rather than chastise her as she anticipated, he grimly and deliberately proceeded to recall the painful events of that evening long ago. He and her mother had been out at a party in a neighboring town about twenty miles away from the farm. Driving home late, his wife napping next to him in the pickup, he had became increasingly groggy. Although he had tried to force himself to keep alert, his exhaustion after a hard workweek and "the few beers" he had "shared" at the party were too much. The car swerved off the road toward a tree. He awoke at the very last instant and yanked the steering wheel, but it was too late. As her father completed his grim story, Janie recounted how he turned his face away from her to hide the fact that he was crying. Afterward, they had sat together in speechless silence.

Janie's sad story alerted Dr. Slufay to the meaning of his own baffling experience, opening his eyes to an impending danger in the therapy. He immediately understood that his drowsiness had a very specific meaning, that it was an element in an unconscious staging of a treatment disaster that mirrored the tragic events in Janie's childhood. This realization literally woke him up—his torpor vanished! The immediate therapeutic road was clear again, to help her find the words to understand and express the anguish, despair, and rage at the parent/therapist who fell asleep on his watch.

An experience such as this may be disquieting. It seems alien, at least until we begin to recognize points of articulation in the patient's behavior or material. Bewildered by the elusiveness and specificity of such unconscious influence, many analysts have seriously toyed with the idea that certain patients are capable of putting psychic contents directly into our minds (or emotions under our skins) through telepathic channels. While such explanations may account for the uncanny subtleties of mutual influence and apprehension in a sustained intimacy, they risk endorsing ways of knowing that warrant more reserved skepticism. It is more useful to believe, and more reasonable to assume, that some subtle mode of evocative communication has escaped our attention. Often enough, a supervisor or study group reviewing the same clinical process can clearly identify the suggestive innuendo and covert instruction embedded in the interpretive dialogue that takes place. We do not believe that analysts or patients read each other's minds, or know each other's feelings and fantasies directly, except in extremely fragmentary and inconclusive ways. Idealizing empathic identification, or clinical intuition, or telepathic clairvoyance, either in the analyst or the patient or the dyad, is as unsound as elevating logical deduction, sequential inference, or diagnostic correspondence as conclusive ways of knowing. To be sure, each has a place in analysis, but none by itself holds promise of unimpeachable certainty.

The preponderance of our countertransference experience is neither arcane, disruptive, nor terribly elusive. As an accompaniment of our receptive listening we encounter a host of relatively transient and predictable fantasies, feelings, impulses, and moods. With experience, an analyst comes to appreciate the extent to which all these internal events have something to tell us if we know how to listen. These understandings can generally be integrated with formulations already built up regarding the patient's dynamics or the process of the moment. They are so numerous as to defy categorization, but there are some predictable forms worth noting. For example, feeling pressured to come up with a solution to a patient's current dilemma may cue the analyst to the emergence of rescue fantasies in the patient–analyst interaction. An experience of defensive tension, on the other hand, can direct attention to off-target attacks on the therapy or therapist that we have preferred to deny. When we experience an urge to accommodate a patient's perceived need, rather than analyzing it further, we may question whether we are caught up in our own wish to preserve a blissful union uncontaminated by frustration and discord. Such countertransferential phenomena, though not always agreeable to look at or free of anxiety, guide us to favor particular ways of understanding the material. Predictably, when the meaning of the reactive experience is grasped, its evocative strength will diminish along with its hold on the analyst's behavior.

Some countertransferential enactments, on the other hand, draw us completely off balance. They seem to require more than interpretive engagement in order to safeguard or repair the analytic breach. The analyst's actions or experience needs to be brought into the treatment as a way of concretizing a destructive transference dynamic that has been acted out blindly. Falling asleep on the patient, a display of uncontrolled temper, a cruel slip, being chronically late or forgetting a session altogether, talking to a third party without the patient's permission, and other acts that violate a foundation of safety compromise the patient's trust in a fundamental way. When such breaches occur, we need to depart from our interpretive stance and take personal responsibility for our error or loss of control. It is best to acknowledge our mistake as soon as it occurs, certainly before any attempt to analyze its implications in terms of transference–countertransference. A simple declaration, "I realize that agreeing to speak to your father was an error" or "There's no excuse for falling asleep," makes the point. In many instances a sincere apology—"I'm terribly sorry!"—is in order. Human error is excusable when one is dealt with humanely. It is rare that a patient will try to press for deeper explanations or acts of expiation. Confronting the reality that we are all human and that the analyst will inevitably make mistakes has its value and place in treatment as well. We may judiciously choose to reveal some of the motivation behind our action, but we must be careful that our explanation is not covertly intended to exonerate our acts, indirectly blame the patient, or deflect the patient's legitimate grievance. We generally do better to return to the primary focus of the analysis—understanding the experience of the patient—after receiving a definite sign that the patient is ready to get on with the work. Inevitably, there will be many fears and fantasies that will originate in such acts, many of which pass unnoticed by us, if we try to slough off the impact of what has occurred. Using the analyst's behavior as a springboard to accessing these reverberations remains vital.

The area of clinical events encompassed by the term *counter-transference* is both broad and varied. As analysts have become more comfortable acknowledging their countertransference responses, clinical discussions have taken on a level of frankness that would have been unthinkable twenty years ago. To the extent that this allows contemporary clinicians to explore the interactive dimensions of transference–countertransference phenomena with a nuanced specificity that may have been lost in the past, this represents a great step forward. However, we would be foolish to believe that our generation invented the wheel. Psychoanalysts have always known that their fantasies and emotional responses were crucial sources of clinical insight about patient's dynamics. Furthermore, all countertransference is not equally useful for purposes of analysis. Indeed, it requires considerable discernment, maturity, and sophistication to filter the idiosyncratic or frankly pathological elements of one's countertransference responsiveness so that it can be employed as a subtle tool of exploration or discovery. Naive assumptions and applications of the information that countertransference provides can be as disruptive and unhelpful as the "wild" application of any other interpretive strategy. Balancing the various sources of interpretive hypothesis is always essential in arriving at a valid approach to any clinical situation.

SUMMARY

As we welcome a wider range of emotional engagement in the analytic process, guidelines for integrating countertransference-derived knowledge into our technical practice become more integral to psychoanalytic technique. Psychoanalysis is an emotional involvement that stimulates and provokes both partners of the relationship but maintains as its primary goal the explication of the internal world and adaptive struggle of the patient. In this view, countertransference is one of several important sources of deeper knowledge about the patient or the analytic process. We most appropriately meet countertransference as a challenge—an opportunity to constructively transform the inevitable tensions that accompany psychoanalytic work. Countertransference reactivity can serve a priceless signal function, directing our attention to emerging phenomena that might otherwise be overlooked. A prerequisite for maintaining our emotional balance while working with countertransference is a highly sophisticated self-analytic consciousness. This function rests on a complex emotional/cognitive integration that acts as a general restraint against impulsive action. However, we understand that our ability to be optimally responsive will fall along a continuum of interpretive efficacy—ranging from mild disturbances that we can use effectively to intense disruptions that seem to use us. We caution that patients do not cause or create regressions in the analyst, though they may well stimulate and provoke them unconsciously. At these times, the restoration of neutrality, empathy, and a balanced interpretive perspective becomes the primary function of the analysis of countertransference. We have elaborated the crucial differences between the patient's transferences and an analyst's countertransference, which are mandated by the asymmetrical structure of the analytic situation. Transference–countertransference dynamics are never reciprocal. In considering when the analyst's actions or experience may require direct acknowledgment in order to defuse a destructive transference–countertransference dynamic that has been blindly acted out, we encourage the flexibility to depart from an interpretive stance and take personal responsibility for our error or loss of control.

6

Hearing the Unconscious

No intervention or interpretive action can be considered apart from our understanding of a patient's meaning. Understanding begins with a type of listening that establishes the foundation for all technique. Psychoanalytic listening is a highly disciplined professional activity, bearing little resemblance to the ordinary listening one encounters in friendship. It is, in fact, a complex skill employing many modes of apprehending and attending to the breadth and depth of human experience. We track the explicit, denotative lines of meaning in a discursive or fragmented narrative, screening out clumsy grammatical construction, tangential asides, and false starts that distract from what the patient intends to be saying. We also attend to connotative meanings by "unpacking" figurative speech. The emotional loadings of expressive forms as registered in tonal inflections, verbal cadences, and vocal rhythms is another key to discover how the person feels about what he or she is telling us. We may inwardly stage the dramas that are brought before us in sketchy word texts, recasting their action in ways that permit us to empathically enter into the experience of each protagonist. Perhaps the most stressful and elusive dimension of analytic listening revolves around the need to discern from meager clues what patients are thinking about, feeling toward, and wanting from the person they are confiding in. In effect, the scope of analytic listening is large. It encompasses the entire range of human experience and influences every dimension of clinical technique.

This chapter focuses on the essential premises and orienting ideas that uniquely empower analytic listening, enabling us to hear the disguised dynamic themes and unconscious elements of fantasy embedded in expressive language. This mode of listening facilitates exploration of various covert forms of enactment and dramatization that permeate interpretive dialogue, as well as the identification of other representations of archaic intensity and desire. It is a specifically psychoanalytic mode of listening, conducive to tracing those mental pathways that lead to unconscious memory, fantasy, wishes, and fears. The ability of language to speak to us from a place beyond the patient's subjective awareness is the dimension of psychoanalytic technique for which Theodor Reik (1948) coined the memorable expression, "listening with the third ear," to indicate a special listening function that, attuned to the extraordinary subtlety of human language, with its malleable allusive and symbolic expressive potentials, gives access to our secreted inner life.

Psychoanalysts have long understood that conventional distinctions between rational modes of organizing and representing reality, and the highly condensed, symbolic, and allegorical thinking reflected in dreams and fantasy formations are less clear-cut than many of us prefer to recognize. The tapestry of expressive language, upon close examination, is seen to be woven of multiple associative threads and emotional colorations, each of which has points of deeper attachment in the unconscious recesses of the mind. For descriptive purposes, the intricate narrative contents and/or mental images that compose the complex texture of the mind's self-observed surface are known as the *manifest content*. The underlying thematic structures, affective currents, implicit fantasies, and/or archaic wishes and fears from which these derive their intensity are known collectively as the *latent content*. To analyze the unconscious basically means to explore the ways in which the manifest content that a person consciously avows is linked with a diversity of disowned intentions, intolerable feelings, and unexpected contexts of memory. Sometimes the link is almost self-evident, as in a spontaneous disavowal, "It's not that I'm envious!" or in the awkward slip of the tongue, "I'll expose . . . explain that later." In the latter case, we witness the self's willful vigilance, swiftly deleting its own words at the very instant it has awoken to an unintended meaning.

The earliest generation of psychoanalysts, in the first flush of wonder and excitement at discovering the ubiquitous evidence of unconscious influence in daily life, was prone to employ these sources of meaning recklessly, without proper regard for the patient's sense of plausibility or relevance. It often set up an unnecessarily contentious dialogue in which analysts arrogantly presumed certain knowledge about aspects of their patients' inner life for which skeptical patients could find little subjective validation. Gradually psychoanalysis compensated for the clumsy errors of "wild analysis," evolving a finer appreciation of the exquisite tact and timing that direct approaches to unconscious content require. Patients in analysis, similarly to students of analysis, need time to become conversant with archaic forms of representation before they can give full credence to this evidence. Until this occurs, otherwise invaluable tools for infusing psychoanalytic discourse with unforeseen intensities of feeling and fantasy, can easily degenerate into exercises of cleverness or technical bravado. Our communications to patients are always bound by considerations of tact, timing, and phenomenological plausibility. Above all, contemporary analysts appreciate the narcissistic centrality of autonomous subjective experience, judiciously nurturing a foundation of understanding before attempting to introduce symbolic allusion or reference to unconscious fantasy into their interpretive repertoire. An analyst who is adept at listening with a "third ear" can afford to be patient; opportunities are never far off to deepen the analytic dialogue in unexpected and productive ways.

In analyzing the manifest content of a psychoanalytic session we are thoroughly dependent on a simple though ultimately quite radical premise: there is nothing arbitrary in mental life. Much psychoanalytic technique and interpretive inference is anchored in this assumption. As leverage to expand fault lines beneath the composed surface, everything a patient says (or does), intended or unintended, becomes relevant to understanding psychic meaning in a particular context. It is not the patient's semantic error alone that invites interpretive conjecture. Correct and appropriate language choices do, too, just as surely. Words and figures of speech come "packed" with associative baggage (Bruner 1990) that lends specific weight to their denotative content. Grammatical structure, the form and rhythm of sentences, the choice of active or passive voice, personal and impersonal pronouns, and so on, all serve to represent the latent meanings and intentions of the mind in the manifest surfaces of narrated experience. There is no "verbal static" that can be safely tuned out. This foundational assumption, that every aspect of linguistic form and content contributes to meaning, is familiar in our approach to a poet's literary creation. Psychoanalysts have discovered that it is an equally illuminating way of interpreting a patient's free associations. Within this framework, ordinary language is regarded as serving a poetic as well as a denotative function by condensing meanings in metaphorical, allegorical, and/or symbolic[1] verbal forms that dramatize and elaborate, vary, or contradict the conscious themes being developed in the manifest narrative. Loewald (1988) captures this dimension vividly:

---

1. It should be noted that here we are using *symbolic* in its original psychoanalytic sense as a manifest image, phrase, or word that has a nearly invariant relationship with a specific element of unconscious content. When used in conjunction with an appreciation of the more individualized power of personal metaphor and figurative language to concretize the subjective concerns of a person's unique experience, we believe that there is little danger of reductively truncating levels of meaning that amplify, rather than negate, one another.

I view words and sentences as symbolic expressions that in their genuine function conjure up or evoke persons, things, events, and relations between them, and this on multiple levels of meaning. Words have the potential of awakening memories and fantasies that bring back to life, more or less vividly, the persons or things they name, thus arousing the listener. In derivative forms of verbal language, used in daily life much of the time, this more genuine function, here called symbolic, is deeply hidden, as good as lost, not intended or heard as such; the merely ideational, cognitive content of what is said is what counts. . . . In psychotherapy we try to set off a movement in which that kind of code is deciphered, revealed as symbolic, that is condensing multilayered meanings rather than abstracting from them. [p. 53]

Clearly, we want to guard against jumping to definitive conclusions from a few allusive details. Consistent repetitions of words, phrases, or thematic refrain, on the other hand, are generally confirmatory. Although there is multiple interpretive potential in any single associative element, we learn to have confidence in context, sequence, consistency, and repetition as especially trustworthy guideposts:

Rhonda made a spontaneous and enthusiastic observation as she came into her female analyst's office: "Oh, somebody gave you some beautiful flowers!" Manifestly, her opening remark was presumably intended as a complimentary pleasantry. If, however, we consider her casual assumption, "somebody gave you," an unelaborated fragment of a fantasy about the analyst in relationship to a significant other, we are led to consider other possibilities. Flowers, symbolically associated with genital activity or its consequences, lead to a conjecture that this patient is preoccupied with the analyst's love life in some as yet unclarified way. Thus, when she "formally" begins her session with the reflection, "I don't know if I'm feeding my depression or if I just can't get out of it?" we feel prepared to generate a hypothesis. For unless we consider what has already transpired a non sequitur, the invidious comparison with her analyst's presumed good fortune can be plausibly construed as a feeding of her depression.

Subsequently, when the manifest theme of the unfolding session elaborates feelings of powerless, depressive entrapment, and anticipatory fears that her poignant longing for a husband and children of her own will never be fulfilled, our freedom to conjecture loses many degrees of freedom. Ending the session with bitter reflections about her own mother's procreativity—the patient was one of eight children—and how she had been deprived of the childhood love and attention she craved, Rhonda provides an artful symmetry to her contrapuntal narrative. With a remarkable economy of means, she has told us a tale of barren sorrow and helpless deprivation while her language simultaneously gestured toward an underlying transferential drama in which Rhonda is forced or forces herself to bear envious witness to the fruitful sensuality of another.

Although this brief synopsis condenses a wealth of detailed content, our confidence in its interpretive integrity is sustained by a confluence of thematic, affective, and symbolic contents. Salient wishes, fears, fantasies, and attendant affects are intertwined in a shifting configuration of object/self relationships. In abbreviated summary, it might seem as if the analyst has arbitrarily imposed a meaning on the patient's material, yet the requirement that every element in the session find a meaningful place in the encompassing interpretive framework stands as an exacting standard that checks against arbitrary and fanciful interpretive flights. Within this disciplined structure, treating the patient's language as a highly condensed metaphorical, allegorical, and/or symbolic communication that embodies, dramatizes, and elaborates a subset of organizing themes greatly enhances the power and precision of analytic listening.

We recognize an almost textual inevitability to certain linguistic forms and choices that encourages interpretive inference when the patient fails to follow expected rules. By mentally completing the unfinished sentences or omitted words of our patients, we invariably see that they have broken off the thought before an anticipated but unwanted conclusion. A patient couldn't find the right word: "Bunker . . . no . . . trench? . . . no . . . Oh, you know!" Can we surmise he felt some misgiving about the word *foxhole*, which contains a symbolic genital allusion—Oh, you know without my having to mention the unmentionable. When John says, "I'm fighting to understand what you just said to me!" is it sensible to inquire, "Just whom or what is John doing battle with?" There are a number of possibilities. Yet if he were to respond defensively, "I *only* meant I was wrestling with your ideas!" the possibilities begin to collapse around the inference that the analyst's interpretation represents a threat. To insist on the validity of our conjecture would move us from dramatization to enactment, by actively engaging John in a verbal struggle over whose intentions—the analyst's or the patient's—should prevail.

In employing an analytic approach to listening, we assume that multiple levels of meaning intersect in any intense subjective experience. Insight into these multiple contexts and their complex relationships shows us how meaning is structured in the analytic process, often making it possible to address issues that impede progress:

Roger was particularly adept at elaborating any interpretation his analyst could make. He obligingly sought current-day parallels, as well as genetic connections, which were largely corroborative. Nevertheless, his analyst was often left with an uneasy sense that all this diligent effort was yielding considerably less than seemed to meet the eye. By what sleight of hand was Roger turning gold into base metal? Attending carefully to nuances of his expressive language, his analyst noticed a linguistic idiosyncrasy that had escaped his attention: none of this patient's sentences ever ended with a full stop. Rather, they ran together, hastily cemented by a se-

quence of conjunctives—"and," "also," "as well as,"—uttered
in an urgently expectant inflection that suggested that the
very next thought would clarify all the preceding ideas. The
result was an unbroken narrative that couldn't be broken into.

After observing the consistency of this grammatical pattern,
and realizing that his verbal eagerness conveyed a false
promise—the subsequent clause or sentence rarely illuminated what came before—his analyst intervened by describing this entire pattern in detail. Not unexpectedly, Roger
found all this "interesting." A discussion ensued in which he
speculated, plausibly enough, that in speaking this way he
"might be employing a stratagem" to prevent the analyst from
forcefully breaking into his monologue, and to forestall unexpected expressions of emotion. Yet the pattern continued
unabated. The only evident impact of this discussion was that
Roger began to come late for his sessions.

One day a few weeks later, when his analyst was delayed
with an emergency telephone call, Roger found himself, despite his lateness, having to wait a few minutes in the waiting
room. When his session finally began, he reported that he
experienced a sudden onset of anxiety while waiting. This had
built to a sense of acute dread when his analyst finally came
out of his office to greet him. He immediately went on to say
that he felt "as if I were facing a test." He was, in actuality, in
the process of studying for his licensing exam and was worried
"that the facts I was cramming into my head would fall out
before I sat for my exams." After an extended pause, he
commented that the dread he experienced in the waiting room
recalled to him the dread he used to experience each morning
of his childhood before going to school. He would be too
nervous to eat breakfast. It was the very same feeling.

His analyst intervened, sharing a speculation: "Perhaps as
a child you were afraid to eat out of a concern that something
would fall out of you in school—that you would have a fecal
accident?"

Roger: I do recall a scene that made a great impression on me. I still shudder when I recall it. I was in third or fourth grade, Mrs. Stillman's class, I think, and we were lining up at the end of the day to march in size place from our classroom downstairs to the dismissal area. And little Eric Lessor, who should have been at the front of the line, kept shifting nervously toward the back of the room, looking very uncomfortable. Then I noticed an odor . . . shit . . . ugh . . . and saw a stain on the back of his pants. He was standing with a load in his pants hoping no one would notice. No one else seemed to or we were all pretending not to. Stillman had left the room. Anyway, we had to wait until she came back to lead us out of the building. It seemed an eternity to me. Poor Eric! Poor me! I think I had nightmares about that situation. Standing there, pretending not to notice his shame, waiting for the teacher to come through the door.

Analyst: All these situations you've been anxious about today—your dread waiting for me in the waiting room, your worries about the licensing exam, and this childhood fear of going to school—share a common root. They connect to the fear that something will come out in an uncontrolled way leading to a humiliating disaster. Perhaps you've been trying to control this fear in here for a long time, covering your ass so to speak, by plugging up all the holes in your thinking, making sure nothing messy and poorly controlled falls out of you.

In Roger's case, the manifest structure of a resistant interaction, his anxious effort to hold in the shameful contents of his inner life by covering the holes in his narrative only became a compelling interpretation when it was linked with a childhood context of bodily control and social mortification. Before this connection was discovered, the understanding of the defensive process remained relatively inert. After these connecting links became evident, Roger began to "loosen up."

Much as we attend to what our patients say, we listen as well to what they do not say—silence speaks eloquently. Learning to identify and give shape to the "negative space" in our interaction with the patient is an essential aspect of understanding the whole person. Being prepared to hear omission registers aspects of experience that carry feelings, fantasies, or fears that have been split off or repressed. If we listen carefully for the "unthought known" (Bollas 1987) and the unspoken thought, we add a third dimension to our picture of the person with whom we work. What patients choose not to talk about reveals as well as conceals. Sherry, for example, has little compunction exposing the most graphic descriptions of her sexual life but rarely mentions having feelings (sexual or otherwise) toward her analyst. She feels safe projecting an idea of extraordinary sexual power yet wards off the vulnerability of needing anyone. Lisa, on the other hand, engages her analyst in passionately angry struggles, while circumventing more tender feelings with acerbic ingenuity. In a similar vein, when a patient talks about the past to the exclusion of the present, about the present to the exclusion of the past, or about reality to the exclusion of fantasy, we are being told something as surely as if it is being said directly. As we attend to the entirety of the patient's communication, noting areas that are in shadow as well as in bright light, we gradually sketch a chiaroscuro portrait of the patient's vulnerable soul.

As patients advance in their treatment, they gradually learn how to listen to themselves as carefully as we have been listening to them. This familiarity with archaic means of representation is a central element of the identification with the analyst's "observing ego" that Sterba (1934) emphasized as a crucial element in a productive treatment situation. When we see patients using this understanding without our prompting and direction, we recognize that they have taken an important step toward independence in the journey of self-discovery. They have incorporated tools to explore the manifestations of unconscious motivation, fantasy, and feeling, apart from our guidance.

Brenda was describing her discomfort at a big family gathering Christmas day, when she found it increasingly difficult to make "small talk." She recognized that she felt both diminutive and childlike compared to her older cousins. "It's a one-way street," she observed. "They ask about me and how things are going in my life, but I rarely inquire about them." She was perplexed by this reticence, however, since in her ordinary social and professional life she considered herself anything but inhibited. At this point in the session, to her analyst's surprise and pleasure, she spontaneously associated the expression *one-way street* with the specific block she had actually lived on when growing up in Newark. Her family was "the poor relations," she recalled, living in a small apartment in the rear of a modest private house. Her mother was particularly sensitive about the fact that her own brothers, Brenda's uncles, always preferred to host family gatherings at their more spacious homes in affluent suburbs and rarely visited Newark. Brenda's associations to this figure of speech made it clear to her that in a quiet and inhibited way, she was going to redress this offense to her family by making sure the next generation of relatives, in conversation at least, met her more than halfway.

What has come to be known as "evenly hovering attention" is a figurative description of an openness in attitude that is receptive to seemingly insignificant nuances or details. Free-floating listening is not always as unfocused or random as might be imagined. Essentially, all we are attempting to free ourselves of is a premeditated or exclusive focus of attention. Once we are cued to a relevant context by the patient's narrative, our attention takes direction. Identifying subtle contextual cues is an important aspect of analytic listening, for it enables us to elicit intersecting layers of meaning. When, for example, a patient announces, "After I left your office Monday, I had a fight with Henry" by way of introducing a detailed episode of marital disharmony, we have been explicitly told that everything we are

about to hear will have a connection to something that transpired in Monday's session. The manifest episode of marital
disharmony should be heard in the context of this, as yet
undefined, "something" that occurred in that previous session.
Thus, in the back of our minds, the issue of linkage with
Monday's session will be implicitly raised with regard to everything we hear. If no subsequent clarification emerges, either in
the patient's material or our memory, we would have grounds to
pose the question directly: "Perhaps there is some way that this
argument with John was triggered by something that happened
here Monday?"

When clear contextual cues are absent, we allow our attention
to float, taking in passing details as well as broader themes and
linguistic patterns. This will entail focal shifts—from close up to
sweeping overview—as well as movement between simulta-
neous auditory, visual, or even tactile sensory modalities. We
may visualize figures of speech, reversing a process that is
implicit in all figurative imagery. "I'm sinking into depression!"
or "The bottom fell out from under me!" virtually demands visual
transcription. Silent parroting of the phrase "I feel sky high!"
may amplify a vocal echo ("aihheee!") distilling the thrill of
psychic abandon accompanying an unstable mania. By playfully
disturbing the organized thought structures of the patient's
language the analyst may succeed in finding emotionally condensed visual metaphors and verbal puns that hover between
and within the lines. More often, we are taken by surprise.

Ralph was in the termination phase of his analysis when he
began a session with the statement, "Since Wednesday I feel
myself sinking into a depression. I'm afraid I won't be able to
get out of it." He went on to connect this mood with a specific
precipitant, his pregnant wife's imminent departure on a
short vacation with her mother. He spoke of his inability to
willfully "climb out of the dark, enveloping mood." "It's like
being trapped in quicksand." He recognized that he was
having morbid thoughts that something terrible might hap-

pen to his wife while she was away, far beyond his protection. If she were to die, he reflected, "what a mess my life would become." How much work and commitment and love had gone into this relationship; how solid it all seemed now! Yet he went on to confess that the thought of all that insurance money got him excited. He couldn't deny it, however shameful a feeling it was. He'd be free to run around, indulge himself sexually, drink and get high all night. He reflected somewhat ruefully, that this exciting fantasy was really just a part of "the old pattern." He had understood through analysis that this had been the way he had tried to comfort himself as a small boy after his mother died, and at every significant loss since that time. Wallowing in self-indulgence, "like a pig in shit," had distracted him from unendurable misery and utter emptiness. He really knew there wasn't anything on earth that could assuage his pain if he were to actually lose Jane.

Ralph's associations moved from this painful anticipation back in time to a particularly forlorn period of his adolescence, a time when his father had been preparing to remarry. A specific memory emerged: One afternoon Ralph and his friend Shawn had gone out in the fields looking for groundhog holes. When they found one, they poured a bucket of water down one end and then caught the groundhog in a bag as it scrambled out the other end. After describing this scene in some detail he fell silent for a while. As his analyst sat puzzling over this memory, trying to find some context of significance within which to understand it, Ralph suddenly declared, without any overt transition, "I really think I'm prepared. If I had to, I could deliver the baby myself!"

His analyst was startled. He had been immersed in the manifest content of Ralph's associations, empathizing with his fear of separation, loss, and irreparable despair. He was even more startled to hear himself respond, without a moment's pause, "Oh, I see, all you have to do is be ready to catch the baby as it comes out of the hole!"

His analyst had been following the denotative line too closely to recognize that Ralph's opening statement signaled an unconscious link between a fantasy of anal birth (entrapment in a pit of quicksand/a pig in shit/a groundhog flushed out of its dirt hole), his depressive affect, and a reparative fantasy reunion with his departed mother/wife in the grave (a fetus in a fecal womb). This latent thematic development had surface points of attachment in the manifest narrative anchored by the familiar symbolic equation, feces = money = baby, and culminating in the specific memory of flushing out the groundhog, which unites the manifest theme of loss and death with the latent theme of hope and rebirth. Retrospectively, Ralph's "shitty" mood is understood as a place of refuge, a literal depression or dark womb-like enclosure, in which he withdraws to escape the dreadful risks of committed love and paternal obligation. His startling declaration, "I think I'm prepared. . . . I could deliver the baby" (for my child's birth, to be finally adult, to live on my own without my analyst's protection) may be interpreted most saliently as a hopeful reaction to the painful rebirth trauma of impending termination—"it's in the bag."

Jacob Arlow is the contemporary psychoanalyst who has made probably the greatest contribution to our understanding of the way unconscious fantasy manifests its ubiquitous presence in the conscious experience and linguistic expression of the patient. He argued that metaphor is an "outcropping into conscious expression of a fragment of unconscious fantasy" (Arlow 1969a, p. 7). The most profound levels of understanding become possible when we are both comfortable and conversant with these more primitive psychic strata and their expressive manifestations. We do not equate depth with profundity, yet it is undeniably a dimension of profundity. Analysts develop the technical dexterity to integrate unconscious contents into higher-order interpretations. In clinical terms, the significance of our understanding is always determined by its relevance and saliency within a specific context. Much solid and valuable psychotherapy can and often must take place without active attempts to engage the unconscious.

Free association is never a solipsistic event. If a person's language becomes incomprehensible for any sustained period, we know that a defensive and/or regressive withdrawal is in progress. At least a distant echo of the analyst's attentive presence reverberates through patients' minds, even when they appear lost in reverie. A slight intake of breath before we speak, the creak of our chair, a faint scratch of pen on notepad are ambiguous cues that often register as definitive markers of shifts in our attention. And patients experience our attention as a palpable entity; it has a substantive, definable quality, which mediates consciousness of our presence. Even our silence speaks with a unique voice; it may seem keen, restless, approving, or enthralled. Of course, this does not mean that patients are clairvoyant. Attributions regarding the nature and content of our attention locate many emerging transference fantasies.

The subtleties of expressive language provide a way for us to listen to a patient listening to us, even before we venture into an interpretive dialogue. Overt reference to the listening analyst, sometimes takes the form of an unquestioned attribution, as in "I know you think I'm being defensive when I say that I'm not angry about your vacation," or "You're going to like this dream I had about my mother," or, more distantly, "I suppose one might consider this a selfish idea." More often, the analyst must infer the emotional disposition of the implicit listener from subtle details of form and tone of the patient's expressive language. What we are listening to, in effect, is the patient's listening to us. Do they believe we are a bored, anxious, judgmental, irascible, or erotically excitable listener? What theories, values, prejudices, and knowledge have they assumed we possess and how did they infer these "facts"?

We listen intently therefore to indirect communications: to the off-hand comments, "door-knob" remarks, and "innocent" asides that patients assume are outside the analytic purview. As Gabbard (1982), citing Stoppard (1967), has adroitly pointed out, "Every exit is an entrance to somewhere else." We know that this positioning marks these extra-analytic comments with a special significance. It is as if patients act out their ambivalence by bringing in and keeping out pieces of themselves that they cannot own explicitly. Attending to these seemingly insignificant interactions as valid communications worthy of exploration is often a shortcut to the transference. To listen in this way, one must overcome the polite discretion that governs ordinary social discourse. We take seriously what we are not supposed to notice.

Our analytic ear is specially tuned to disguised expressions of emotion, whether originating outside the analytic interaction (in descriptions of involvements with others; in reactions to particular books or movies; in response to cultural events) or within the analytic process itself. Recalling the sensory primacy of our earliest years, that emotion is quintessentially a physical experience, we "think body" as we listen to the patient, even as we attend to other patterns of interaction. This directs our attention to bodily metaphors and allusions in speech and to the continual emotional expressiveness of the living body before us. References to body parts, orifices, and functions saturate expressive language. Patients speak of "blowing off" a friend who made them angry, of being "left high and dry" by a loved one, of an interaction that left a "bad taste." We note how the body is used to punctuate what is being said—the patient's "body language," as it has been aptly named. At appropriate times, we call the patient's attention to (see Chapter 7) the way in which she turns away from us, flushes, or impatiently twitches when attempting to contain her anger or hide desire. We coordinate the evidence of our ears, our eyes, and our gut reactions to what patients communicate with their bodies. How patients enter or leave the consulting room, posture in the chair, or lie on the couch is never arbitrary or accidental. These become ritualized and intelligible acts. They telegraph emotional significance, invitation, and warning. We do well to pay attention.

It is important to recognize that as analysis gets under way and patients become familiar with these modes of revealing meaning in expressive language and action, they turn this new awareness upon *our* speech and behavior, employing the same principles of inference that we have demonstrated through our interpretive interventions. They listen between the lines and within the lines, with an acuity amplified by transferentially powered anticipation, contemplating our word selection, timing, phrasing, and tone. Many fruitful explorations of transferential themes and fantasies begin, not with the content of the patient's fantasies or dreams about the analyst, but when we identify the patient listening to ourselves with specifically charged attention. When Anne says, "I'm amazed that you were able to recall so many details of my dream from last week," we are less flattered than curious that our powers of memory should be the source of such amazement. It may give us the first hint that dream work is proceeding under a spell of magical expectation in which the analyst is being experienced as an exciting wizard who possesses arcane knowledge of mysterious secrets, or that the patient's expectations of being truly listened to are very low. Patients' expectations of us are often communicated subtly, through inflection, tone, or movement; these expressions of their subjective experience can be easily glossed over. They offer us, however, a starting point for the exploration of feelings and beliefs that have been molded by unconscious forces. Attending to patients' attributions of us enables us to productively actualize and explore aspects of transference and resistance activity.

SUMMARY

In this chapter we have formulated some of the empowering principles of analytic listening. Many of the specific techniques and interpretive strategies we have illustrated have their origin in the radical assumption that there is nothing arbitrary in mental life. If there are no irrelevant details, then we are charged with the interpretive task of discovering how the whole and its smallest parts form an integrated unity. How does the manifest denotative line of meaning relate to the symbolic and metaphorical resources of the language used to express it? Such questions, when carried through consistently, instruct us to listen to sequence, detail, style, content, and theme with an ear to how each dimension amplifies a coherent psyche. Although human meaning is inevitably ambivalent and inconsistent, these incongruities are structured by conflict between conscious and unconscious intention. Multiple contexts of seemingly inconsistent, tangential, or contradictory meaning must find a higher integration through the analyst's interpretive art. This is one of the allusive connotations of the expression "to conduct an analysis," for we strive to hear and interpret an underlying order within the patient's "music," a secret harmony within the affective cacophony of subjective experience. We listen with our ears through our eyes, and to our guts, to what is in the room as well as to what has been left outside. We listen to the strings of meaning and the stirrings of the heart. Through a creative synthesis, the analyst's understanding of the patient's living aspires to an ideal of coherence in which neglected intentions, wishes, fantasies, and feelings find balanced expression. Although seldom achieved in a given session, or an entire analysis for that matter, we still recognize that this ideal of comprehensive understanding stands as a crucial safeguard against errors of reductive simplification.

7

Interpretive Activity:
A Contemporary Integration

As the type of therapeutic intervention in which the analyst's understanding of the patient or the therapeutic process is communicated to the patient, interpretation is understood to have a central, mutative role in psychoanalytic treatment. "Making" and "giving" interpretations is what a psychoanalyst does; it is an activity that distinguishes an analyst from other kinds of therapists. Exactly what it means to make or give an interpretation, however, is subject to considerable disagreement among practicing clinicians. This ambiguity is due in part to the fact that our conception of the interpretive act has evolved—more, perhaps, than other aspects of technique—in hand with new understandings of the psychoanalytic process and psycho-dynamic structure. Over time, our interpretive models have accrued substantive dimensions as well as subtle nuances without entirely superseding or integrating earlier forms.

The original meaning of interpretation was intimately connected with the art of unraveling the disguises and complexities of manifest dream structure in order to reveal the underlying thoughts and warded-off wishes in a patient's mind. At a period when psychoanalytic understanding of the complex dynamic structuring of psychic life was still rudimentary, the art of dream interpretation was largely synonymous with psychoanalytic technique. Through a long, and often contentious evolution, subsequent generations of psychoanalytic thinkers have substantially enhanced our understanding of the complex role, content, and function of the analyst's interpretive activity (Bergmann and Hartman 1976). Interpretive technique has expanded well beyond so-called id analysis, incorporating advancing theoretical models of defense and resistance, character rigidity and structure, ego functioning and ego/superego relations, object relations, the structure of self experience, and the dynamics of narcissistic equilibrium. This chapter does not attempt an extensive review of the evolution of the concept (the interested reader is referred to Blum 1983, Cooper 1987, Etchegoyen 1983, Halpert 1984, Levy 1984, Ramsy and Shevrin 1976, Rothstein 1983). Rather, our goal is to elucidate a practical integration of contemporary understandings of interpretation.

Essentially, the analyst's interpretive activity is an extension of a unique way of listening and thinking about clinical process that emphasizes the *context*—as much as the *content*—of the patient's experience. There are a number of relevant though shifting contexts, which the listening analyst must take into account in arriving at an interpretation. At a given moment, the narrated sequence of spontaneous associations, the transference–countertransference field of emotions, fantasies, and actions, or the adaptive drama of the patient's past and present extra-analytic life may claim the forefront of our attention. Ultimately, the analyst's interpretative activity culminates in a deliberate attempt to make explicit connections between disparate fragments of the patient's experience. An interpretation suggests or posits a dynamic linkage between two or more elements of action, memory, thought, or emotion. Linking these elements helps the patient become aware of continuities of experience that were, at best, at the edge of consciousness.

Although one of these elements may be an inferred aspect of the patient's unconscious experience—a fantasy, a wish, an archaic fear—this is in practice the exception rather than the rule. Analysts have come to appreciate the efficacy of interpreting within the reach of the patient's subjective experience, as it strengthens the therapeutic alliance, encourages the analysand's experience of personal agency, and facilitates dealing with resistance. The ultimate goal of uncovering and explicating the role of unconscious forces in the lives of our patients is best viewed as an evolutionary process, one that gains momentum within an analytic climate conducive to change and discovery. Cathartic breakthroughs, lightning assaults on character armoring, or incisive dynamic illuminations of hidden unconscious meanings, however gratifying to our pride, are rarely fateful occurrences in an extended course of treatment.

INTERPRETING AS DESCRIBING

Contemporary epistemological theories in the social sciences emphasize that our way of seeing, experiencing, and describing the world are intrinsically interpretive. Inevitably, they reflect culturally mediated acts that structure the "facts" of our senses. This understanding forces us to recognize that even when we believe that we are merely stating what is empirically observable—"You are dressed entirely in black today!"—or only echoing words already spoken, these interventions are inherently interpretive. From this perspective, many activities traditionally considered subsidiary modes of analytic intervention, such as clarification, observation, questioning, active exploration, or confrontation, are better understood as integral elements of a more broadly conceived interpretive activity.

Indeed, the argument for this point of view is as much clinical as philosophical; most patients behave as if they believe it to be true. Our patients, especially those with heightened narcissistic sensitivities, have taught us that an analyst's descriptive or summarizing remarks are rarely experienced as purely "neutral" statements.[1] Seemingly innocuous observations are re-

---

1. Here we are not speaking of our "technical neutrality." Rather, a neutral act is one that does not attempt to argue/assert one thing over another. Some

butted with guarded qualification: "But there's purple in my socks!" Every summary or description, however true to subjective experience, reduces material according to some principle of priority that patients will attempt to infer. Inevitably, the analyst's interventions serve to clarify something observed from within our independent framework (Schwaber 1986, 1990). That perspective, however benign, may prove threatening to patients' agendas of having control over how their self is represented to another. What does wearing black mean to the analyst, after all?

All meaningful interpretive strategies begin with careful descriptions of the psychological events or phenomena one is beginning to address. Freud's (1909) "pursuit of the particular" (Levenson 1988, Sharp 1937) in the Rat Man case vividly demonstrates the efficacy of developing a thorough description of the patient's actions and experience. Indeed, apt description in itself often serves an interpretative function, as it allows patients to apprehend elusive aspects of hitherto bewildering phenomena. Simply naming an ambiguous emotional experience—"You felt mortified!"—can sometimes galvanize diffuse awareness around an entirely new percept. With emotionally isolated or disorganized patients a good deal of therapeutic work is accomplished at this preliminary level of interpretive effort.

At times we will find simple description problematic. This alerts us to the possibility that a foundation for explicit interpreting has not been adequately established. The difficulty may be traced to feeling a pressure to interpret before hearing enough detail. Often, that foundation will be filled in if the analyst can sit back and listen to the multiple meanings of the patient's free associations. Descriptive difficulty also arises when we press too hard to "connect" with a patient's experience in the absence of adequate clinical evidence. Such forced empathy overworks a naive assumption of similarity—"I would feel

---

contemporary adherents of perspectivism conflate these two separate meanings in a way that forces them to challenge the whole viability of technical neutrality as a clinical construct.

that way if I were in that situation"—in an attempt to simplify the painstaking task of finding one's way into an alien sensibility. Even experienced therapists, who have mastered the complex listening skills necessary to substantiate their conjectures, can succumb to this reductive universalization. Disciplined listening, which is the basis of all reliable description, demands that we disabuse ourselves of many of our conventional preconceptions about how other people feel, think, or react. When an analyst truly describes what is heard rather than what is expected, interpretive work assumes a creative edge that frequently yields quite astonishing results. As a working principle, whenever we feel pressured to respond, whether it emanates from indirectly expressed demands of the patient or internalized expectations within ourselves (often it is both), we do well to resist until we restore a sense of interpretive autonomy.

Samantha, who had been in analysis for two years, greeted her therapist's return from vacation with characteristic aplomb. She graciously inquired how his holiday had been, exuding a warmth and interest that was immensely appealing, especially in light of the resentment radiating from some of his other patients. The therapist found himself responding to her with genuine warmth. He allowed himself to be drawn into the exchange, but chided himself for a reluctance to go along with her implicit overture to share more specific details of his vacation. Don't be so stuffy! he remonstrated inwardly. After all, we are two real people in addition to everything else. Why not acknowledge that by sharing a snippet of my life with her?

Yet, enticing as this invitation seemed to him on this first day back at work, he was also aware of another, less comfortable feeling: an almost distinct pressure to respond to Samantha in kind, as if any other type of interaction would be hurtful or unthinkable. Buying more time to understand this pressure, he continued to respond personally yet refrained from revealing explicit details.

As he listened to his patient's associations in the unfolding session, the theme of shutting off emotions kept surfacing. He found himself realizing, not for the first time but with a conviction born of emotional connection, that the "ordinary" human exchange that took place at the beginning of the session was in fact an example of the way Samantha achieved this distancing in the analysis with him: seductively engaging "outside" the session but suppressing her feelings and fantasies about him "in" the session itself. Reflecting on this experience and the context of her subsequent associations culminated in an interpretation linking the two observations: "This splitting we've been talking about today also applies to us. Have you noticed how engaging you are with me before we start or as you leave, but that you rarely mention feelings or thoughts about me during a session?" Resisting the pull to engage until he understood more specifically how Samantha's actions and words related to his own complex experience made it possible for him to open up a subtle dynamic: the paradoxical way in which Samantha tried to hide her desire for a more intimate connection with her therapist through superficial affability.

There are situations in which the fragmentation of personal experience serves unconscious defensive functions and open-ended listening will yield little that seems trustworthy. In these cases, a more focused exploration of the "who-is-doing-what-to-whom" particulars of patients' actions, fantasies, and impulses in regard to the analyst's interpretive activity provides us with hidden clues to what is obscuring the analyst's vision. We should be prepared to discover that the process of being understood can take on pernicious or intensely stimulating meanings that the patient actively subverts.

Michelle, an intelligent young woman in her late twenties, came into treatment after a performance review at work revealed problems with authority that had eliminated her from consideration for a promotion. Stymied, Michelle was determined to resolve the obstacles that were interfering with her professional advancement. Initially treatment proceeded without undue difficulty, but gradually her analyst noticed a resistance to anything he said with even a hint of authority. Even hypotheses qualified as possible connections were disturbing to her. Indeed, any statement that carried even an implication of seeming to know more than the patient about the patient generated intense anxiety and rage. Every interpretive act—regardless of content—seemed to stimulate a fantasy of malevolent intrusion that was desperately evaded. Michelle's analyst suspected that his interpretive activity itself had come to embody childhood humiliations suffered at her mother's hands. Turning the interpretive lens reflexively back upon the interpretive process was a vital preliminary step in helping Michelle understand her issues with authority. Careful examination of Michelle's experience, especially her understanding of the meaning of the analyst's actions, began to defuse the terror and rage that was infiltrating the analytic situation. Analysis of the interpretive process was aided by the analyst's attention to the importance of maintaining a therapeutic alliance, explicitly requesting that the patient let him know when she felt he was becoming intrusive or critical so that these experiences could be examined collaboratively. Feeling safer and more in control, Michelle was able to sustain an exploratory look at the interpretive dialogue that was repeatedly infused with malevolent potential.

Generally, patients are reasonably receptive to the suggestive inferences, encouragements, and directives embedded within our descriptive takes. "So, you emerged from the meeting feeling expansive—in command—until you recalled that one question that called for a more complete answer; then your mood began to plummet" may represent a reasonably succinct and accurate summary of a more extended narrative. It also advances an implicit interpretive suggestion. The patient's depressive mood swing has an implied cause: an overly constricted focus on a detail of remembered performance. Furthermore, the linguistic gesture "So!" seems to attach a subtle directive to the entire intervention: the patient is supposed to find an obvious implication in the words that follow. The analyst's tone of voice, whether eagerly attentive, dryly objective, exasperated, or ironic, will put a further spin on its content. "Gee, I guess I expect a lot of myself!" might be a predictable response. Alternatively, "So you think I'm hard on myself!" In our view, it is wiser to acknowledge "It had crossed my mind!" rather than debate the imputed authorship of the idea.

Clearly, the preliminary descriptive phase of our interpretive activity is far more complex and demanding than one might suspect. Indeed, it calls upon powers of observation, dramatic visualization, and compressed expression that are literary in scope. To distill a useful verbal representation of the patient's inner and outer world, the analyst must strive to identify and descriptively isolate salient details, significant patterns, and encompassing themes from an associative text that is often obscure and defensively elaborated. Furthermore, these representations must be framed in a manner that the patient both recognizes and is prepared to consider.

It is especially important that we learn to construct our interventions without arousing unnecessary narcissistic resistances. Pine (1985) notes that with fragile patients, affectivity carries the potential for disorganization and debilitating anxiety, transforming the interpretive moment into a moment of heightened vulnerability. Presenting interpretations in a way that supports positive functioning, "with functions relevant to good object relationships, benign aspects of the superego and support for flexible defenses" (p. 150) increases the probability that such patients will be able to receive them. In effect, he holds considerations of safety paramount; increasing the psychological "hold" of the therapeutic environment may prove essential. Attending carefully to our tone of voice, phrasing, and tact makes it possible for any patient to better hear what we are saying. Increasing the patient's degree of active participation with regard to interpretive content often ameliorates the tension that develops when the interaction is fused with panic, anger, or resistance. Undoubtedly, the art of interpretation is a higher-order integrative faculty that matures slowly, nurtured by years of training and experience. (Although the current literature tends to discuss this faculty under the rubric of *empathy*, we feel that this term can obscure rather than explain the complex imaginative and emotional functions that come into play in the apprehension and construction of another person's inner world.) Fortunately, patients will forgive occasional clumsiness and inaccuracy when they are confident that the animating spirit of our interventions are kind.

The artistic dimension of the analyst's interpretive activity has been compared to a stage director's task (Loewald 1975). A course of understanding clarifies and refines motivational intentions that are initially only implicit in the text. The momentum of description moves from action to dynamic explication; the "who does (or wishes to do) what to whom?" becomes "why does X do (or wish to do) what to whom?" Our apprehension of dynamic motivation becomes simultaneously more elemental and elaborate, just as in a well-staged psychological drama. In treatment, however, the course of revelation is less predictable. Dynamically intensified relational configurations, archaic fantasies, and depressive states emerge, disappear, and reemerge, with greater or lesser clarity than before. Pursuing a spiraling sequence of repetitive themes, memories, and emotional vicissitudes, the interpretive process very gradually distills a clarified picture of the dynamic organization that integrates the patient's inner world.

The tempo and rhythm of this interpretive process, unique to every analysis, has to be respected. Every treatment encounters periods of obscurity and stasis, as well as unexplained detours, which must be endured by both participants. At other times, there is a give-and-take momentum to the interpretive flow that instantly amends, expands, or substantiates the observations advanced by either analyst or patient. When things go well we find ourselves in a position to hypothesize more elaborate motivational descriptions that augment fundamental observations. Substantial evidence must accrue for favoring one particular dynamic proposition over a number of plausible alternatives. The patient above, for instance, might object: "I can tolerate triumph fine, but I have to know that it's deserved!" Taking a lead from the affective valence of the patient's protest, we would be redirected to the meaning of "un/deserved triumph." Overt interpretive activity would be bracketed for the moment, as we listened very carefully to succeeding associations for indications that would amplify the meanings for the patient of feeling undeserving and/or triumphant. At a later time, this entire sequence may be connected with other elements in the patient's experience: a competitive rivalry with a sibling remembered from childhood, a fantasy about the destructive consequences to others of ambitious success, or, perhaps, a pattern of mood fluctuation over a lifetime.

INTERPRETIVE COLLABORATION AND DIALOGUE

Contemporary analysts increasingly acknowledge that valid interpretive frameworks must be arrived at collaboratively through much painstaking, precise, and empathically mediated descriptive/exploratory experience. Ideally, the patient who is meaningfully engaged in an interpretive dialogue actively amends and clarifies each of the elements in a carefully monitored interactive process. Each party must acknowledge the other's reservations about important areas of mutual attention before confident formulations can be established. Agreement is not achieved through direct appeals to the analyst's authority, even though the process rests on an implicit assumption that the analyst's interventions draw upon a special body of relevant expertise. Rather, we seek to make inferences plausible (Gill 1982) by directing the patient's attention to the immediate evidence of experience, including the obviously inconsistent or reluctant ways in which the patient entertains that evidence.

The encompassing goal of this collaborative dialogue is to further the conscious integration of the patient's experience, including the remembered remote and recent past. The quality of integrated awareness we strive for—what has come to be spoken of somewhat imprecisely as insight—includes intrapsychic and extrapsychic dimensions. It can be meaningfully assessed along a number of descriptive/metaphorical lines. We speak in terms of the depth, complexity, comprehensiveness, affective vividness, psychological plausibility, and relevance of insight. A clinician's assessment of these criteria will be affected by theoretical commitments, but sound interpretive work is always embedded in a meticulous consideration of the specific personal nuances of an ever-shifting psychic reality illuminated through detailed observation. Generalizations and speculations have little therapeutic weight in psychoanalysis. Although one can retrospectively conceptualize an area of interpretive focus as a didactic exercise (e.g., work on a drive conflict, a transference paradigm, a relational configuration, a characterological attitude, a defensive configuration, or a genetic reconstruction), such judgments are mostly irrelevant in the turbulent intimacy of a clinical encounter. Interpretive activity is imbued with the rich ambiguity of life rather than the sterile precision of a laboratory procedure. It is better to recognize simply that the generic purpose of all interpretive intervention is to increase the patient's awareness of the continuity and interconnection of a uniquely organized psychic life.

It follows that the success or usefulness of our interventions must be apprehended in the course of an extended interpretive dialogue, the duration of which may be measured in sessions rather than sentences. Brief extrapolated excerpts, which are employed illustratively in this and other analytic texts, have limited utility in conveying this dimension of clinical process. One of the advantages of this conceptualization, however, is that it deflates unrealistic expectations regarding the impact of any specific intervention, however elegant or timely. Contemporary psychoanalysis is moving away from the model of an analyst as one who "makes" or "gives" finely crafted interpretations that fulfill ideal technical criteria, toward the idea of an analyst engaged in more or less continuous interpretive activity. Most of this activity remains private conjecture, while some is revealed to the patient verbally. As we have seen, nonverbal and implicit communication through context has a significant place in this process. We never lose sight of the fact that the meaning of our interpretive activity can only be assessed as we observe precisely what the patient is doing with it.

THE INTERPRETIVE DIALOGUE AND THE THERAPEUTIC ALLIANCE

The interpretive dialogue must be recognized as a representational medium of considerable importance, on a par with dreams or associative sequence. It affords the patient creative opportunity to enact, as well as to describe, the crucial dramas of a neurosis. The mutual elaboration of the impact of the analyst's interpretive activity and the patient's reactivity provides a refractive analytic surface through which memory, fantasy, archaic fearfulness, and wishfulness are rendered visible as constituents of subjective experience.

The patient's response to the analyst's interpretive activity is always a major part of the salient content that needs to be elucidated in the course of an analysis. Interpretation involves developing an appreciation of the implicit premises and psychological operations that patients employ in ascribing meaning to our interventions. Clarifying the process a patient goes through in finding meaning in the analyst's words concretizes the fantasies, habitual attitudes, and beliefs that fix transferential experience. If, for example, a patient greets our interpretive activity with a consistent attitude of belittling denigration, we make this predisposition our subject: "You display a great deal of ingenuity in paraphrasing my comments in ways that make them sound silly!" This interpretation abruptly shifts the topic of discourse to an interactive process of disparagement. If our tactic is successful, we are likely to discover that this patient had been experiencing our interpretive activity as subtle belittlement. Indeed, we may realize, retrospectively, that the form of our confrontation had an ironic cast, which might easily be experienced as mockery or one-upmanship. Describing more completely this dialogue of belittlement that has been constructed between analyst and patient becomes a new interpretive focus. This shift, to the interaction as a representational medium, enables the participants to work together on understanding how patients construct the world. In what way does the patient create meaning from the analyst's actions? What is specifically attended to? What is denied? How does the patient collaborate with the analyst? Is seduction or anger the primary route to contact? Is there a need to do it all oneself? Does the patient appeal to the analyst as an omnipotent parental figure, or set up a barrier beyond which we are not to venture? The unique form of collaboration generated by the participants at any given time is a key to the dynamic organization of the patient's experience. Attention to the interaction establishes a context that enables analyst and patient to jointly articulate their specific contributions to the dynamic structures that integrate the patient's experience.

As with other more familiar representational mediums, the overriding interpretive goal remains to describe and connect our discoveries in ever more encompassing integrative configurations. A growing body of literature supports the idea that our interpretive activity is significantly enhanced by attending to our experience of this interaction, generating otherwise unavailable cues to as yet unmetabolized conflicts and contents (Aron 1991, 1992, Boesky 1990, Chused 1991, Gabbard 1996, Gill 1979, 1982, 1994, Greenberg and Mitchell 1983, Jacobs 1983, 1986, 1991, Levy 1984, Lynch et al., 1998, McLaughlin 1991, Renik 1993, Roughton 1993, White 1996).

In addition to serving as a representational medium and a

means of expanding the analyst's understanding, the collaborative dialogue has a therapeutic aspect that facilitates the analytic process as well. The importance of joint collaboration in the analytic endeavor was noted by Freud (1895) and later elaborated by Fenichel (1941), but it was Sterba (1934) who first provided a compelling explanation of the nature of this collaborative effect. He described the analyst as inducing a therapeutic split between observing and experiencing sectors of the patient's consciousness by forming an alliance with the reality-oriented part of the patient. Sterba highlighted the importance of the positive transference in permitting a transitory strengthening of the ego through an identification with the analyst's analyzing attitude. This identification is specifically nurtured by direct references to the collaborative nature of the work, particularly through the use of the bonding term *we*. Fostering an alliance with the patient's "observing ego" facilitates the integration of archaic aspects of experience with higher levels of organization. "Let's try to understand the meaning of that remark" facilitates mutual engagement more effectively than "What did you mean by that?" Likewise, the statement "We need to know more about why feeling close to me makes you freeze up" is more conducive to collaboration than "Why did you stop talking?" or "What made you freeze?"

Attention to the development of a therapeutic alliance is an integral part of effective interpretive collaboration. Freud attested to the therapeutic importance of this relationship in his *Introductory Lectures on Psychoanalysis* (1916/1917). He noted that the patient, struggling through the conflicts uncovered in analysis, is in need of a powerful emotional enticement to recovery. "What turns the scale in his struggle is not his intellectual insight—which is neither strong enough nor free enough for such achievement—but simply and solely his relation to the doctor" (p. 455). In the course of an analysis, patients inevitably endure multiple losses and tumultuous disruptions as long-standing protections, compromises, and dynamic equilibria are modified or relinquished. During a period characterized by lack of connection to earlier modes of relating or defense, connection to the analyst serves as a bridge spanning the void created by these processes of change. The therapeutic alliance provides vital containing functions (Bollas 1987, Modell 1976, Pine 1985, Winnicott 1956), as patients gather courage to confront that void. Winnicott's (1954) holding environment, Kohut's (1971, 1977) selfobject functions, and Stone's (1967) necessary gratifications all speak to the same idea from different perspectives.

It stands to reason, therefore, that the development of the alliance is a primary concern of the analyst (Meissner 1992). Initiating an awareness of the importance of working together is a central task of early analytic work. We have a vested interest in facilitating a working collaboration. In this regard, the analyst cannot be passive. We must structure and safeguard the integrity of the psychoanalytic situation, for without attention to cementing a treatment alliance we may feel the patient slip through our fingers. Describing how the analyst experiences the patient's collaboration is often a useful first step and can serve as a model for future interpretations. "I've noticed that it seems important to you that I just listen and not say anything. How can we understand this?" "Are you aware that you tend to turn to me as a child turns to a parent, with an expectation that I will know better than you what is best for you? Let's work on exploring why you tend to leave yourself out of this process." "Arguing together seems to be easier for us than relating in a more positive way. We need to understand how this mode of relating becomes so easy for us to fall into." These interpretations deal not only with the interaction between the participants, but specifically focus on that aspect of the interaction that impedes the development of a therapeutic alliance. The value of joint collaboration is communicated through consistently focusing on the patient's understanding and organization of the interaction. Helping the patient to understand the difficulties that impede working together connects difficulties in the present with the issues and conflicts that brought the patient to treatment, providing an immediate emotional resonance with broader problems in living.

It is essential, however, that the therapeutic alliance not be understood as operating apart from the analytic process itself. As Brenner (1979), Langs (1975), Levine (1993), and Kanzer (1975) have pointed out, the alliance cannot be exempt from examination or isolated from the analytic process. Unlike earlier formulations of the working alliance (Greenson 1967, Greenson and Wexler 1969) that were based on the distinction between "realistic" and "nontransference" aspects of the analytic relationship, contemporary understanding acknowledges that transference inescapably infuses every dimension of that experience. There is an inherent risk that in deepening the therapeutic alliance, the emotional enticement of gratifying union will draw the analytic couple away from the rigors of further interpretive work. As the place of love in analytic treatment is ubiquitous, and the pull to live out, rather than analyze, relational dynamics is ever compelling, the analytic injunction to sublimate experience through understanding is an essential safeguard of the patient's autonomy.

It is important to realize that the analyst's interpretive effort to describe and connect elements of the patient's internal experience defines a particular mode of relationship, rather than an alternative to a relationship. We are committed to being understanding, though not in any conventional sense of the word. Expressions of sympathy, support, or validation of the subject's personal representations of experience are generally less pertinent than a specific appreciation of the patient's actual dilemma—a situation inevitably compounded by internal, unconscious complexities. The analytic ambition to reveal the dynamic structure of this experience in depth does not, however, preclude appropriate and sincere expressions of compassion. Unless the patient's pursuit of such comforts becomes a focal point of resistive struggle, we must acknowledge acute personal suffering brought on by neurotically compromised living. Such acknowledgment reinforces the conviction that the rigors and sacrifices of an analysis are worth the effort. Our support of the patient, moreover, extends beyond explicit expressions of compassion. It is indicated in the way in which we diligently sift a profusion of clinical impressions searching for an angle that enables the patient to see a potential for growth in confronting a fear. It is there in our reliable presence, which encourages the patient to reveal what is true without fearing judgment. And it is there in our willingness to make the patient the center of our efforts. Although much of the time it is this implicit support built into the structure of the analytic situation (Adler and Bachant 1996, Pine 1993) that conveys our benevolent intentions, ideally every interpretation embodies an element of this benevolence as well.

On the other hand, if we are forthright, we will acknowledge that there are times when a patient's apparent suffering simply is not poignant. In these situations, we often can discover a subtle form of subjective split, in which dramatized representations of suffering are simultaneously witnessed and enjoyed by a part of the patient's self that stands apart as audience. A careful description of the kinds of internal pleasures that such performances yield is more useful than bearing witness to this suffering. In time, appreciation of the gritty integrity that informs our interpretive activity is extracted from benefits sustained. For the best of us, self-knowledge will always be an acquired taste.

INTIMACY AND INTERVENTION

The analyst's individuality stands revealed most clearly through our interpretive activity. Although we may sit behind a patient and speak with restraint, our personal voice will be heard. As in any complex creative activity, no two analysts conduct analysis in quite the same way. Unique qualities of imagination, empathy, interest, tact, self-confidence, and intelligence cannot—and should not—be expunged from our interventions. Our intimate presence, as an emotionally responsive person who laughs, displays excitement, experiences a range of emotion—including, at times, irritation or anger—is not in conflict with an attitude of interpretive neutrality, except in caricatured renditions of analytic demeanor. As long as the analyst's display of emotion is not used to manipulate the patient's experience (i.e., to intimidate, seduce, persuade, etc.), there will be adequate scope for the organization and expression of transference. Moreover, a profound concern for the patient's well-being will be evident in the tact and compassion that we try to bring to all our interpretive efforts.

Inevitably, the patient's experience of our relatedness is an essential element of an interpretation (Freud 1905a, Greenson 1967). Therefore, we tailor our interventions individually, speaking to each patient in a voice suited to that person and that personal situation. An interpretive dialogue is a very intimate exchange. In the intimacy of this encounter, we greet indications of the patient's erotic stirring with *acknowledgment*. This word implies both a knowledge of and acceptance of desire—in both its sexual and spiritual forms—as a dimension of analytic relatedness. As Freud (1915a) recognized early on, it is one of the more difficult and odd things about psychoanalysis, that love and desire are encouraged in an intimate human relationship for purposes other than physical or romantic gratification. Yet that is the course we must negotiate, carefully steering clear of suggestive enticement or rejecting discouragement. While discussions of this aspect of analytic technique have traditionally been cast almost exclusively in deprivational terms, our experience convinces us that the analyst's readiness to recognize and describe the patient's desire—without judgment, condescension, or reciprocation—is one of the most reassuring and affirmative acts in the interpretive repertoire. Tacitly recognizing the urgency of bodily desire as an elemental driving force of human intimacy sanctions the verbalization of the most excited—and exciting—elements of the patient's essential nature. By carefully leaving unanswered the implicit question of reciprocal desire, the analyst keeps open the most compelling issue in every enduring human relationship: How and in what ways are two people to love one another?

June, an overweight woman of 35, came into treatment after she was fired from her job by a boss with whom she had become entangled in a web of mutual recriminations. Initially, June thought of her female boss as the perfect mentor, someone who could teach her and be there for her in a way that her alcoholic mother never had been. She set herself to the task of making herself invaluable, cheerfully volunteering to tackle unpleasant tasks and "selflessly" giving her time, regularly staying at the office until late into the evening. She was flattered when her boss suggested that they get together with their husbands socially, but although the personal involvement was initially gratifying, it led to considerable confusion and agonizing conflict as time went on. June couldn't explain it, but she recognized a pattern in which her relationships with authority, especially women, would be wonderful at first but inevitably degenerated into discord, only to be resolved by June's leaving to find another position. This was the first time that she had been fired, and because June was profoundly invested in her competence, it was a severely debilitating blow: her call for a consultation came after several weeks of being "afraid to be alone" that was beginning to try the patience of her friends and family.

When June came in for her sixth session, she was inconsolable. Tears streaming down her face, she chronicled the difficulties of getting through each day as thoughts about what she had done wrong consumed her.

"I don't know what I'm going to do," she sobbed. "I feel like I can't do anything. I'm used to being the one other people depend on and now I'm the burden. I can't stand it! I feel like nothing is ever going to be right again."

"Let's try to understand why you feel so hopeless about getting through this."

"Your saying that makes me feel better, as if there might be some way out. . . . but I feel like I'm a burden on you, too. . . . I really can't imagine getting through this. I feel like . . . like I'm inside a glass bubble, able to see and hear what goes on around me but isolated and cut off from human contact. . . . I can talk to people and they can talk back but there's always this wall. . . . Always . . . I can't imagine anything that would make it better . . ." (silence)

"What's coming to mind?"

"Well, I never realized it before, but there is one thing that gets through the wall . . . (pausing, then hesitantly) . . . touch makes the wall melt."

"It was hard for you to tell me that."

"Yes. . . . I feel very embarrassed about this . . . but I . . . I found myself thinking that . . . if you would give me a hug, it might get through the wall. I might feel better."

"My giving you a hug feels like it would get through to you in a way that my words don't."

"Yes . . . I feel like I can trust a touch, whereas words are just words. I don't think I've ever really trusted anyone. At first it seems like this will be a person I can trust, but it never works out. I'm always disappointed."

"So a hug is a way of assuring yourself that you're cared about. If I give you a hug you feel safer that I won't disappoint you, whereas if I don't, you feel very unsure of how I feel."

"Exactly. I really don't know how you feel. You might think that I'm a pathetic blob that you dread having to see."

"Why would I dread seeing you?"

"Because I need so much."

INTERPRETATION AND AFFECT

Psychoanalysts have recognized from early on that emotions are the elements of subjective experience least subject to defensive distortion, representing reliable pathways to a patient's intimate concerns. Freud (1900) observed that the patient's affects are "always appropriate" (p. 461), though he allowed for variations in intensity and displacements onto related ideas and objects. The affective thread in the tapestry of the patient's associations can be quite subtle, manifesting itself in an insistent tone of voice, a particularly evocative phrase, gesture, or allusive symbolic motif. Often it is embedded in elements that simply "shine" with significance. At other times the patient's emotion intensifies like a squall over warm waters, threatening everything in its path. Finding a way to navigate these rugged seas poses a therapeutic challenge. Emotional currents rip through the associative process, gathering its contents into a swelling narrative of dynamic significance. When we succeed, however, in holding a course through these emotional storms, we enable the patient to link action, thought, and memory with the driving forces that carry subjective experience.

Stephanie came to her session boiling with rage. She was incensed over what she believed was her roommate's "demand" that she do more than her fair share of the chores. Her analyst noted a discrepancy between the intensity of the anger and the particulars of the situation she was describing. Wondering if her wrath was intensified by a hidden flame, she asked Stephanie to tell her more about the quality of the anger she was experiencing. As Stephanie described her feelings in detail, something—she couldn't say exactly what—made her recall that Stephanie had recently increased the frequency of her sessions. Could Stephanie's feeling of being pressured represent a transference displacement from her experience of the analyst or the recent intensification of the treatment? She commented:

"So your roommate is making unfair demands on you, pressuring you to do more than your share. Perhaps you also feel more is expected here, now that you are coming so frequently? Could it be that you feel pressure from me?"

Stephanie hesitated and then blurted out, "I do feel pressured by you. . . . I know it was my idea . . . but coming more often makes me feel more pressured . . . like I'm never good enough. I thought by coming more often I would feel like I was finally getting it right, but I don't. I just feel like no matter what I do it's never enough."

"Never enough?"

"Yeah, like at that singing audition I told you about. When I told my parents that I didn't win a place in the choir they were really disappointed. I just didn't want to sing anymore, after that."

"You seem to be demanding a lot from yourself."

Powerful emotions follow pathways that originate in core dynamic structures. Following these emotional currents links disparate experience into a coherent, thematic whole. In Stephanie's case, the projection of internalized expectations onto others, in the face of her ambitious tensions, dovetailed with her deeper (never satisfied) longing to win and hold her parents' love. The exploration, understanding, and engagement of the affective core of experience is essential and sought out even when the patient is unaware or resistant (Fenichel 1941). Our interpretive activity with regard to the patient's emotions is necessarily complex. We interpret attitudes to reach unavailable feelings, but we also interpret feelings to reach unavailable fantasies, and vice versa. In doing this, we ask the patient to explore the determinants of experience as fully as possible, especially compulsive and automated modes of being whose importance may be hidden from awareness.

Although Marcia had shown little patience for exploring the relationship with her analyst, she had been able to acknowledge that the analyst's vacation the previous year had left her with devastating feelings of abandonment. It evoked an emotional withdrawal that took months to work through. Eternally preoccupied with testing her desirability to attractive men, the session before the analyst's approaching vacation was, characteristically, involved with expressions of ambivalence about the man she was currently seeing. The analyst considered it likely that her overt ambivalence was an indirect allusion to unexpressed feelings toward herself on the eve of another vacation. Marcia, an exceptionally beautiful young woman, had to go to extraordinary lengths to ensure that she would be rejected by men. During this particular session, dominated by concerns that the man she had just started seeing wasn't going to like her, Marcia suddenly picked up an object on the side table next to her chair. She spontaneously remarked that if she could take this object home with her, she would feel better about the ensuing separation from her analyst. After acknowledging the patient's desire to stay connected during this break, the analyst also commented on the way in which her request turned the analyst into a rejector: "You want to stay connected to me during the break, but you do it in a way that ensures that I, too, will reject you." Although Marcia typically saw herself as the object of others' rejection, on this occasion she reluctantly entertained the relevance of her analyst's observation. The sense of personal agency that this awareness engendered enabled Marcia to approach the ensuing break with an enhanced experience of her own power and a correspondingly greater ability to avoid devastating feelings of loss.

Contemporary analysts are aware, however, that we feel things for many different reasons. While some feelings may represent the center of the person's experience and initiative, other feelings—or the same feelings at other times—may defend against feelings, ideas, and fantasies of a more painful nature. Feelings also may serve as agents of self-punishing or self-shaming tendencies, as well as crystallizing a patient's terror of change:

Elaine came to treatment possessed by her rage. Her relationships were inevitably turbulent, and marked by expectations that people were always trying to "get something" on her in order to have the upper hand. Her anger was passionately

felt and at times viciously acted out, supplying her with
sadistic gratifications that far exceeded the pain she experienced. Elaine's anger was so consuming that contact without
it was boring to her, devoid of the "excitement" that made her
feel alive. During one particular session she spoke of her
difficulty loving the man who seemed to love her. He treated
her with affection, kindness, and understanding. Her reverie
about his ability to accept her was suddenly shattered by a
bolt of rageful fury at an apparent humiliation she had recently experienced at his hands. She then turned this destructiveness upon herself and the analyst, loudly lamenting the
time she had wasted in treatment getting nothing accomplished. The analyst asked if she noticed how easy it was for
her to find some reason to move into rage and how difficult to
stay with her more tender feelings, whether they were about
her boyfriend or about the therapist. Elaine stopped, unchar-
acteristically, and acknowledged that she could see what the
analyst was talking about. For a moment she allowed the grip
of rage to relax, while she briefly contemplated the sequence of
her emotional process.

This session was distinct only in that Elaine was able to stand
outside her compulsive tendency to blind herself with whipped-
up passion. The principal function that this lashing out at self
and others served had been observed and described to her on
numerous occasions. She could give lip service to the idea that
she was protecting herself from the dangers of intimacy, engaging in overheated encounters that did not threaten the vulnerability of her longing to be loved. In this session, however, the
irruption of her rage was directly and dynamically connected to
the contemplated fantasy of love fulfilled. Elaine was able to
grasp that she was using rage actively as a means of avoiding a
more painful experience—the terror of allowing herself to risk
love without the certainty of fulfillment.

The accumulation of such reflective moments of understanding introduces deliberation and choice where automatic and impulsive action had prevailed. The language of interpretation is full of phrases that call upon the patient to exercise forms of deliberation, delay, and reflection in the face of emotional upheavals, even as the structure of the psychoanalytic situation encourages spontaneity. "Are you aware that X . . ." "Have you observed (considered, recognized, noticed, etc.) Y . . ." "What do you make of Z . . ." are often repeated phrases that announce the analyst's interest in having the patient stop, look, and listen. These phrases, with their intonations of curiosity, interest, or surprise, are calls to reasoned deliberation.

A patient spoke exuberantly about a job opportunity in another city for much of a session without mentioning any feelings about ending treatment with his analyst. His analyst intervened, "I notice that you haven't indicated whether you have considered the impact of this choice on the fate of your treatment!" raising the question of the patient's mode of deliberation, without directly challenging either the conclusion or the patient's right to make such a choice. It is an observation that focused attention on the most relevant immediate context from the point of view of the analytic relationship—Is it to endure? Within a framework of neutrality it is a question that only the patient has the right to decide, but it is the analyst's obligation to attempt to expand the internal perspectives that will enter into the debate. Of course, the patient may construe this intervention as a covert demand, especially if his overt excitement has been serving to ward off any feelings of loss, or anger about the analysis and/or the analyst: "Oh, you think I should give up this great job just to stay in this treatment with you!" His analyst responded with sincerity, "Even if it was my wish, I would never presume to tell you what's best for you. But I do feel entitled to speak for what's best for the treatment. What weight you give that in this deliberation is, of course, up to you."

The structure of the analytic situation encourages the patient to use a broader understanding of the determinants of experience to integrate feelings into a framework that considers the whole person. In effect, we treat the mind to reach the soul. In the course of things we invite love, hate, pride, greed—virtually all the passions of the human soul—to a party, where reason stands as host.

TOWARD INTERPRETIVE CLOSURE

The call to reasoned deliberation inherent in our language of interpretation begins at the surface of an analytic encounter. By tradition, we are enjoined to explore the surface to find pathways to the depths. Levy and Inderbitzin (1990) portray the delicacy of this attitude of hovering alertness metaphorically; they write of the analyst's exquisite sensitivity to "the ripples, waves, or glass-like calm that appear and catch our attention, often with an element of surprise" (p. 374). Contemporary analysts are, as we have seen, extending the idea of the analytic surface beyond the edges of the patient's conscious mind to embrace subtle textures and patterns of interactive engagement within the analytic relationship itself. One consequence is a greater willingness to prolong our immersion in surface phenomena as a place of analytic interest in its own right. Not in quite such a hurry to "peel the onion," we are intrigued by the juxtaposition of surfaces and depths, the interpenetration of past and present, as well as the intricate interplay of fantasy and reality, at all levels of psychic experience. While we still seek to understand the irrational fantasies that organize subjective attitudes, we also struggle to unravel how an attitude may serve to structure our world of fantasy.

The idea of multiple analytic surfaces (Levy and Inderbitzin 1990) is a useful way of thinking about the fluid contexts of meaning that alternately capture and engage our interpretive attention. At the experiential level, transference, resistance, and countertransference must be revealed in a configuration of multiple clinical surfaces. We can never say, except by way of shorthand summary, this is the transference, here is the resistance, that was my countertransference. Rather we trace their ubiquitous influence in elaborate embellishments of fantasy and dream, the uneven contours of emotional engagement, the content and form of narrative development, the unseen bridge-work of associative continuity, the rhythmic cadence of interpretive dialogue, or the feints and passes of interpersonal adaptation. Each will become the focal point of our attention in the recurrent figure–ground play of interpretive activity. What we attend to in a given moment is often an intuitive choice, as much a hunch as a considered judgment, suggesting a workable surface of dynamic significance may be at hand.

Defining and technically exploiting varied surfaces of interpretive opportunity is an aspect of maturing craft that draws on a host of sensibilities. We must train our ear to identify the linguistic encoding of archaic fantasy or to hear the unspoken continuities that anchor a fragmented narrative. We become attuned to the emotional nuance caught in a fluttering vocal timbre, facial coloring, or nervous gesture. We recognize situations that emerge with repetitive regularity in a particular treatment, learning to monitor complex sequences of action and reaction even as we are drawn to repeat these enactments. We attempt to ground our interventions in observations that are accessible to the patient's immediate awareness, and, when possible, close to the patient's emotional experience.

Theory plays a significant part in this education. Good theory is persuasive because it is the residue of meticulous observation. As such, it empowers us to return to our own work with a heightened awareness of psychological dimensions that were the focal point of another analyst's vision. All analysts have had the experience of going from a book to an analytic session and finding in the living material precisely what we had just been reading about. Recent theoretical developments have pointed an intense spotlight on interactive and intersubjective dimensions of transference, vividly detailing relational configurations, misunderstandings, and enactments between patient and analyst, as well as mapping the thematic organization of the patient's subjectivity. From an interpretive stance that recognizes the clinical importance of multiple analytic surfaces, the impact of ongoing theoretical evolution can only expand our interpretive skills, enhancing our capacity to define varied analytic surfaces with greater precision and flexibility. This flexibility is a hallmark of contemporary psychoanalytic practice. With particular patients, new developments will augment our understanding of crucial processes significantly, contributing to the eventual success of the psychoanalytic enterprise.

Contrary to popular stereotype, interpretive closure is something an experienced analyst approaches cautiously. Provisional conviction has been an established, though frequently neglected, principle of analytic interpretation since Freud (1900) first warned that the appearance of complete understanding does not preclude equally inclusive interpretations of a dream from subsequently coming to light. When Freud first wrote this, it was an extraordinary achievement to have established any reliable meaning to dreams, symptoms, or neurotic behavior. For contemporary psychoanalysts, our facility at generating alternative meaning is both a blessing and a burden. Equipped with so many interpretive models and hypotheses (or narrative story lines, as Schafer [1983] has expressed it), there is little danger that we will need to force a patient's experience into a rigid formula. But being aware that there is always a multitude of alternative ways to interpret each psychic phenomenon we attend to challenges us to await compelling contextual evidence before committing our authority to any one understanding. As Shengold (1988) has eloquently put it, "Optimal clinical work demands a flexible ability to balance an awareness of the limitations of knowledge with a transient certainty" (p. 5).

Indeed, fragmentation of process and diffusion of focus are technical dangers that are the complement to our contemporary flexibility. These are likely to occur when a heightened attention to multiple clinical surfaces is not balanced by a hierarchical sense of clinical significance. Not every facet of transference or resistance or countertransference is equally weighty or strategically germane to the analytic process. Unless our choices are cogently informed by a comprehensive and coherent theoretical framework, we run the substantial risk of generating a diffuse and fragmented psychoanalytic process.

Conjecture is that part of the analyst's analyzing activity that remains private. An interpretation is simply a conjecture in which we have gained enough confidence to share with a patient. This simple distinction represents an important demarcation defining a psychological space within which the most creative analytic thinking can take place. The freedom to conjecture boldly (Brenner 1976) is an essential attitude that informs our interpretive activity. An analyst's imagination cannot be confined by constraints of ordinary good taste, formal logic, conventional morality, theoretical and supervisory allegiance (or rebellion), or the preferences and sensitivities of our patients. One needs to be unencumbered to pursue the unconscious resolutely.

At what point and in what form a conjecture is verbalized is a complex clinical judgment that must take into account a host of considerations. Timing, tact, plausibility—from the patient's perspective—are all determinations that require subtle discriminations. Guidelines can only be roughly approximated. As with so many clinical matters, it is easier to define than to assess the potential risks and benefits of a particular intervention. The virtues of spontaneity—an analytic atmosphere of liveliness or surprise—have to be balanced against the dangers of therapeutic traumatization with accompanying defensive failure or rigidification. Analysts differ markedly, some preferring to wait for considerable corroborating material. Others are comfortable with intuitive assertions that arise seemingly straight from their unconscious. Although interpretive statements can be voiced with a range of formality and designated confidence— from "a hunch" or "idea" to a definitive certainty—their impact on the patient cannot be calibrated in advance. It is of overriding importance, therefore, that we track the impact of our interventions closely. As opposed to the conjectures we formulate in our own minds, we can only be certain what interpretation has been heard through the chains of thought and affective reaction traced in the patient's associations.

There are abundant ways to stimulate conjecture. We may consider sequencing of associations, symbolic equations, established theory; we consult our empathic identifications, our unbidden fantasies, and emotions, to name some of the more familiar.

Betsy came to her session and was immediately in tears, informing her analyst that she was going to have to stop treatment. It was now just over two months since treatment had begun and she just felt "compelled" to stop. She spontaneously commented that she had left her previous therapist after seeing him for 2½ months also. Surmising that the time period might be symbolically significant, her analyst asked her what came to mind with regard to the time 2½. Betsy began to sob even more despairingly and told the analyst that she had stopped talking for an entire year when she was 2½. This was also the period in which she had recurrent nightmares of a child's drawing of a man's face getting bigger and bigger, pulsating in intensity as it filled her entire field of vision until she awoke screaming in terror. The therapist's conjecture that the symbolic meaning of 2½ might be relevant to the patient's compulsive desire to cut herself off from the intensities of treatment led her to actively explore this possibility with Betsy. Archaic fears and automatic strategies of flight triggered by the current analytic interaction were accessed by attaching symbolic meaning to a distinctive detail (2+ months of treatment) of the narrative surface of the patient's associative flow.

Naturally, many emotionally compelling ways of stimulating conjecture are centered in the relationship between patient and analyst. Some analysts are stimulated almost exclusively by the activity of the analysand in the immediacy of their interaction (Busch 1995, 1997, Gray 1994), using blockages in the associative flow as a primary cue to explore the patient's experience—particularly manifestations of resistance and defense—more carefully. Other analysts (Arlow 1969a,b, Greenson 1967, Grossman 1982, Heimann 1950, 1956, Isaacs 1952, Kernberg 1976, 1985, Klein 1957, 1958, Ogden 1986, 1989, Reed 1987, Richards 1981, Stone 1961, 1967) emphasize the emergent revelation of fantasy in the context of the analyst–patient interaction. Implicit transference fantasies infuse every therapeutic encounter as continually transforming derivatives of early wishes and fears. The ever-present availability of these fantasies and their intimate connection with early experience mark them as a treasure trove of information about the patient's relation to body, psyche, and others.

Cindy, a student at a local college, came ten minutes late to her early morning session. "Sorry," she murmured as she flopped down on the couch, "I just couldn't get out of bed this morning." After a long pause, she yawned, dramatically. "Excuse me! I don't know what's the matter. I can't seem to wake up this morning. I actually turned off the alarm and went back to sleep."

"Perhaps your bed seemed more appealing than my couch."

"Oh no. No. I'm fine about this. If it's anything, I have that Chem Lab right after this. I acted like such a jerk last week. We had to do a simple experiment, but I felt so helpless. I kept asking the T.A., 'Where do I find this. How do I do that.' He must have thought I was a silly girl, a helpless child. It was as if I was making a fuss and waiting for someone to come and save me. If I'm like this in a stupid college laboratory, what kind of doctor would I make?"

"What makes the lab work feel so problematic?"

"I don't know, it's *science*! It's about *doing* things, *proving* things, there is actually a real world, limits, you're studying the facts of life. The humanities are all opinions. You don't have to know anything to do well, just make a good case for yourself. Thinking, reading, writing papers, I can do all that with my eyes closed."

"You're studying 'the facts of life' in lab?"

(Blushing) "I heard it when I said it. I was hoping you wouldn't notice."

"Mm. You'd rather close your eyes and go back to sleep than confront something alarming and real that you're reluctant to face."

"I did realize something the other day that upset me terribly. If I do get into Med School, I'll probably have to leave town. That means leaving Eric . . . or marrying him. But I'm not ready for all that. I'm not that grown up. You know how scared I am of commitment!"

"And leaving me?"

"I'm stunned. It never crossed my mind. I actually feel sick. I think I must have believed that you would be with me wherever I would have to go. That I would be lying here, sharing my life with you forever."

"Like before your father and mother split up."

"He didn't have to leave town, just because he left my mother. (Beginning to cry convulsively.) He didn't have to abandon me like that!"

In this interpretive dialogue, the analyst connected elements of fantasy organized around the wish to go on sleeping by juxtaposing them to external demands to wake up and confront the facts of her life, creating a broad metaphor of avoidance. In this context, her intrusive and disturbing recent experience of feeling like a helpless child in lab class is revealed as a piece of wishful enactment. "If I am a child, I won't have to face these grown up tasks and make these difficult choices. Someone will come and save me." In Cindy's associations the locution "the facts of life" is a nodal point of avoidance. She actively attempts to hide her awareness of this meaningful figure of speech, with its links both to current and early childhood experience. When this avoidance is unmasked, Cindy's thoughts move from intellectualization toward emotional themes of separation and loss as well as fear of commitment to marriage. These conflictual issues seem to be organizing this patient's experience of both the analysis and her immediate life circumstances. However, when the analyst draws attention to an obvious omission of thoughts about their relationship terminating when Cindy moves on to Med School, a deeper, more painful reality confronts her with visceral force. Cindy feels sickened. The impact of this recognition gathers weight from an unconscious fantasy of union with the analyst which begins to find articulate form here for the first time, a fantasy of an inseparable parent–child bond that need never be ruptured.

Though her analyst did not feel the need to make explicit reference to the historical fact, she was aware that when, at the age of 5, Cindy's father left her mother and moved away from the city they had lived in together, the despairing and frightened mother took her daughter into her bed at night for comfort. Clearly, only a few elements of the more extensive preconscious and unconscious fantasizing that can be discerned in her material could be developed in any one session. Fantasy is not an isolated event but ongoing activity that informs and contributes to the organization of all experience. Understanding the wishes and fears represented in these fantasies helps us to identify the core issues that organize the patient's relationship to reality. Arlow (1969a,b, 1979, 1987) has compellingly elaborated the reciprocal relationship between unconscious fantasy and external reality, contending that every moment of experience involves a complex intermingling of perception and fantasy. Often implicit in the patient's off-hand comments, unconscious fantasies are easily glossed over. Indeed, they are meant to be glossed over, as patients act out their efforts to simultaneously conceal and reveal themselves to us. We deepen the process dramatically by attending to these implicit transference fantasies, connecting through conjecture what the patient is invested in keeping separate.

A patient comes to the therapist's office and impatiently asks if the workmen are ever going to finish renovating the lobby. An indirect reprimand, "Why can't you get this job (i.e., the analysis) done faster," underlies the comment, suggesting an anger born of an excessive dependence on the therapist (this is your job, not my job). Interpreting here would focus on attending to the details that the patient would have us ignore by highlighting the transference allusion implicit in the comment:

"Perhaps you're getting impatient with this process as well, wanting me to make it happen for you?"

Attending to the fantasies that guide the patient's perception of the analyst, or specifically elaborating the implicit fantasies the patient expresses about us are sources rich in material for analytic conjecture. But evidence for the analyst's interpretive activity is by no means restricted to transference-based fantasies, reactions, and enactments, however important these may be in our current conceptions of analytic effectiveness (Blum 1983, Leites 1977, Stone 1967). Indeed, valid interpretive frameworks are complex structures built up piece by piece, much like work on an elaborately detailed puzzle. Coherence and connection achieved in one area may for long periods remain isolated from other areas and levels of organization. In this work, narratives about experience that occur outside the analytic situation, both in the remembered and recent past, must be integrated with evidence that arises inside the analytic situation. The interconnection between these sources often proves extremely complicated. Just as in completing any puzzle, however, the analyst's efforts are predicated on an essential assumption: as more connections are made, and the forms that these linkages make cogent are revealed, an overall pattern will articulate in a comprehensive whole.[2] There is an irrational logic to be deciphered, patterned on a coherent deep structure of the psyche. Like a fingerprint, it leaves its distinctive mark on all the surfaces with which we work.

THE LIMITS OF INTERPRETATION

The patient's experience of the analyst's interpretive activity will be selectively attended to, ignored, or otherwise transformed and elaborated. That this phenomenon is so regularly observed is the basis of the central place of transference analysis in psychoanalytic treatment. There are, broadly speaking, three patterns of response that one can expect: Patients who devalue and negate the analyst's involvement, asserting that it is not as passionate or unlimited as would be wished; those who deny it altogether, because it stimulates unbearable, deeply dreaded longings; and more frequently, those who invest it with fantastical meanings and hidden intentions.

These predictable forms of response may be pursued with remarkable persistence. This should not, however, cloud the analyst's recognition that our interpretive activity is a mode of relatedness that is palpable, real, and uniquely helpful. The urge to embrace technical departures that go beyond interpretation, often justified as efforts to reach the patient through more direct and powerful forms of relatedness, may be rooted in

---

2. This puzzle analogy serves to illuminate one aspect of interpretive activity, and is certainly not meant to be taken as a model. For one thing, in analytic work, the solution or partial solution of a problem area often leads to a reconfiguration of the entire pattern; for instance, the successful understanding of a particularly aversive meaning of depending on the analyst as an emotionally evocative presence will profoundly transform the nature of experience and evidence that is tolerated in the analytic situation, as well as the narratives of outside experience that are recounted in the analyst's presence. Nonetheless, we believe there is a leisurely and patient state of mind that is evoked by this analogy, which can fortify the analyst for the often tentative and repetitively frustrating rhythms of interpretive work.

an essential misunderstanding. Interpretation is not the antithesis of relationship, but a particular mode of relationship organized around the analytic task of explicating the dynamic
structure of the patient's inner life. Describing and connecting
the ways this relationship reflects the patient's core conflicts is
one of the central tasks of analytic work. By abandoning the
framework of neutrality, we give up on the task of collaboratively understanding the strategies, attitudes, and postures
through which a patient negates or denies an immanent reality—the analytic relationship—in favor of a mode of relationship that holds a compromised equilibrium in place.

We do not want to idealize the analytic process or the efficacy
of our interpretive efforts. There are times when the ongoing
interpretive dialogues within an analytic process seem to exhaust their possibilities, becoming routinized, predictable, and
stale to both parties. Sometimes this reflects a lack of technical
resource on the part of the analyst. Supervisory consultation
may get the process back on track, though not always. Interpretive dialogues, like relationships, are of necessity constrained by
many factors. The analyst brings to the interpretative process
his or her own internal life—the unique identifications, fears,
adaptive strategies, wishes, and conflicts that structure character and inform personality. However unintentionally, implicit or
explicit theories about development, pathogenesis, mental functioning, and therapeutic action (Bachant et al. 1995a, Greenberg
1991, Kris 1982) will necessarily influence and reductively
determine the analyst's choice of what to address. Each patient
will uniquely challenge the emotional and imaginative resources
of a particular analyst in ways that cannot be easily predicted or
controlled.

These constraints brought to the analytic situation by the
analyst are real. They must be recognized as limitations that
organize the interpersonal field of analytic work in a particular
way, and give a distinctive coloration to the interaction of each
analytic dyad. That limitations exist, however, is inescapable.
We are all both continually constructing our experience and also

limited by that experience (Bachant 1995). The unique individual slant on understanding that is brought to the analytic situation by each participant provides an opportunity for patients to grapple with issues of differentiation and separateness that pervade relatedness. We hold it as a given that no psychoanalysis ever completely exhausts the relevant ways in which a patient's experience can be meaningfully apprehended. It is a predictable and sometimes formidable postanalytic task for the former patient to amend and complement the perspectives achieved in the formal period of analysis.

SUMMARY

The analyst's interpretive activity entails a primary focus on describing and connecting disparate aspects of the patient's experience through the process and the content of the analytic interaction. Interpretation aims at positing dynamic linkages between two or more elements of action, memory, thought, and emotion. The intrinsic interpretive aspect of many activities traditionally considered subsidiary modes of analytic intervention was stressed. Our investigation of interpretation highlighted the importance of balancing an ability to maintain an empathic focus on the affective core of the patient's experience with an awareness of the centrality of reasoned deliberation. We emphasized that interpretation is not the antithesis of relationship, but a particular mode of relationship organized around the analytic task of explicating the dynamic structure of the patient's inner life. The integration and interdependence of insight and relationship factors, including the multiple functions served by the therapeutic alliance, were elaborated in an effort to examine the primary influences that facilitate an interpretive process.

8

Therapeutic Action

Every clinical generation is faced with the task of formulating some essential statements about the therapeutic action of psychoanalytic therapy. Although our collective professional experience convinces us that our treatment is powerful, the very diversity and richness of that experience makes simple generalization difficult. Analysts who subscribe to widely divergent ideas about psychoanalytic therapy effect substantial results, which they quite naturally explain in accord with the premises and theories of their school's particular traditions. Does this imply that our theories of therapeutic action are merely decorative ornamentation unrelated to the real nitty-gritty structure of therapeutic engagement? If we have confidence in the effectiveness of our treatment and we can specify our methods clearly, why even bother with the thorny issue of spelling out how they are achieved?

There is undoubtedly some pragmatic appeal in this posture. A little reflection, however, convinces us that even if we fail to find a language to contain the multitude of therapeutic possibilities and theoretical tastes, we are better off for having made the attempt. For no matter how evolved, a methodology on its own cannot dictate the infinite number of choices and potential directions that a clinician faces in a living psychoanalytic encounter, let alone an entire treatment. Rather, we look to method for guidelines and constructive ways of thinking about what transpires. We hope for a rough set of clinical tools to help cut our way through the psychic underbrush that obscures our trail. Yet we are continually reminded that every clinical intervention or therapeutic response occurs in a unique context. "We never," as the philosophers instruct us, "step into the same river twice!" Guidelines, rules of technique, and therapeutic clichés may get us started on the trek but cannot be counted on to bring us home safely. In such a situation, a theory of therapeutic action functions like a compass, an instrument to orient clinical vision and ground intuitive inspiration. It reassures us that we are moving toward a destination, even when we seem lost in the forest.

Before we can meaningfully address the question of how change comes about, it is necessary to have some notion of what constitutes the desirable changes that psychoanalysis can hope to engender. Psychoanalytic therapy holds a more ambitious and fateful promise than its original concern with symptomatic cure. Indeed, psychoanalysis emerged, almost from its inception, as a vehicle of personal revolution and renewal. The optimum results of a psychoanalytic process are to be found in an internal freedom to aspire to the most meaningful life and the highest development of innate potentials of which a person is capable. It is far more appropriate, in this regard, to speak of integrative and maturational achievement rather than of symptomatic relief or cure when evaluating the outcome of psychoanalytic therapy.

Studying the evolution of psychoanalytic technique, we recognize that most of the earlier formulations of therapeutic action, however dated by the theoretical and technical preoccupations of the particular period in which they were formulated, continue to have something useful to teach us: making the unconscious conscious, excavating an infantile neurosis, interpreting resistance and defense, confronting and undermining character armoring, softening the superego, restoring the autonomy of the ego, resolving a transference neurosis, holding out the potential

of a new object—or selfobject—experience. Surveying even
this abbreviated list, one may sense that though none of these
would be wholly sufficient to a sophisticated clinician in contemporary practice, each offers some inspiration to our current ways
of working and thinking. Certainly, the more proximate goals
of ameliorating excessive anxiety, guilt, and shame as a means of
building personal agency has continued resonance. And viewed
broadly, each speaks to the challenge that psychoanalysts of
every generation have confronted as they sought to find a key to
unblocking structured rigidities that inhibit emotional freedom.

The goals of psychoanalysis are not static in the sense of being
definable end points. They are not embodied in a specific ideal
type of character or way of being human. Psychoanalysts have
every reason to know that full maturity and completely integrated selfhood are fictions, even though they may have popular
currency as social ideals. We are rightfully wary of authorizing
ideal mental health criteria, as they are so easily abused by
moralists and moral masochists alike. We are too familiar with
the tenacity of conflict and the allure of regression. From the
vantage point of the psychoanalytic situation, the impact of
therapy is more accurately observed in an internal reorganization of ongoing conscious and unconscious psychic processes. As
an outcome of successful analysis, we envision human beings
whose movement toward expansive affirmation of self is not
rigidly foreclosed by unnecessary restrictions. A person's potential for self-renewal may be obstructed by a host of observed
psychic conflicts, adaptive disharmonies, inflexible ideals or
attitudes, distorting fantasies, unacknowledged object ties, self-
tormenting introjects, self-limiting compromise formations, confining identifications, as well as the recurrent pull of regressive
or repressed potentialities. Either alone or in consort, consciously or unconsciously, such "fixedness" stands in the way of
a person's negotiating an optimal balance between their preconditions for emotional safety and the risks of vitalizing adven-
ture.

Perhaps we are in a position to propose an inclusive definition that might serve to anchor our discussion of therapeutic action: Psychoanalysis is a procedure, undertaken within the context of a relatively stable object relationship, that sets in motion a complex array of integrative and maturational processes that reorganize the structured qualities of the patient's subjective experience and motivational initiative. Psychoanalysis reorganizes experience and initiative. The psychoanalyst's primary function within this definition is twofold: first, to construct, maintain, and safeguard a psychoanalytic situation that serves to facilitate crucial integrative and maturational processes; and second, to engage in an intricate human relationship that can absorb and crystallize the centripetal tensions emanating from this destabilizing endeavor within the analytic frame. This unique relationship is, as Friedman (1997) has enjoined, the "crucible" of psychoanalysis, an ephemeral product of attitudes that warrants our protection. A peculiar laboratory of the mind, it is "dedicated to research on the pathway of desire, the nuances of interaction, the limits of freedom, the relationship of cause and reason, the nature of meaning, the meaning of responsibility, and all the special paradoxes of humanness" (pp. 35–36).

The analyst is both object and agent, a catalytic figure for animating and enacting the repressed contents of the unconscious. Simultaneously, the analyst exists for the patient as a reliable foundation of emotional sustenance during what can be painful disruptions of existing equilibria. Psychoanalysis is unthinkable without this human contribution. A "maternal matrix" (Chasseguet-Smirgel 1992), "holding environment" (Winnicott 1945), or "real relationship" (Greenson 1971), as it has been variously called, is the dimension of the analyst's relatedness that is often implicit in the formal gestures, actions, and strategies that define psychoanalysis as a method. But analytic endurance is fundamentally an expression of an analyst's capacity to love, nurture, and promote growth in the objects of our love over an extended period of time. The painful mastery and artful exercise of this disciplined, difficult, and eternally frustrating craft would be inconceivable without this basic ingredient. This assertion does not contradict in any way the observation that a host of less reputable (libidinal, aggressive, and narcissistic) motives may be fulfilled through the exercise of our professional activity.

The centrality of transference experience within psychoanalysis rests on the analyst's unique place at an intimate crossroad between the external world and the patient's inner world. Within this extrapsychic space, bounded by analytic neutrality, transference becomes possible as a psychic creation. Like a dream (Lewin 1955) or a work of dramatic art (Loewald 1975, McDougall 1991), it uses the person of the analyst as a pliable, representational figure to animate or embody fantasy, to regulate or contain tension, and to anchor the longings of heretofore split-off parts of the self. To serve in this capacity, the analyst should not be formless, like a lump of putty, but must maintain a sufficiently amorphous presence that can be shaped in accord with the patient's shifting needs and purposes. It is through this evocative ambiguity that the analyst gains—and retains—a privileged and influential place near the subjective center of the patient's emotional life.

In specifying an array of integrative and maturational processes in our definition of psychoanalysis, we are indicating our belief that an authentic psychoanalytic experience does not inhere in one particular subset of processes—for example, the unfolding and resolution of a transference neurosis—however optimal this may be with a given patient. Rather, we see that the therapeutic action of psychoanalytic therapy has multiple temporal locations in both psychological or material space. The primary site of this action is not exclusively in the here-and-now transference, however much this dimension is emphasized in contemporary accounts of psychoanalytic technique, including our own. Nor do all the maturational processes set in motion by a psychoanalysis necessarily have their focal point in the affective dimensions of the transference relationship with the analyst. An interpretation, for example, of the patient's resistance to emotional experience may reverberate throughout the patient's living, impacting on important object relations far beyond the analytic situation in remembered time and place.

We suggest that "Where is the action?" may be as important a clinical question as the more familiar "What is the transference?" Different at different times in an analysis, the therapeutic action may be taking place for one patient in the library as she struggles to persevere in her studies despite crippling anxiety, for another in the waiting room as he averts his eyes from the patient who precedes him in his analyst's office, or for a third in the hallways and bedrooms of a long-abandoned family dwelling. At one moment, the analyst's therapeutic contribution may be centered in the role of an appreciative listener, and at another in the actions of an incisive observer, strategically positioned to decode complex mental maneuvers of disguise. At still another time, it lies in the capacity to contain, without impulsive discharge, the tumultuous wrenching of the patient's discordant desires. Although we know that all such events can be revealed to have a comprehensive unconscious order, this is not identical to their therapeutic import. Keeping an eye on the "action," while listening with a third ear, establishes a counterpoint to the often languid rhythm of psychoanalytic discourse.

In effect, we are advancing the idea that the therapeutic action of psychoanalysis is not a unique property of the psychoanalytic situation or method. Maintaining a clear distinction between the analytic action and the therapeutic action contributes to technical clarity. It reminds us that the profound processes of growth and maturation engendered by analysis are not always synonymous with an interpretive process immersed in the vicissitudes of transference or the obscurities of resistance and defense. As we know, significant psychic reorganization and emotional growth can take place in the absence of any psychoanalytic intervention whatsoever. Even transference, in both its adaptive and archaic dimensions (Chapter 3), arises spontaneously in everyday life, reaching intensities and complexities of transference-neurotic proportion. It is, ultimately, the greater likelihood of all these processes reaching a sustained intensity and constructive resolution that distinguishes the psychoanalytic situation. Informed by this perspective, a psychoanalyst is more likely to honor the fact that it is the patient's process of growth, acknowledging that an optimal sequence and location of therapeutic events unfolds according to a program given by the patient, however obscurely or indirectly announced. We strongly believe that the methodological centrality of free association and analytic neutrality serves as guarantor of this principle (Chapter 2). We create a channel but refrain from forcing events to flow in a particular direction. Analytic neutrality is an essential piece of this framework.

At the subjective center of personal awareness, where our interpretive efforts are mainly directed, people strive to construct consistent and condensed descriptions of their motives, intentions, and emotional responses. Encouraging free association outside the organizing framework of face-to-face exchange defuses the patient's attention and temporarily thwarts the active effort to efface discordant tendencies. Reflexively turned back upon his or her self, passively focused, as it were, upon the thoughts, feelings, and fantasies constructed in the presence of an analytic auditor, discordant lines of feeling and thinking take on a definition that would normally escape notice. Contemporary analysts recognize many more clinically relevant levels of personal awareness than are subsumed under the broad topographic trichotomy of conscious, preconscious, and unconscious. Since the analyst is, we must hope, the most evocative external object in the immediate surround, many, if not all, of these associations contain some point of reference to our person, if only as silent auditor of the patient's private mental reflection. This does not imply that every association can be interpreted as a disguised reference to the analyst (Gill 1979).

We are prepared by experience to expect that our ambiguous subjectivity will be constructed along both wishful and fearful lines. We will be experienced as both a comforter and a disturber of the peace, in turn, aversively intrusive, omnipotently protective, coercively judgmental, seductively overstimulating, and soothingly nurturant. Our comprehension of the indirect modes of representing and disguising meaning, including symbolism, metaphoric allusion, sequential cohesion, dramatization, and enactment, allows us to map unconscious vulnerability and excitement (Chapter 6). It also presents a transferential flash point, as we serve warning that the patient's intricate labyrinth of protective illusion is not inviolate. This intersubjective field constitutes the dimension of relatedness within which the most crucial interpretations of transference begin. We continually monitor the patient's attributions and draw attention to the myriad ways that these constructions restrict the patient's full expressive spontaneity. It is the principle of safeguarding the patient's potential spontaneity above our own comfort that assures that we do not derail these transferences toward self-serving ends. We are obligated to inquire relentlessly into the multiple determinants of transferential construction, the actualities and fantasies they express, and the intrapsychic and interactive equilibria they preserve. When a patient is willing to work associatively with this material, the lines of exploration will move fluidly between adaptive and archaic dimensions of transference, illuminating the deeper structure of a temporal actuality by freely transposing the past into the present and the present into the past.

The parameters of analytic methodology as codified in our technical literature represent the distilled wisdom of our profession. They have been passed down and reworked by many independent contributors of diverse temperament, who have found in them the elements of a durable framework. As such they have a claim to our respect—though not necessarily our allegiance—as tested ways of managing the numerous tensions of the analytic relationship over the long haul. They have proved remarkably serviceable in helping patients and analysts work through the daunting intensities of dysphoric and euphoric emotion—the anxiety, guilt, shame, mania, and depression—that are the recurrent affective obstacles to achieving deep-seated analytic change. The various instrumentalities of psychoanalytic technique, especially interpretation (Chapter 7), should be viewed as but one means of facilitating, stimulating, or managing those integrative and maturational processes that can lead to growth, a specifically analytic way of encouraging momentum in the direction of more advanced levels of unconstricted functioning.

Interpretation is, in this light, the foundation of a uniquely analytic—as opposed to more inclusive therapeutic—strategy of influence. Inevitably, this value is rooted in a Western ethical tradition that prizes individualism organized by self-knowledge and anchored by reason. We are aware that the hierarchical preeminence of reason is currently being contested at many levels of cultural and intellectual discourse. It may run counter, as we know, to other respected paths of spiritual and personal enlightenment, and in some minds has been tainted by association with sexist and elitist political agendas. In all of this, it is important to keep in mind that what is consensually sanctioned as a "rational" course of action is generally dictated by conventional standards that may confine the protean individuality that psychoanalysis seeks to nurture through reasoned deliberation. Ultimately, valuing reason is a choice. It represents a commitment to a particular means of weighing and deciding what makes best sense or is most true; it does not prescribe specific behaviors, conduct, or goals. In accord with this ethical tradition, psychoanalysts—as opposed to other kinds of psychotherapists and healers—have remained committed to the idea that reasoned deliberation should bear the pivotal role in the analyst's mode of influence upon the patient's inner life.

Reasoned deliberation is central to analytic work because it integrates feeling, thinking, and acting. Each of these vital functions contributes to the development of understanding in numerous ways, but the synthesis required by reasoned deliberation guards against a defensive imbalance that prioritizes one to the exclusion of the others. For example, a person who comes to treatment tyrannized by an archaic feeling of being

242

WORKING IN DEPTH

unlovable may have to understand that there are many reasons for this intractable emotional state, in addition to his early experience with significant others whose capacity for love was stunted. Reasoned deliberation may help him recognize that feeling unlovable serves current psychic imperatives such as the need to punish himself, to protect loved ones from his destructiveness, or to avoid engaging in perilous acts of love in his current life. The effectiveness of our interpretative activity ultimately depends on incorporating intransigent and/or impulsive modes of functioning within the larger scope of a person's conscious aspirations and ideals. An analyst who believed it was obligatory to get a patient to behave "rationally" would be mistaking reasonable behavior for reasoned behavior—a legitimate goal of our interpretive activity. Experience speaks persuasively in favor of the view that reasoned deliberation, because it facilitates an integration of subjective experience, is the mode of influence most consistent with an individual's inviolate autonomy and emotional independence. Its effects are more enduring, even though there can be no guarantees in the face of unforeseen frustrations and disappointments. Psychoanalysts are united in their belief that influence by exhortation, seduction, or manipulation will prove less resilient as a vehicle of change. When a person falls out of love, falls out of grace, or loses his faith in an awesome authority, the tenuous nature of transferentially inspired "cures" are cruelly exposed.

The fixing of change through insight is the specific achievement of reasoned deliberation. When psychoanalysts express ambivalence about the clinical importance of insight, as most of us do from time to time, we are generally frustrated with the limitations of our own interpretive facility. An interpretation, however insightful, is merely an instigation to insight. For insight implies a personal vision—perhaps but a glimpse—into the true nature of one's psychic reality. Therefore, it cannot be given to a person. Nor are all insights equal, or equally helpful. Some are more sophisticated, mature, encompassing, or pivotal. Furthermore, patients may be more or less articulate in expressing this dimension of their subjective experience. Whether in a moment of subdued reflection or sudden drama, an insight that fixes change in analysis is itself already a manifestation of incremental change. It is a thing—neither wholly of intellect or emotion—that expresses a higher-order integrative achievement of heart and mind. It may subsequently be obscured but rarely washed away by life's ceaseless tides. On this basis, insight claims a persuasive power unlike other forms of experience, and authorizes a level of responsibility that no other form of knowledge can bestow. In this sense insight makes an essential contribution to that foundation of knowledge on which genuinely autonomous judgment and conduct must be based. Alternative schools of psychoanalysis may predispose patients to have insights into various dimensions of reality— for instance, interpersonal reality as opposed to intrapsychic reality—but this doesn't mean, as is often argued, that our self-understanding is a mere reflection of our analyst's theories. Reasoned deliberation is primarily an effort to be guided and grounded through authentic experience rather than received wisdom.

Complex insights into psychic reality are built up slowly, a result of long and frequently painful deliberation over disparate elements of experience. This sorting through the chaos of experience, making order of daily details and fragments of subjectivity, constitutes the bulk of ordinary psychoanalytic work. Although an insight is "complex" in this sense, its formulation is often elemental. "I see now that my mother never *really* loved me!" or "I've always envied my sister!" may represent the fruits of arduous collaborative effort. Subsequent analysis may forge a more elaborate composite: "Though my mother really never loved me, she did seem to care about my sister. What I envied most was, at bottom, my sister's possession of my mother's love." The often-debated question, Is some action necessary in addition to insight in order to produce meaningful change? is from this perspective unproductively framed. Insight implies a change in regard to psychic reality. The better question is, What is the relationship between the integrative achievements of insight and the maturational advances that fulfill the implicit promise of an analysis?

Insight often stimulates maturational advance because it prepares a person to view and encounter the world in new ways that have fateful impact: "I no longer feel compelled to win the love—and conquer the body—of every indifferent woman I meet. I choose instead to pursue love in a place where it might be returned and in a body that I might truly cherish." Each significant maturational advance simultaneously elevates individual experience to a new psychological plane that promises far more refined perspectives and mature insights. "Now that I've found love with a woman, I realize that my mother may not have been as unloving as I presumed. She wasn't entirely unloving. She just didn't love the part of me that I felt was most aggressive, the part of me that was central to my feeling of myself as a man like my father." Vivid insights such as these are compelling. They cannot be confused with the obsessive intellectualization that attempts to subdue emotion by imposing arbitrary order.

Although such understandings generally emerge in the context of a dynamically charged relationship, without the integrative cement of insight, the analytic encounter would become simply another, more or less successful, relational experience (Strachey 1934). Transference interpretation, by describing and connecting the ways the patient's infantile past is being kept alive in the present, places the wishing, fearing, and elaborate fantasizing that unconsciously organizes repetition phenomena within the realm of the individual's integrative reach. Although this analytic action certainly does not depend on patients' behaving reasonably, we do encourage them to be reasoned with regard to their behavior in the analysis. Our intention is always to expose and clarify the unique dynamic framework of the feeling, thinking, and acting person. We give special emphasis to elucidating the way present action is being shaped by unconscious fantasies constructed in the past (Reed 1990). A therapeutic consequence of this analytic focus may be that the person is able to struggle more effectively with internal conflicts and replace automated modes of experiencing with the capacity for more considered judgment and unencumbered action. As internal forces and fantasies previously enacted in a passive and unconscious mode are progressively integrated, a willingness to engage a broader, more precisely differentiated reality will be expanded (Arlow and Brenner 1990, Loewald 1971). This, in turn, provides the patient with sustained opportunities for ever more complex integrations and refined maturational initiatives within and outside the analysis. When things go well, not only one's self but the world itself can be said to have found renewal as a place of unexplored mystery and potential fulfillment.

We see that the most powerful therapeutic effects emerging from these new connections and thoughts about self and other are not exclusively the result of analytic insight. They are as much the residue of awakened passions and unbound fragments of personal forcefulness afforded new mobility, coherence, and direction. This confluence of uncovered forcefulness generates a powerful synergy capable of destabilizing the fixedness of inhibiting structure. It simultaneously generates turbulent extremes of mood—desire and shame, impulse and guilt, fantasy and anxiety—all of which must be weathered repeatedly as the patient takes hesitant steps to move through the world in new ways.

As psychoanalysts, we are mindful that there are many experiences that might "shake us up," potentiating integrative processes that can lead to growth. Major life events and crises, births, deaths, divorces, business reversals—almost any intensely evocative experience—will put stress on a person in ways that may temporarily destabilize accustomed forms of emotional containment, thought, and action. In general, analytic opinion has sided with Freud's decision to leave such interventions in fate's hands, not to contrive through provocative design, as opposed to interpretive evocation, to arouse the sleeping dogs of transference (Freud 1937). Admittedly, contemporary analysts are less confident that they are always in a position to determine where the line between provocation and interpretation can be drawn. As Kohut (1977) has taught us, an unempathic or untimely interpretation carelessly worded in regard to the patient's subjective reach can have the impact of an intentional injury within the transference–countertransference field. But these disruptions and their repair are not intentional technical maneuvers intended to break through, break down, or rile up the patient. To the disciplined psychoanalyst, safeguarding the psychoanalytic situation always takes precedence over the allure of beguiling "targets of opportunity." Treatments melodramatically represented and conceived in terms of cathartic breakthroughs and critical turning points seldom hold up to careful scrutiny.

It is necessary, therefore, to specify and differentiate the integrative and maturational processes that we place at the core of our therapeutic action. Simply stated, an integrative process occurs as previously unnoticed, newly available, or defensively warded-off elements of experience are recognized and gradually assimilated into the subjective center of personal awareness. We are, in our thinking, drawn to the metapsychological proposition that a fundamental tendency of mind toward unity, what Nunberg (1931) has called the "synthetic function of the ego," mediates this therapeutic action of psychoanalysis. The mind, psychoanalytically observed, gives abundant evidence of being engaged in multiple integrative tasks, day and night, at various levels of consciousness. Obviously not all of these integrations are equally significant or relevant to psychoanalytic therapy. The psychotherapeutic issue must eventually be joined at the juncture of the most irreconcilable psychic realities. Much painstaking effort—interventions that both disrupt and clarify the defensively structured analytic surface—has to be expended before the underlying dimension of this neurotic fragmentation will stand revealed and open to integrative processes.

A maturational process, on the other hand, occurs when a person succeeds in finding a new or more effective way to harmonize a wish, fantasy, or subjective need with the external world. Such adaptive harmonies may be structured in many ways and do not always represent maturity in the conventional moral sense. A potentially destructive engagement with the external world along sadomasochistic lines may represent a maturational "advance" for a particular patient, attaining access to previously unavailable erotic reserves. Similarly, a narcissistically vulnerable person who has only risked social intimacy from a position of assured superiority may be taking a courageous initiative by applying to a snobbish club that may not welcome her. Just as intrapsychic conflict and personal fragmentation are the pivots around which integrative processes form, adaptive imperatives and impasses in the external world form the crux of maturational striving.

Early Freudian thinking, at least in its metapsychological preoccupation with the developmental impact of drive evolution, tended to paint this external object world in reductive terms. Objects were broadly classified as gratifying or frustrating, loved or hated, incorporated or extruded, mostly in regard to their suitability for meeting drive-specific psychosexual criteria. As psychoanalysts began to map the enormous diversity of higher-level organization, it became increasingly apparent that rather nuanced qualitative aspects of the child's object world had tremendous consequence for development beyond its potential for gratification. Winnicott (1945) and Hartmann (1956) anticipated these implications, pointing the way to our contemporary understanding of the impactful way that reality is represented to the developing child in the person of a maternal interpreter. Subsequent observation and research has amply confirmed the hypothesis that a child not only discovers reality for himself—bumping into it, so to speak, in his search for bodily gratification—but is also introduced to it through the intersubjective medium of his mother's psychic reality. In short, the mother's, the parents,' and the culture's subjectivity, from the beginning, is a salient dimension of external reality encountered at every orifice and interface with the world. Meth-

odologically, contemporary psychoanalysts are still coming to
terms with the technical implications of a corollary insight: our
own subjectivity is the ultimate embodiment of external reality
within the psychoanalytic situation. In some very basic sense,
maturation, as a goal of analysis, still means coming to better
terms with reality, just as integration means coming to terms
with one's self. We are finding the concepts *reality* and *self* far
more elusive than we had once imagined, however, as our
positivist foundation is increasingly challenged. Accordingly, we
are developing a greater sophistication with regard to the
analyst's subtle and influential role in facilitating maturational
advance, both as observer and as participant.

In our usage, the harmonies achieved through maturational
initiative within the analytic situation always involve mutual
conscious and preconscious adjustments. A patient who integrates a previously inaccessible murderous hostility toward
dismissive rivals is challenged to find new ways of both mastering rage and asserting anger competitively. Rather than dissolv-
ing in tears, he or she may find an articulate voice for the
displeasure in something the analyst had just said that sounded
demeaning. Presumably, such a confrontation reflects a reorganization of self experience as well as an emerging capacity to
assume motivational initiative with regard to aggression. It also
announces the possibility of a maturational advance within
the analytic relationship. Our challenge is to respond to the
specific accusation in a way that addresses the patient's sense of
grievance, without necessarily validating the point of grievance.
Understandably, we are reluctant to meet the patient with the
full weight of a personal subjectivity that could compromise the
protective framework of restrained neutrality. On the other
hand, to remain placidly within a studied technical posture of
unperturbed curiosity would surely seem patronizing and com-
pound the patient's sense of injury. There are times when
technical facility can prove a hindrance to therapeutic momentum and a flexible analyst must weigh alternative perspectives
and goals. The response to such situations is perhaps best

informed by a spontaneous sense of the entire context and emotional texture of the patient's action. Any programmatic formula might seem contrived or encourage us to represent our own experience in a disingenuous manner. Often enough, our apparent willingness to explore the content of the patient's concerns, accompanied by a subtle shift in the quality of our immediate attention provides sufficient evidence that the protest has been taken seriously. Clearly, if we know that we have acted badly, there is no alternative but to apologize. More often than not, the situation is more ambiguous. Whether there is a reasonable way of deciding if the patient has legitimate cause for sensitivity is less significant, however, than establishing the legitimacy of grievance as a dimension of the analytic relationship through a spontaneous encounter.

As we see, integrative and maturational processes interact in highly complex ways. Advances in either direction put new pressures on comfortable habits and ritually structured ways. While intrapsychic defenses inhibit integrative processes primarily by warding off alien elements of experience, successful character defenses interfere with maturational advances by reductively truncating the adaptive imperatives that a person will tackle. Reality, or significant segments of it, is simply ignored or flattened to cartoonish dimension. This serves to avoid the necessity of making the ever more refined adjustments through which we continue to construct the external world in our ceaseless effort to discover what is real. From this defensive position, situations of criticism or rebuke, however gentle, become annihilating attacks; opportunities for gratification, however innocent, are represented as perverse temptations; and collaborative interactions are construed as exclusive occasions of domination and/or submission to another's will.

The direct instigation of maturational initiatives outside an analytic situation has long been a staple of supportive or time-limited focal psychotherapies that do not aspire to move in the direction of analysis. Although such therapies, variously structured around assertiveness training, personal modeling,

cognitive reframing, or the manipulative engineering of correc-
tive emotional experiences may be skillfully executed and significantly helpful in many ways, often they do not attain the
depth of understanding offered by the analytic process. Maturational initiatives not carefully balanced by reciprocal integrative
advances often backfire as therapeutic events. Patients who are
encouraged by enthusiastic psychotherapists to "get their anger
out" find that the cathartic expression of long-suppressed intensities seldom serves them well in the world outside an artificial
therapeutic environment. In large measure this is the reason
that advice giving is so rarely effective—in therapy or in life. If
only we could attach enough conditional qualifiers: "Say this to
your boss, but say it in just this tone at just this moment, and if
he responds in just this way, you should say X or Y or maybe Z."
Instead, like Shakespeare's Polonius, we fall back on portentous
maxims of the "Buy low/Sell high!" level of specificity.

Imposing an exclusively instrumental framework of expedient
execution upon human motivation may help a person get to
where they think they want to go; but getting into an elevator, a
vagina, or a marriage, however fervently desired, only forestalls
a larger maturational opportunity. Its very success is achieved
by further isolating psychic reality and strengthening character
defenses. In a one-dimensional world of good and bad people,
actions and opportunities, this purely expeditious vision of a
managed health care priority may get by, but it should not
distract those who persevere in more ambitious exploration of
the deeper potential harmonies of the intra- and extrapsychic
realms.

Metapsychologically, most theorists have seen maturation
riding on the back of an inherent human drive toward mastery,
variously referred to as a self-preservative instinct (Freud
1915a), a drive for self-actualization (Maslow 1962), or an effec-
tance drive (Greenberg 1991). We must always consider, however, that spontaneous maturational initiatives not launched
from a securely prepared foundation do not always have benefi-

cent outcomes.[1] Rather than representing an advance toward emotional maturity, they may simply lead to more efficient consolidations of constricted functioning. Adaptive efficiencies can be purchased with very dear spiritual capital. Certainly informal observation often supports the sad conclusion that without some exceptionally fortuitous life events, many neurotically compromised people simply ripen into more eccentric and dogmatic versions of their former selves. Psychoanalysis must justify its existence as therapy. Quite obviously, psychoanalysis exists on the premise that the things that happen within the analytic situation will provide specific impetus to our patients' general well-being and constructive conduct of life. Yet we must be prepared to work for very long periods while such "growing" takes place surreptitiously, at a remove from the convoluted twists within transferential reality. We may hear only faint echos of emerging maturity reflected inconsistently in the fragmentary comments of friends and relatives carried incidentally into session. At other times, however, steps toward maturity virtually clamor into the foreground of our awareness, almost entirely drowning out the integrative struggles that lie at the heart of transferential enactment. Treatments differ in this regard, and we must respect these differences.

Despite our reservations about the wisdom of instigating maturational advance through active techniques (Frank 1993) within the context of a psychoanalytic relationship (Adler 1993), the recognition of emergent maturational initiatives, as well as the acknowledgment of genuine advances, is an important dimension of all analytic work. Recognizing potential or emergent maturational initiatives has both an organizing and inspi-

---

1. We are quite familiar with the developmental fact that the superego as a maturational achievement often succeeds in increasing the harmony of a young child with his or her external environment at the cost of an intrapsychic split of damaging proportions to future vitality. Similarly, a "false self" adaptation imposes severe restrictions on potential emotional spontaneity and evolving subjective integrity.

rational aspect. It serves, from the very first session, to position the analysis with regard to the patient's aspirations in life; it defines roads that eventually must be traversed. Without this perspective, analysis can take on a surreal inwardness that has no apparent point of contact with everyday concerns.

The specific form our recognition takes is too varied to catalogue here. It may be as subtle as a softly murmured "Mmmm!" or the timing, intonation, and soothing vibration of a well-placed "Uh huh!" Even a more formal interpretation, which describes and connects the specific meaning of an idea, experience, or anticipated situation within a broader context of the person's unfolding psychosocial history, arrives freighted with supportive innuendo. Consider, for instance: "The excitement you feel in anticipation of that project must be related to your deeper understanding that it represents the fulfillment of a very old dream, the dream that was thwarted for so many years by devotion to your father's insecure authority." Or, "Naturally your heart was pounding when you went through the door to that interview. You were leaving behind a part of yourself, the part that has always sought to avoid the implicit threat of competing with your envious siblings." Having an event placed within a narrative of maturational advance makes the attendant anxiety more tolerable by balancing pain against potential gain. In laying out these stakes, the analyst cannot fully escape a burden of moral authority, an authority immanent in the declaration of fateful action. We will most certainly confront our patients' awkward chagrin if they beat a sudden retreat or fail to meet the challenge that has been framed. Similarly, we must acknowledge their courage if they succeed. As should be apparent, we do not view such actions on the analyst's part as conflicting with a role of analytic neutrality, even if the patient rightly concludes that we are eager for his or her success. Consistently recognizing and acknowledging growth involves a tension between helping patients confront painful aspects of self experience and finding ways to reveal, organize, and nurture nascent germs of progress.

In observing narrative accounts of maturational advance outside the analytic situation, analysts employ complex intuitive criteria that distinguish authentic steps from manic renditions of unbelievable "new beginnings." Inevitably such judgments express and are circumscribed by the analyst's personal appreciation of the opportunities and ironies of fortune. As Loewald (1951, 1960, 1975) has taught us, the somber view of cold reality as a graveyard for renounced childhood dreams represents a disillusioned realism that psychoanalysis need not endorse. We may seem to be doubly disadvantaged, inasmuch as our view of the patient in real life is also obscured by what we recognize to be highly subjective and schematic presentations of persons and events. Yet analysts who also work with couples are aware that even when one has a ringside view of a relational impasse, the intersubjective complexities may bewilder the naked eye. Therefore, we resist that specific eagerness on the patient's part that would enlist our hasty commitment to a definitive view of an interpersonal conflict, an eagerness that may disguise a demand for a gift of unconditional love posing as a need for validation.

The psychoanalytic situation itself imposes a notoriously stringent adaptational challenge that makes it a natural arena for many maturational impasses, initiatives, and advances. Its radically open-ended structure—"Express whatever you think or feel"—as well as the ambiguity of the analyst's subjective presence throw into bold relief the entrenched hierarchical structure of any person's maturational organization. Thus, in addition to our role in recognizing and acknowledging initiatives set in motion by the analytic situation, we find ourselves participating in them. Our awareness of this reparative dimension informs our analytic stance.

We know that the neurotic patient routinely adapts to the challenges of the psychoanalytic situation by falling in love with his or her analyst. This of course, is a sign of relative health, in the sense that it demonstrates a capacity to "re-find" in an ambiguous object the beloved outlines of an earlier one (Bergmann 1987, Freud 1905a). We also know, that as long as the analyst resists the temptation to impose a reparative emotional experience, the neurotic patient will be capable of re-finding all the conflictual elements of that original love—the wishes to please, seduce, eliminate rivals—that give rise to anxiety, guilt, and shame. We do not want to sidestep these impasses, nor are we too eager to encourage new initiatives, before we have had the opportunity to analyze in sufficient depth. Again, acknowledgment rather than instigation is our guide. The crucial maturational initiatives of neurotic patients are structured around the risks and vulnerabilities of expressing love in its more and less mature oedipal and preoedipal forms. This thematic complex provides the essential context in which ambivalent striving is played out. The tendency toward enactment, when successfully analyzed, reveals the patient's unconscious longing to engage us in disguised erotic scenes or complex unconscious fantasy scenarios that are themselves compromise formations constructed around conflictual resolutions of the wish to express love and to be loved in return. This was, we believe, what Loewald (1960) meant when he referred to the transference neurosis as "the patient's love life."

With the "less than neurotic patient," things don't line up quite as neatly as we have been describing them. A little less than neurotic will not pose insurmountable dilemmas for the skillful and experienced analyst. One might say that the autoplastic adaptations undertaken in early development were so extreme that they involved significant constrictions in the capacity to trust, to risk love, or sometimes to even acknowledge the evocative elements of external reality, as embodied in the analyst's subjective presence. These patients don't so much fall in love as fight their love for the analyst. Ultimately, it's only a variation on a theme.

Within the transferential reality, an intimate interpretive dialogue unfolds through the medium of words, symbolic displacements, and intricate emotive gesture harboring abundant possibility. To the extent, for example, that a patient experiences the analyst's interventions on an oral level, his or her words become milk, an intoxicating ambrosia, bypassing other levels of symbolic representation. The analyst who encourages the patient to free-associate invites expressions of longing, fantasy, and wish through verbal and symbolic exchanges that potentially afford a measure of oral gratification—to the analyst as well as the patient. Our welcome of these less disguised expressions of the patient's eroticism, as well as our comfort and unfeigned pleasure in the explicit description of desired acts of tender and erotic exchange, allows for a series of new harmonies to emerge in step with the existing limits of psychosexual development. It is essential that the analyst be emotionally prepared to enjoy the symbolic intimacy of the patient's wish-fulfillment, without undue encouragement or discouragement, once the analysis has proceeded to a depth where patients can risk owning this level of desire. This is the challenge of a neutrality that seeks to acknowledge what is true in the patient's experience without insisting that things be otherwise. The analyst has the paradoxical task, however, of continuing to speak for alternative realities outside the scope of the immediate transference fulfillment (Modell 1991). This points, to follow our example, in the direction of a potential harmony in mutual understanding of the patient's orality. In the fullness of analytic time we say to the patient, "Yes, you would prefer to continue to drink in my words and to remain my nursing child, but these are interpretations and I am your analyst! Let us try to understand why you take in only the pleasure of my words, rather than their meaning." When transference gratification becomes too secure, we may have to assume the initiative of introducing an analytic dialogue about the anxieties and fantasies that make orality the only reliable mode of achieving pleasure in the world.

SUMMARY

In this chapter we have made some systematic observations about therapeutic action within the framework of an understanding of the psychoanalytic situation bounded by the parameters of free association and analytic neutrality. We have

proposed that the goals of psychoanalysis are best conceptualized in terms of the spontaneity and flexibility of maturational
and integrative processes rather than in terms of static or ideal
qualities of personality. Our definition of psychoanalysis "as a
procedure undertaken within the context of a relatively stable
object relationship" placed emphasis on the analyst's function as
both a protector of the analytic situation and a provider of
emotional sustenance. We proposed that differentiating an analytic from a therapeutic action of psychoanalysis is conceptually
and clinically useful. It guides the therapist to respect the
patient's unique program of psychological growth, as well as to
recognize that an analytic process, governed by the pursuit of
interpretive clarity through reasoned deliberation, is not the
exclusive means of fostering psychodynamic gains within a
contemporary psychoanalytic paradigm.

Our discussion of the role of emotional insight in the context of
the adaptive and archaic dimension of transference presented it
as a specifically analytic means of fixing change that can serve
as a foundation of autonomous motivational initiative. We
believe that our way of addressing the question of therapeutic
action has the virtue of appreciating what is unique to psychoanalysis, while acknowledging its place within a continuum of
other therapeutic modalities. Finally, we have attempted to
define and illustrate the maturational and integrative processes
that we believe to be at the core of therapeutic action, and to
demonstrate how a contemporary psychoanalyst may foster
these events without violating the essential structure of a
psychoanalytic stance defined by neutrality.

9

The Analyst's Growth and Maturation

Psychoanalysis is a professional activity that, when practiced at the highest levels of craft, merits the name *art*. As such, it offers all the potential satisfaction of any creative enterprise. Fully absorbed in the passing moments of an analytic session, a therapist is capable of experiencing an exhilarating sense of resonant meaning and emotional coherence that is indisputably aesthetic. It is, in practice, a healing art that draws compassion and power from the most profound response to our own life's inevitable entanglements; the impact of love, rivalry, and loss quickens the springs of apprehension. In the exercise of this empathy we may earn a rare trust that grants access to private places and circumstances far removed from our own. For all its formality and apparent one-sidedness, psychoanalysis comprises forms of intimacy that transcend the warmest friendship. We learn secrets, are guided through intimate scenes, and are privileged to commune with other human beings in ways that nourish our insight and fundamental knowledge of the larger world we inhabit.

Yet despite these extraordinary gratifications, there is a toll that analytic work exacts from its practitioners. In a typical day we must engage a daunting sequence of scenes, attitudes, and emotions, all the while struggling to honor the ubiquitous claims of human narcissism. We are confronted with harrowing images of abandonment and abuse or are absorbed by narratives of passionate love, betrayal, and revenge. A psychoanalyst witnesses all this, not as a member of an audience contemplating a psychological drama from a comfortable distance, but as a protagonist, drawn onto a stage of turbulent emotion and dreadful anxiety. Alternately elevated by worshipful blandishment or dismissed in contemptuous defiance, we may be swept on buoyant waves of hopefulness only to precipitously crash on the shores of despair. Within the psychoanalytic situation, there is an ever-present pull toward less disciplined involvement or a push toward isolating distance. Just about every patient seems to draw us in, or box us out, often at one and the same time. We must constantly monitor and adjust our responsiveness. Keeping one's balance can be tricky, for by validating the perspectives of psychic reality, the constant coordinates of our everyday experience—past and present, reality and fantasy, self and object—lose their assured fixedness. Assigned parts in our patients' dramatized reenactments, we experience the unique tension of inhabiting transferentially organized versions of our selves, unfamiliar to personal experience. We confront our own features reflected in other people's eyes, rearranged as in a fun-house mirror—bloated here, compressed there, the whole twisted and turned and lit with alien menace.

To our dismay we may not always be quite certain whose mirror has caught our true likeness. For in setting out to treat patients from a position of technical neutrality (Chapter 2), we invite a problematic relationship. Encouraging the emotional chips to fall where they may declares our determination to go the distance in sorting out whatever disorders and entanglements ensue. It always requires a leap of faith for both patient and analyst to accept such uncertain terms. After all, experience does not foretell exactly what will happen in the specific case, it only gives us a measure of confidence that we can eventually see our way to a fruitful conclusion. Considering the length of analytic treatment, the frustrating obstacles along its circuitous path, and the unsettling doubts created by an absence of unambiguous markers of progress, we may wonder just how an analyst finds the resources for this arduous enterprise. Even this rough accounting does not include the emotional burden of an intimate involvement with our patients' real-life tragedies, for which there is no analytic solace.

When we leave our office and retire to home and family, we are expected to re-enter ordinary life as ordinary people. A professional must strive to separate and protect one's personal identity. For a psychoanalyst, this boundary between profession and person is a hard-won and ever-vulnerable achievement of formal training, personal analysis, and accumulating experience. It is never to be taken for granted. Our inspiration is sustained by processes that touch and engage our most intimate being. Even seasoned analysts can call up vivid recollections of utterly bewildering encounters with the more malignant forms of transference–countertransference, encounters that left them uneasy for days and nights thereafter.

The comforts of family life, friendships, athletic activities, even mundane chores and occupations, constitute a welcome refuge from the taxing demands of analytic relatedness, helping to restore a sense of proportion and commonsense measure. Taking the long view, however, in the day-to-day, year-to-year willingness to return to the ongoing and eternally problematic struggles of this work, reserves of analytic endurance, patience, and inspiration seem fundamental. Endurance implies dedication, though it connotes something gritty and less high minded, which draws upon all our instinctive resources of love and toughness and pride. There is a muscular element to be reckoned with, sinews of strength and stamina built through repeated strenuous exercise. Indeed, an analyst may feel the tension of the first day at work after an extended vacation in the gut, or lower back, like an athlete in training camp. Endurance encompasses the stubborn refusal to give up, or give in, the will to resist the seductively beckoning conclusion that *this* particular patient is unanalyzable or *that* obdurate resistance insurmountable.

Muscle must be tempered by flexibility. The grace of analytic patience is apparent in a readiness to take things as they come, without judging how welcome new developments may be or worrying what energy they may cost. One learns to appreciate the deeper erratic rhythms of growth behind the plaintive cry and clamor of the moment. Acceptance of the ambiguity of the analytic process is balanced by a growing confidence in the patient's responsibility for change. We ultimately recognize that no matter how conscientiously we may try to do our part, we must find a collaborator willing to seize the opportunity and take maturational initiative. Here, patience is our ally, as we await a deepening process that inevitably takes time to emerge out of a welter of conflict, fear, and catastrophic fantasy.

Without periodic flashes of inspiration, undertaking the sheer labor of analysis with its ceaseless emotional wear and tear would surely exhaust the most resolute soul. Inspiration is a necessary spark to ignite our imagination and fire our vision. Although an analyst always seeks to find meaning, at these rare moments, meaning seems to stand forth with clairvoyant edge. It illuminates the underlying pattern and meaning of our effort, leaving a residual glow of enlightened hopefulness to sustain us through long hours. Things dulled by familiarity or repetition are reanimated with the aura of luminous significance as we reawaken to the symbolic and metaphoric richness of analytic events. How does one cultivate and replenish such sources of inspiration and conviction? Just how does one prepare adequately for the rigors of an analytic life?

There are no textbooks on endurance or inspiration. Lessons in patience, which every analyst must study in abundance, are conveyed only incidentally. Supervisors remind younger colleagues that working through takes time and repetition, or that there are always unrecognized resistances to be uncovered. We are tactfully cautioned to restrain our therapeutic ambition, that every hypothesis and explanation we arrive at, however compelling, is only a partial understanding to be augmented by currently unforeseen meanings. We learn to wait for the patient to catch up to our sure knowledge and then, humbly, to retrace our steps to find the correct path we had bypassed entirely. Above all, we are directed and redirected to explore what is happening in the analytic encounter—to consider the full range of what the patient is asking of us and what we can legitimately give in return. We are schooled to listen acutely, and to see in nuanced detail the intricacy that is before us in process as well as content. Gradually, we come to appreciate how much an analytic stance is fortified when we feel secure in our grasp of appropriate tools for finding out what is happening in the room.

Students facing the enormous complexities of an analytic relationship for the first time rely upon borrowed sources of encouragement and wisdom. In their need, idealizing respected supervisors, personal analysts, and particular schools of thought may mitigate some of the anxieties that inevitably emerge as the consolidation of one's own way of working analytically is tested and developed. Through introducing an irrational component to analytic education, these ties facilitate a complex dependence that is emotionally sustaining during that difficult period when one's commonsense understanding is being reorganized along psychodynamic lines.

Embracing a truly dynamic perspective on human problems that fully recognizes the inescapable reality of unconscious forces in our living does not come easily. There are ties of mutual frustration, as well as love, in student–mentor collaborations. Lectures and readings can illustrate the technical parameters of analytic work, define the appropriate structure, scope of action, and cast of mind that makes possible an unfolding analytic process. This establishes a framework within which to make sense of one's clinical experience, as well as a set of constructs such as transference, resistance, and countertransference to organize one's thinking. Nevertheless, each new generation, in its impatience to answer urgent questions, will be frustrated with the guidance that can be extracted from this knowledge. Indeed, the teachable aspects of psychoanalytic technique—its theories, concepts, technical principles—cannot adequately deliver knowledge in the integrated form a therapist requires to feel confident in the psychoanalytic situation. This is the fruit of mature experience, not the provenance of a prescribed course of study, however extended or carefully presented.

In actuality, the "rules" of analysis, or even a supervisor's custom-tailored advice often comes off with clumsy effect. Nevertheless, taking on the manners and mannerisms of one's personal analyst, supervisor, or teacher, however self-consciously, can be helpful in getting started in the right direction. We are more disposed to have patience with the awkwardness of beginning when we fully appreciate the magnitude of our undertaking. An aspiring analyst is faced with the challenge of assuming an unfamiliar, demanding, and, in some respects, mysterious role whose subtle dimensions are quite elusive. Conventional prototypes that one might think to draw upon, such as the sympathetic friend or the benevolent parent, do not truly instruct us in the intricacies of analytic relatedness. Nor can we study it from the outside, since it can only be observed in the privacy of the psychoanalytic situation, where our position as patient provides notoriously unfavorable sight lines. Besides, the better part of what an analyst does is unspoken; it is a role defined as much by what one does not say, do, or respond to, as by any manifest gestures and statements that can be recorded. There is always a swim-or-sink threat in this kind of learning; we are thrown in over our heads and left to learn from our mistakes. Alone in uncharted depths, behavior that can look at times like a straitjacket from the outside may feel much more like a life jacket to the struggling analyst. Psychoanalysis, practiced nervously according to "the book," protects, as well as constricts, a bewildered beginner. Feelings of unease, even fraudulence, abound. These may recur throughout training—and beyond—whenever the clinician strives to consolidate a new professional equilibrium that undermines the security of previously held beliefs. Yet yielding to the temptation to evade the discomfort of initial approaches to an analytic stance by seizing upon more congenial roles involves a purchase of immediate relief at the cost of future sophistication. The trouble taken to master fundamentals of technique contributes to a reliable framework of safety and flexibility to face the psychological risks that will follow.

There are, to be sure, many categories, levels, and nuances of observation that one must integrate before arriving at the sophisticated analytic attitude that gives life to the analyst's "involved restraint." Attitudes that are virtually instinctive must be carefully rethought. Nurturing a variety of interpretive modes is a primary task, as it offers a uniquely analytic alternative to conventional relational forms (Chapter 7). Working in depth requires us to make sense of the interactions, communications, and emotional events that take place in a psychoanalytic encounter from multiple points of view. We learn how to refine emotional and imaginative responses to the material in ways that further reliable understanding, and to correlate these observations with existing theoretical and diagnostic models. The heart and mind must be educated to see with clarity what has been avoided in fear. Through these didactic exercises, we not only discipline our faculties of observation but put life onto the skeletal structure of theory by cloaking it with the tissue and blood of living experience. Since analysts accentuate different ways of using what takes place in a psychoanalytic session to formulate their understanding, a variety of supervisory experiences are useful when starting out. One quickly comes to see that supervisors rely on different cognitive strengths, as well as models, in processing their clinical experience. Compatibility between a supervisee and supervisor involves a complex fit that goes far beyond theoretical orientation.

It is essential that interpretive fluency be established and continually cultivated by exposing oneself to new ways of conceptualizing and expressing psychological understanding. As a reliable dimension of an analyst's repertoire, it is the foundation of a technical dexterity that propels crucial processes. Through interpretive fluency the mounting psychic intensities generated in the analytic field are transformed, contained, or defused.

When this function is working well enough, an analyst may hope to approach working hours in a mood of unperturbed calm. No matter how demanding, our work is rarely fatiguing, and equally important, it can safely be left behind in the office. At every level of experience, however, we are never free of the danger of being temporarily thrown by the complex intellectual and emotional demands of an analytic encounter. At these times, analytic endurance suffers a relentless test. Whether unsettled by the patient's material, or by anxiety arising from unrelated issues in the analyst's personal life, internal conflict scrambles those sublimatory channels that allow free discourse with one's most elemental and responsive self. Professional time becomes tiresome when this occurs, and our leisure is prey to disquieting preoccupations that betray unconscious efforts to cope with the fantasies and emotions stirred in the office. In less impactful instances this drama may not be disruptive, confined instead to idle reverie or dramatized in a vivid dream. However, if usual homeostatic measures fail, there is a possibility that these pressures may erupt, causing disturbing discontinuities in ordinary self-experience. In choosing psychoanalysis as a career, therefore, an individual is making a commitment to a lifetime of continuing self-analysis. To fail to do so puts oneself, one's patients, and even one's loved ones at emotional risk.

The young analyst embarking upon a career is typically an intrepid explorer, energized by the dazzling new psychic vistas opening ahead. Each new case is a privileged journey of discovery; every resistance overcome, dream interpreted, emotional catharsis, is an awakening. Like seeing exotic places previously encountered only in a guidebook, the clinician is amazed that the reports he or she has read are true. Not that the early going is always easy. On the contrary, inexperience results in avoidable and painful blunders. Still, there are usually helpful guides at hand when one gets discouraged and there is the comforting expectation that in time everything will get easier. Of course, this is not an entirely illusory expectation. Many things do get easier: we make fewer and less costly mistakes; we handle potentially problematic situations more gracefully. If all goes well, our skills and knowledge continue to ripen in a most gratifying way. We become expert.

There is, however, a bittersweet price exchanged for this expertise. The innocent thrill of discovery is muted as our attention is gripped by the unyielding persistence of many of the irrationalities we have come upon—that concatenation of incongruous motivation that makes significant change such a painstaking process. If, as Melanie Klein (1957) has suggested, the deepest resources of human hope are unconsciously connected with the triumph of love over hate, a more sober appreciation of the corrosive and ubiquitous effects of human self-destructiveness is perhaps the most difficult understanding an analyst must confront. For with this knowledge comes the obligation to reassess the scope of initial ambitions in the light of substantive achievements. Practically speaking, the mature psychoanalyst has made peace with the fact that profound analytic effects come about only through meticulous and repetitive attention to subtle nuances; that in mental life even small changes can make a significant difference; and that the road to maturity is traversed in many desultory steps that take some persons more than a lifetime.

Our readiness to view the proverbial glass as "half full" will be influenced by the complex psychological factors that predispose a person to a sanguine disposition. Like most individuals who engage in exceedingly demanding creative activities with ambiguous standards of success, psychoanalysts are prone to fluctuations of expansive and depressive self-assessment. Certainly the bottom-line vicissitudes of personal destiny—harmony in love relationships, physical health, financial prosperity, and professional esteem—have to be factored into this equation. And any estimate of our contribution to the welfare of our patients is not immune to the general regard that psychoanalysis enjoys in the community within which we practice. Increasingly, psychoanalysts must be prepared to defend their convictions and views in a society disposed to hasty and uninformed judgments regarding faddish and/or economically expedient new therapeutic approaches.

Although prosperity does provide a lift, the springs that feed a reservoir of analytic optimism and determination are drawn from deeper strata of compelling personal experience. We must have intimate awareness of the ennobling effect that psychoanalytic ways of discovering and pursuing meaning eventually impart to the effort to create a life of significance. It is here that we find recurrent and irrefutable confirmation of the lasting importance of our work. Although such conviction rarely comes into existence without benefit of a reasonably thorough personal treatment, posttermination achievements in self-analysis are indispensable in assuring continued access to archaic sources of instinctive vitality and potential. For it is only after analysis has ended that one can assess the staying power of the integrative and maturational processes that have been set in motion. Sometimes we learn, to our dismay, that without an impetus of transferential urgency the striving for emotional mastery cannot be sustained. Freeing oneself repeatedly from inevitable states of depressive and anxious discouragement through self-analytic effort is a trial of independence that will consolidate a steadfast conviction regarding the special value of psychoanalytic modes of change. But consolidating the gains of a therapeutic analysis is a more exacting challenge for a practicing psychoanalyst, who must terminate treatment without ever leaving the psychoanalytic situation. Somewhat like the child who grows up to take over the family business, our work may be haunted by the looming shadow of a former analyst peering over our shoulder. Internal conflict and resistance to self-knowledge are seemingly inexhaustible opponents, as are—to a surprising degree—the transference constellations that have been born of these in therapy. The complicated process of finding one's emerging voice as an analyst can trigger psychodynamic struggles of individuation and oedipal emancipation with considerable ferocity.

The recently certified analyst is often uneasy with this new identity. Although graduate attorneys seem eager to announce their appointment to the bar, psychoanalysts display a curious diffidence about introducing themselves as psychoanalysts. Feelings of competence are still transitory. Many of the rules, theories, and procedures of the profession have been adopted with provisional commitment; there are still ways in which the role seems larger than life. The decade after graduation is a period during which we come to fully embody our professional identity, while refining technical skills to a stage of comfortable fluidity. Personal analyses are terminated. Supervisors and teachers may still be sought out, but with much greater selectivity. Liberated from the obligatory scrutiny of institute supervision, the limitations and rigidities of the ground rules of technique will be reevaluated against the perplexing ambiguity of clinical experience.

If maturing analysts are to derive lasting inspiration from the school of technical practice in which they have been trained, an integration of various identifications will be undertaken in an attempt to match what is best in that tradition with what is best in one's self. Theoretical knowledge must be transformed into personal vision. One cannot expect simple, unambivalent, linear development. Indeed, these processes are often characterized by moments of anguish and troubling doubt, as well as times of confidence and genuine pleasure in our skillful accomplishment. During this unsettling transition, comforting idealizations of authority—heros and mentors from one's student years—must be reluctantly surrendered so that one's own analytic identity can emerge with mature integrity. If personal treatment and training has prepared us to grapple adequately with the anxieties and opportunities of this period, it is likely that we will evince continued allegiance to the broad technical and theoretical traditions that have guided our maturation. It is, however, at this juncture that qualitative limitations in the analyst's personal analysis may throw up obstinate roadblocks. As we have suggested, the fate of the posttermination transference will prove especially crucial. Therapists whose work is dominated by a passionate wish to prove a former analyst wrong, or to win his or her love through selfless surrender, must pay dearly in terms of professional autonomy.

The most important outcome of this initial decade of professional evolution is the maturation of a unique amalgam of learning and sensibility constituting an analytic vision of the psychotherapeutic process. This residue of virtually thousands of clinical hours slowly gains the structural dimensions of durability and consistency. It is at once less specific and yet more complex than any elaborated theory of analytic technique or model of personality. Although bearing the stamp of theoretical commitments, these formal influences have been refined and subtly transformed by our unique way of experiencing clinical events at the quite personal level of a clinical encounter. Bion's (1967) aphoristic advice, to enter each session without desire, intention, or memory encourages us to place our full confidence in this integral vision rather than relying on intellectual structures, or technical programs that have been sanctioned by our education.

A personal vision is, of necessity, less orthodox than the programmatic blueprints debated in the contemporary literature. One is free to draw inspiration from disparate and even incongruous sources, when the rigorous standards of logical argument are relaxed. Alone with one's patient, the echoing of contentious rhetorical voices subsides, and one's attention is absorbed by the challenge of hearing and seeing and feeling the unfolding events of the moment. This imbues our clinical choices with a greater flexibility and individuality that will be palpable to our patients, but frustrating to articulate precisely to colleagues. It is so very difficult to take an accurate measure of one's own vision; rather, like looking at oneself in a mirror looking at a mirror, the eye can't study itself in the act of seeing. With effort one can specify some of the orienting concepts or experiences that are shaping our vision of the psychoanalytic encounter. These ideas, when formulated in conceptual language, seem pale reflections of the vivid experiences that they make possible; at the experiential level one's vision is always empowering.

Ideally, of course, our analystic vision will continue to evolve and mature. Yet, once it has achieved a sufficient complexity and subtlety, it serves to shelter our practice against the swirling winds of theoretical fashion. We are more prepared to rely on the evidence of our own clinical experience, rather than on the opinions and pronouncements of others who are regarded as authorities. In this sense, we are ready to navigate the waters of psychoanalytic exploration securely in control of our methods of inquiry, and not needing to know in advance the destinations to which our patients will lead us. Curiously, as we begin to speak with a clinical voice of increasingly confident timbre, we are ready to find our way without a map that details every turn. We are finally in position to search for the genuine riches of analytic discovery, to earn our own opinions rather than to live off the wealth of our inheritance.

References

Adler, E. (1991). The eye of the storm: psychoanalytic reality and the analyst's vision. In *The Psychoanalyst: The Interplay of Work and Identity, a Monograph of the Westchester Center for the Study of Psychoanalysis and Psychotherapy* 1(1):3–19.

———— (1993). Commentary on Frank's "Action, insight and working through" from the perspective of Freudian Analysis. *Psychoanalytic Dialogues* 3:579–587.

Adler, E., and Bachant, J. L. (1996). Free association and analytic neutrality: the basic structure of the analytic situation. *Journal of the American Psychoanalytic Association* 44:1021–1046.

Arlow, J. (1963). The supervisory situation. *Journal of the American Psychoanalytic Association* 11:577–593.

———— (1969a). Unconscious fantasy and disturbances of conscious experience. *Psychoanalytic Quarterly* 38(1):1–27.

———— (1969b). Fantasy, memory and reality testing. *Psychoanalytic Quarterly* 38:28–51.

———— (1979). The genesis of interpretation. *Journal of the American Psychoanalytic Association* 27 (suppl):193–288.

———— (1985). The concept of reality and related problems. *Journal of the American Psychoanalytic Association* 33:521–535.

———— (1987). The dynamics of interpretation. *Psychoanalytic Quarterly* 56:68–87.

Arlow, J. A., and Brenner, C. (1990). The psychoanalytic process. *Psychoanalytic Quarterly* 59:678–692.

Aron, L. (1991). The patient's experience of the analyst's subjectivity. *Psychoanalytic Dialogues* 1:29–51.

—— (1992). Interpretation as the experience of the analyst's subjectivity. *Psychoanalytic Dialogues* 2:475–507.

Bachant, J. L. (1995). Freedom limited: discussion of Josephs' *Reanalysis of Mr. Z. Psychoanalysis and Psychotherapy* 12:145–151.

Bachant, J. L., and Adler, E. (1997). Transference: co-constructed or brought to the interaction? *Journal of the American Psychoanalytic Association* 45:1097–1120.

Bachant, J. L., Lynch, A. A., and Richards, A. D. (1995a). Relational models in psychoanalytic theory. *Psychoanalytic Psychologist* 12:71–88.

—— (1995b). The evolution of drive in contemporary psychoanalysis: a reply to Gill. *Psychoanalytic Psychologist* 12:565–574.

Bachant, J. L., and Richards, A. D. (1993). Review essay: *Relational Concepts in Psychoanalysis: An Integration,* by Stephen Mitchell. *Psychoanalytic Dialogues* 3:431–460.

Bergmann, M. S. (1987). *The Anatomy of Loving.* New York: Columbia University Press.

Bergmann, M. S., and Hartman, F. R. (1976). *The Evolution of Psychoanalytic Technique.* New York: Basic Books.

Bion, W. R. (1967). Notes on memory and desire. In *Classics in Psychoanalytic Technique,* ed. R. Langs, pp. 259–260. New York: Jason Aronson, 1981.

Bird, B. (1972). Notes on transference: universal phenomenon and hardest part of analysis. *Journal of the American Psychoanalytic Association* 20:267–301.

Blum, H. P. (1983). The position and value of extratransference interpretation. *Journal of the American Psychoanalytic Association* 31:587–617.

Boesky, D. (1990). The psychoanalytic process and its components. *Psychoanalytic Quarterly* 59:550–584.

Bollas, C. (1987). *The Shadow of the Object: Psychoanalysis of the Unthought Known.* New York: Columbia University Press.

Brenner, C. (1976). *Psychoanalytic Technique and Psychic Conflict.* New York: International Universities Press.

—— (1979). Working alliance, therapeutic alliance, and transference. *Journal of the American Psychoanalytic Association* 27 (suppl):137–158.

——— (1982). *The Mind in Conflict.* New York: International Universities Press.

——— (1995). Resistance, object-usage, and human relatedness. *Contemporary Psychoanalysis* 31:173–191.

Bromberg, P. (1995). Resistance, object usage, and human relatedness. *Contemporary Psychoanalysis* 31:173–191.

Bruner, J. (1990). *Acts of Meaning.* Cambridge, MA: Harvard University Press.

Busch, F. (1993). In the neighborhood: aspects of a good interpretation and a "developmental lag" in ego psychology. *Journal of the American Psychoanalytic Association* 41:151–177.

——— (1994). Some ambiguities in the method of free association and their implications for technique. *Journal of the American Psychoanalytic Association* 42:363–384.

——— (1995a). Do actions speak louder than words? A query into an enigma in analytic theory and technique. *Journal of the American Psychoanalytic Association* 43:61–82.

——— (1995b). *The Ego at the Center of Clinical Technique.* Northvale, NJ: Jason Aronson.

Chasseguet-Smirgel, J. (1992). Some thoughts on the psychoanalytic situation. *Journal of the American Psychoanalytic Association* 40:3–25.

Chused, J. F. (1991). The evocative power of enactments. *Journal of the American Psychoanalytic Association* 39:615–640.

Cooper, A. M. (1987). Changes in psychoanalytic ideas: transference interpretation. *Journal of the American Psychoanalytic Association* 35:77–98.

Damasio, A. R. (1994). *Descartes' Error: Emotion, Reason, and the Human Brain.* New York: Grosset/Putnam.

Ehrenberg, D. (1992). *The Intimate Edge: Extending the Reach of Psychoanalytic Interaction.* New York: W. W. Norton.

Etchegoyen, R. H. (1983). Fifty years after the mutative interpretation. *International Journal of Psycho-Analysis* 64:445–458.

Fenichel, O. (1941). *Problems of Psychoanalytic Technique*, trans. D. Brunswick. New York: Psychoanalytic Quarterly.

Ferenczi, S. (1928). Gulliver phantasies. *International Journal of Psycho-analysis* 9:283–300.

——— (1932). *The Clinical Diary of Sandor Ferenczi*, ed. J. Dupont. Cambridge, MA: Harvard University Press, 1988.

Frank, K. (1993). Action, insight and working through: outlines of an integrative approach. *Psychoanalytic Dialogues* 3:535–577.

Freedman, N. (1985). The concept of transformation in psychoanalysis. *Psychoanalytic Psychologist* 2:317–339.

Freedman, N., and Lavender, J. (1997). Receiving the patient's transference. *Journal of the American Psychoanalytic Association* 45:79–103.

Freud, A. (1936). *The Ego and the Mechanisms of Defense*. New York: International Universities Press.

Freud, S. (1894). The neuro-psychoses of defense. *Standard Edition* 3:41–61.

——— (1895). Studies on hysteria. *Standard Edition* 2:253–305.

——— (1896). Further remarks on the neuro-psychoses of defense. *Standard Edition* 3:157–186.

——— (1900). The interpretation of dreams. *Standard Edition*: 4/5:1–626.

——— (1905a). Fragment of an analysis of a case of hysteria. *Standard Edition* 7:1–122.

——— (1905b). Three essays on the theory of sexuality. *Standard Edition* 7:125–243.

——— (1909). Notes upon a case of obsessional neurosis. *Standard Edition* 10:151–318.

——— (1913). On beginning the treatment. Further recommendations on the technique of psycho-analysis. I. *Standard Edition* 12:121–144.

——— (1914). Remembering, repeating and working through. *Standard Edition* 13:145–156.

——— (1915a). Instincts and their vicissitudes. *Standard Edition* 14:109–140.

——— (1915b). Observations on transference love. *Standard Edition* 12:157–171.

——— (1915c). Repression. *Standard Edition* 14:141–158.

——— (1916/1917). Introductory lectures on psychoanalysis. *Standard Edition* 15:15–239, 16:243–463.

——— (1919). Introduction to psycho-analysis and the war neuroses. *Standard Edition* 17:205–210.

——— (1923). The ego and the id. *Standard Edition* 19:1–59.

——— (1925/1926). Inhibitions, symptoms and anxiety. *Standard Edition* 20:75–172.

——— (1937). Analysis terminable and interminable. *Standard Edition*: 23:216–253.

Friedman, L. (1997). Ferrum, ignis and medicina: return to the crucible. *Journal of the American Psychoanalytic Association* 45:21–45.

Gabbard, G. O. (1982). The exit line: heightened transference/countertransference manifestations at the end of the hour. *Journal of the American Psychoanalytic Association* 30:579–598.

——— (1996). *Love and Hate in the Analytic Setting.* Northvale, NJ: Jason Aronson.

Gabbard, G. O., and Lester, E. P. (1995). *Boundaries and Boundary Violations in Psychoanalysis.* New York: Basic Books.

Gill, M. M. (1979). The analysis of the transference. *Journal of the American Psychoanalytic Association* 27(suppl):263–288.

——— (1982). *Analysis of the Transference,* vol. 1. New York: International Universities Press.

——— (1994). *Psychoanalysis in Transition: A Personal View.* Hillsdale, NJ: Analytic Press.

——— (1995). Discussion of relational models papers. *Psychoanalytic Psychologist* 12:89–107.

Gray, P. (1973). Psychoanalytic technique and the ego's capacity for viewing intrapsychic activity. *Journal of the American Psychoanalytic Association* 21:474–494.

——— (1982). "Developmental lag" in the evolution of technique for psychoanalysis of neurotic conflict. *Journal of the American Psychoanalytic Association* 30:621–655.

——— (1986). On helping analysands observe intrapsychic activity. In *Psychoanalysis: the Science of Mental Conflict. Essays in Honor of Charles Brenner,* ed. A. S. Richards and M. S. Willick, pp. 245–262. Hillsdale, NJ: Analytic Press.

——— (1987). On the technique of the analysis of the superego—an introduction. *Psychoanalytic Quarterly* 56:130–154.

——— (1994). *The Ego and the Analysis of Defense*. Northvale, NJ: Jason Aronson.

Greenberg, J. (1991). *Oedipus and Beyond: A Clinical Theory*. Cambridge, MA: Harvard University Press.

Greenberg, J., and Mitchell, S. A. (1983). *Object Relations in Psychoanalytic Theory*. Cambridge, MA: Harvard University Press.

Greenson, R. R. (1965). The working alliance and the transference neurosis. *Psychoanalytic Quarterly* 34:155–181.

——— (1967). *The Technique and Practice of Psychoanalysis*. New York: International Universities Press.

——— (1971). The "real" relationship between the patient and the psychoanalyst. In *The Unconscious Today*, ed. M. Kanzer. New York: International Universities Press.

Greenson, R. R., and Wexler, M. (1969). The nontransference relationship in the psychoanalytic situation. *International Journal of Psycho-Analysis* 50:27–39.

Grossman, W. (1982). The self as fantasy: fantasy as theory. *Journal of the American Psychoanalytic Association* 59:55–61.

Halpert, E. (1984). Reporter. Panel: the value of extratransference interpretation. *Journal of the American Psychoanalytic Association* 32:137–146.

Hartmann, H. (1950). Psychoanalysis and developmental psychology. In *Essays on Ego Psychology*. New York: International Universities Press, 1964.

——— (1951). Technical implications of ego psychology. *Psychoanalytic Quarterly* 20:31–43.

——— (1956). Notes on the reality principle. In *Essays on Ego Psychology*. New York: International Universities Press, 1964.

Heimann, P. (1950). On counter-transference. *International Journal of Psycho-Analysis* 31:81–84.

——— (1956). Dynamics of transference interpretation. *International Journal of Psycho-Analysis* 37:303–310.

Hoffman, I. Z. (1983). The patient as the interpreter of the analyst's experience. *Contemporary Psychoanalysis* 19:389–422.

——— (1991). Discussion: toward a social constructivist view of the psychoanalytic situation. *Psychoanalytic Dialogues* 1:74–105.

Isaacs, S. (1952). The nature and function of phantasy. In *Develop-*

ments in Psycho-Analysis, ed. M. Klein, P. Heimann, S. Isaacs, and J. Riviere, pp. 67–121. New York: DaCapo, 1983.

Jacobs, T. (1983). The analyst and the patient's object world: notes on an aspect of countertransference. *International Journal of Psycho-Analysis* 31:81–84.

—— (1986). On countertransference enactments. *Journal of the American Psychoanalytic Association* 34:289–308.

—— (1991). *The Use of the Self: Countertransference and Communication in the Analytic Situation*. Madison, CT: International Universities Press.

Johan, M. (1992). Enactments in psychoanalysis. *Journal of the American Psychoanalytic Association* 40:827–841. Reporter: M. Johan, Panelists: D. Boesky, J. F. Chused, T. J. Jacobs. Annual Meeting of the American Psychoanalytic Association, San Francisco, May 6, 1989.

Kanzer, M. (1975). The therapeutic and working alliances. *International Journal of Psychoanalytic Psychotherapy* 4:48–73.

Kern, J. (1987). Transference neurosis as a waking dream: notes on a clinical enigma. *Journal of the American Psychoanalytic Association* 35:337–366.

Kernberg, O. (1975). *Borderline Conditions and Pathological Narcissism*. New York: Jason Aronson.

—— (1976). *Object Relations Theory and Clinical Psychoanalysis*. New York: Jason Aronson.

—— (1985). *Internal World and External Reality*. Northvale, NJ: Jason Aronson.

Klein, M. (1957). Envy and gratitude. In *Envy and Gratitude and Other Works: 1946–1963,* ed. M. Klein, pp. 176–235. New York: Delacorte, 1975.

—— (1958). On the development of mental functioning. In *Envy and Gratitude and Other Works, 1946–1963*, ed. M. Klein, pp. 236–246. New York: Delacorte, 1975.

Kohut, H. (1971). *The Analysis of the Self*. New York: International Universities Press.

—— (1977). *The Restoration of the Self*. New York: International Universities Press.

—— (1984). *How Does Analysis Cure?* Chicago: University of Chicago Press.

Kriegman, D. K., and Slavin, M. O. (1989). *Dimensions in Self Experience: Progress in Self Psychology*, vol. 5, pp. 209–252. Hillsdale, NJ: Analytic Press.

Kris, A. O. (1982). *Free-Association: Method and Process*. New York: International Universities Press.

Kupferstein, L. (1997). *Discussion of Bachant and Adler, "Transference: Coconstructed or Brought to the Interaction? A Consideration of Contemporary Views."* New York Psychoanalytic Scientific Lecture, March.

Kwawer, J. (1995). *Discussion of Aron's presentation: "Whose Analysis is it, Anyway? The Mutual Analysis of an Analyst's Dream."* Paper presented at the Westchester Center for Psychoanalysis and Psychotherapy, Conference on "Boundary Dilemmas in the Psychoanalytic Relationship," March.

Langs, R. (1973). *The Technique of Psychoanalytic Psychotherapy*, vol. 1. New York: Jason Aronson.

——— (1975). Therapeutic misalliances. *International Journal of Psychoanalytic Psychotherapy* 4:77–105.

——— (1996). *The Evolution of the Emotion-Processing Mind: With an Introduction to Mental Darwinism*. London: Karnac.

Langs, R., and Stone, L. (1980). *The Therapeutic Experience and Its Setting*. New York: Jason Aronson.

Leites, N. (1977). Transference interpretations only? *International Journal of Psycho-Analysis* 58:275–287.

Levenson, E. (1988). The pursuit of the particular. *Contemporary Psychoanalysis* 24:1–16.

Levine, F. (1993). Unconscious fantasy and theories of technique. *Psychoanalytic Inquiry* 13:326–342.

Levine, H. (1997). *Discussion of Bachant and Adler, "Transference: Coconstructed or Brought to the Interaction?"* Paper presented at the Spring Meeting of the American Psychoanalytic Association, May.

Levy, S. T. (1984). *Principles of Interpretation*. New York: Jason Aronson.

Levy, S. T., and Inderbitzin, L. B. (1990). The analytic surface and the theory of technique. *Journal of the American Psychoanalytic Association* 38:371–392.

Lewin, B. (1955). Dream psychology and the analytic situation. *Psychoanalytic Quarterly* 24:169–199.

Loewald, H. (1951). Ego and reality. In *Papers on Psychoanalysis*, pp. 3–20. New Haven, CT: Yale University Press, 1980.

——— (1960). On the therapeutic action of psychoanalysis. *International Journal of Psycho-Analysis* 4:16–33.

——— (1970). Psychoanalytic theory and psychoanalytic process. *Psychoanalytic Study of the Child* 25:45–68. New York: International Universities Press.

——— (1971). Some considerations on repetition and the repetition compulsion. *International Journal of Psycho-Analysis* 52:59–66.

——— (1975). Psychoanalysis as an art and the fantasy character of the psychoanalytic situation. In *Papers on Psychoanalysis*, pp. 352–371. New Haven, CT: Yale University Press, 1980.

——— (1988). *Sublimation*. New Haven: Yale University Press.

Loewenstein, R. M. (1969). Developments in the theory of transference in the last fifty years. *International Journal of Psycho-Analysis* 50:583–588.

Lynch, A., Bachant, J., and Richards, A. D. (1998). *The spectrum of analytic interaction: a contemporary Freudian perspective*. Paper presented at the American Psychoanalytic Association Spring Meeting, May 29, Toronto, Canada.

Maslow, A. (1962). *Towards a Psychology of Being*. Princeton, NJ: Van Nostrand.

Mayer, M. (1968). *There's a Nightmare in My Closet*. New York: Dial Books for Young Readers.

McDougall, J. (1991). *Theaters of the Mind: Illusion and Truth on the Psychoanalytic Stage*. New York: Brunner/Mazel.

McLaughlin, J. T. (1987). The place of transference: some reflections on enactment in the psychoanalytic situation. *Journal of the American Psychoanalytic Association* 35:557–582.

——— (1991). Clinical and theoretical aspects of enactment. *Journal of the American Psychoanalytic Association* 39:595–614.

Meissner, W. W. (1992). The concept of the therapeutic alliance. *Journal of the American Psychoanalytic Association* 40:1059–1087.

Mitchell, S. (1988). *Relational Concepts in Psychoanalysis: An Integration*. Cambridge, MA: Harvard University Press.

————— (1993). *Hope and Dread in Psychoanalysis.* New York: Basic Books.

Modell, A. H. (1976). "The holding environment" and the therapeutic action of psychoanalysis. *Journal of the American Psychoanalytic Association* 24:285–308.

————— (1991). The therapeutic relationship as a paradoxical experience. *Psychoanalytic Dialogues* 1:13–28.

Nunberg, H. (1931). The synthetic function of the ego. *International Journal of Psycho-Analysis* 12:123–140.

Ogden, T. (1986). *The Matrix of the Mind: Object Relations and the Psychoanalytic Dialogue.* Northvale, NJ: Jason Aronson.

————— (1989). *The Primitive Edge of Experience.* Northvale, NJ: Jason Aronson.

————— (1992a). The dialectically constituted/decentered subject of psychoanalysis. I. The Freudian subject. *International Journal of Psycho-Analysis* 73:517–526.

————— (1992b). The dialectically constituted/decentered subject of psychoanalysis. II. The contributions of Klein and Winnicott. *International Journal of Psycho-Analysis* 73:613–626.

————— (1994). *Subjects of Analysis.* Northvale, NJ: Jason Aronson.

Piaget, J. (1952). The *Origins of Intelligence.* New York: International Universities Press.

Pine, F. (1985). *Developmental Theory and Clinical Process.* New Haven: Yale University Press.

————— (1993). A contribution to the analysis of the psychoanalytic process. *Psychoanalytic Quarterly* 62:185–205.

Poland, W. (1988). Insight and the analytic dyad. *Psychoanalytic Quarterly* 57:341–369.

Ramsy, I., and Shevrin, H. (1976). The nature of the inference process in psychoanalytic interpretation: a critical review of the literature. *International Journal of Psycho-Analysis* 57:151–159.

Rangell, L. (1981). From insight to change. *Journal of the American Psychoanalytic Association* 29:119–141.

————— (1983). Defense and resistance in psychoanalysis and life. *Journal of the American Psychoanalytic Association* 31(Suppl.): 147–174.

————— (1989). Action theory within the structural view. *International Journal of Psycho-Analysis* 70:189–203.

—— (1990). *The Human Core: The Intrapsychic Base of Behavior. Vol. 1: Action Within the Structural View.* Madison, CT: International Universities Press.

Reed, G. (1987). Rules of clinical understanding in classical psychoanalysis and in self psychology: a comparison. *Journal of the American Psychoanalytic Association* 35:421–446.

—— (1990). A reconsideration of the concept of transference neurosis. *International Journal of Psycho-Analysis* 71:205–217.

Reich, W. (1949). *Character Analysis.* New York: Noonday Press.

Reik, T. (1948). *Listening with the Third Ear.* New York: Farrar Straus.

Renik, O. (1993). Analytic interaction: conceptualizing technique in light of the analyst's irreducible subjectivity. *Psychoanalytic Quarterly* 62:553–571.

—— (1995). The role of an analyst's expectations in clinical technique: reflections on the concept of resistance. *Journal of the American Psychoanalytic Association* 43:83–94.

Richards, A. D. (1981). Self theory, conflict theory, and the problem of hypochondriasis. *Psychoanalytic Study of the Child* 36:319–355. New Haven, CT: Yale University Press.

Rothstein, A. (1983). Reporter. Panel: Interpretation: contemporary understanding of the term. *Journal of the American Psychoanalytic Association* 31:237–246.

Roughton, R. E. (1993). Useful aspects of acting out: repetition, enactment and actualization. *Journal of the American Psychoanalytic Association* 41:443–472.

Sandler, J. (1976). Countertransference and role-responsiveness. *International Review of Psycho-Analysis* 3:33–42.

—— (1983). Reflections on some relations between psychoanalytic concepts and psychoanalytic practice. *International Journal of Psycho-Analysis* 64:35–45.

Schafer, R. (1960). The loving and beloved superego in Freud's structural theory. *Psychoanalytic Study of the Child* 15:163–188. New York: International Universities Press.

—— (1973). The idea of resistance. *International Journal of Psycho-Analysis* 54:259–285.

—— (1976). *A New Language for Psychoanalysis.* New Haven: Yale University Press.

—— (1983). *The Analytic Attitude.* New York: Basic Books.

——— (1992). *Retelling a Life*. New York: Basic Books.

Schwaber, E. (1983). Psychoanalytic listening and psychic reality. *International Review of Psycho-Analysis* 10:379–392.

——— (1986). Reconstruction of perceptual experience: further thoughts on psychoanalytic listening. *Journal of the American Psychoanalytic Association* 34:911–932.

——— (1990). Interpretation and the therapeutic action of psychoanalysis. *International Journal of Psycho-Analysis* 71:229–240.

——— (1994). Review of *Psychic Experience and Problems of Technique. Journal of the American Psychoanalytic Association* 42: 925–934.

Sharpe, E. F. (1937). *Dream Analysis*. New York: Brunner/Mazel.

Shengold, L. (1988). *Halo in the Sky: Observations on Anxiety and Defense*. New York: Guilford.

Smith, S. (1977). The golden fantasy: a regresive reaction to separation anxiety. *International Journal of Psycho-Analysis* 58:311–324.

Sterba, R. (1934). The fate of the ego in analytic therapy. *International Journal of Psycho-Analysis* 15:117–126.

Stolorow, R., and Atwood, G. (1992). *Contexts of Being: The Intersubjective Foundations of Psychological Life*. Hillsdale, NJ: Analytic Press.

Stolorow, R., and Lachmann, F. (1984/1985). Transference: the future of an illusion. *Annual of Psychoanalysis* 12/13:19–37.

Stone, L. (1961). *The Psychoanalytic Situation: An Examination of Its Development and Essential Nature*. Madison, CT: International Universities Press.

——— (1967). The psychoanalytic situation and transference: postscript to an earlier communication. *Journal of the American Psychoanalytic Association* 15:3–58.

Stoppard, T. (1967). *Rosencrantz and Guildenstern Are Dead*. New York: Grove.

Strachey, J. (1934). The nature of the therapeutic action in psychoanalysis. *International Journal of Psycho-Analysis* 15:127–159.

Wachtel, P. (1980). Transference, schema, and assimilation: the relevance of Piaget to the psychoanalytic theory of transference. *Annual of Psychoanalysis* 8:59–76.

Waelder, R. (1930). The principle of multiple function. *Psychoanalytic Quarterly* 5:45–62.

White, R. (1996). Psychoanalytic process and interactive phenomena. *Journal of the American Psychoanalytic Association* 44:699–722.

Winnicott, D. W. (1945). Primitive emotional development. In *Through Paediatrics to Psycho-Analysis*, pp. 145–156. London: Hogarth, 1958.

———— (1951). Transitional objects and transitional phenomena. In *Through Paediatrics to Psycho-Analysis*, pp. 229–242. London: Hogarth, 1958.

———— (1953). Transitional objects and transitional phenomena—a study of the first not-me possession. *International Journal of Psycho-Analysis* 34:89–96.

———— (1954). Psychiatric disorders in terms of maturational processes. In *The Maturational Processes and the Facilitating Environment*. New York: International Universities Press, 1965.

———— (1956). On transference. *International Journal of Psycho-Analysis* 37:386–388.

———— (1960). The theory of the parent–infant relationship. *International Journal of Psycho-Analysis* 43:238–239.

———— (1974). Fear of breakdown. *International Review of Psycho-Analysis* 1:103–107.

Zetzel, E. (1956). Current concepts of transference. *International Journal of Psycho-Analysis* 37:369–376.

Credits

Index

Unconscious (*continued*)
 evenly hovering attention,
  183–186
 fantasy, 186–187
 figures of speech, 188
 free association, 187–188
 language and, 176–179,
  188–189
 manifest/latent content,
  174–175
 multiple levels of meaning,
  179–182
 neutrality, 47–48
 resistance, 97

 self listening, 182–183
 silence and, 181–182

Vocabulary. *See* Language

Wachtel, P., 69
Waelder, R., 45, 98
Wexler, M., 208
White, R., 69, 98, 205
Wild analysis, 175
Winnicott, D. W., 105, 119, 207,
 247

Zetzel, E., 84